EVALUATING SECOND LANGUAGE VOCABULARY AND GRAMMAR INSTRUCTION

Providing a much-needed critical synthesis of research on teaching vocabulary and grammar to students of a second or foreign language, this book puts the research into perspective in order to distil recommendations for language teaching. Boers evaluates a comprehensive range of both well-established and lesser-known research strands and classroom practices to draw out the most effective instructional approaches to teaching words, multiword expressions and grammar patterns. Chapters discuss learning as a by-product of communicative activities, language-focused instruction, diverse types of exercises, mnemonic techniques and more, with a view to building bridges between the available research on such instructional approaches and how they are commonly implemented in actual language courses and textbooks.

This book helps teachers make research-informed decisions regarding their instructional approaches to words, phrases and patterns, and directs researchers to specific areas in need of further inquiry. Boers not only demonstrates how research findings can inform effective teaching, but also calls for a deeper appreciation on the part of researchers of the realities of the teaching profession, making this a worthwhile text for preservice teachers, teacher educators, graduate students and scholars.

Frank Boers is Professor of Applied Linguistics and TESOL at University of Western Ontario, Canada.

EVALUATING SECOND LANGUAGE VOCABULARY AND GRAMMAR INSTRUCTION

A Synthesis of the Research on Teaching Words, Phrases, and Patterns

Frank Boers

Routledge
Taylor & Francis Group

NEW YORK AND LONDON

First published 2021
by Routledge
52 Vanderbilt Avenue, New York, NY 10017

and by Routledge
2 Park Square, Milton Park, Abingdon, Oxon OX14 4RN

Routledge is an imprint of the Taylor & Francis Group, an informa business

© 2021 Taylor & Francis

The right of Frank Boers to be identified as author of this work has been asserted by him in accordance with sections 77 and 78 of the Copyright, Designs and Patents Act 1988.

Library of Congress Cataloging-in-Publication Data
Names: Boers, Frank, author.
Title: Evaluating second language vocabulary and grammar instruction : a synthesis of the research on teaching words, phrases, and patterns / Frank Boers.
Description: New York, NY : Routledge, 2021. | Includes bibliographical references and index. |
Identifiers: LCCN 2020043562 (print) | LCCN 2020043563 (ebook) | ISBN 9780367437664 (hardback) | ISBN 9780367437657 (paperback) | ISBN 9781003005605 (ebook)
Subjects: LCSH: Language and languages--Study and teaching--Foreign speakers. | Second language acquisition. | Vocabulary--Study and teaching. | Grammar, Comparative and general--Study and teaching. | Teaching--Methodology.
Classification: LCC P53 .B637 2021 (print) | LCC P53 (ebook) | DDC 418.0071--dc23
LC record available at https://lccn.loc.gov/2020043562
LC ebook record available at https://lccn.loc.gov/2020043563

ISBN: 978-0-367-43766-4 (hbk)
ISBN: 978-0-367-43765-7 (pbk)
ISBN: 978-1-003-00560-5 (ebk)

Typeset in Bembo
by Taylor & Francis Books

In loving memory of Lucienne Boers-Schroyens, who taught me to question everything.

CONTENTS

AUTHOR BIOGRAPHY

Frank Boers is a Professor in Applied Linguistics and TESOL at the University of Western Ontario, Canada. Before joining Western, he worked at various schools and universities in Belgium and at Victoria University of Wellington, New Zealand. His early publications were in the field of Linguistics, but his current interests stem from his extensive experience as a language teacher and teacher trainer. He now publishes mostly about instructed second/foreign language learning.

PART I
INTRODUCTION

1.

THE AIM, SCOPE AND ORGANIZATION OF THIS BOOK

The Aim of This Book

This book has a two-fold objective. One aim is to help teachers and students aspiring to become teachers of a second or foreign language (henceforth L2) to make informed decisions regarding their instructional approaches to words, phrases and patterns. It does so by evaluating a range of classroom procedures through the lens of published research findings in the discipline of L2 pedagogy. The other aim is to help researchers, including (post)graduate students interested in pedagogy-oriented applied linguistics, to identify topics relevant for vocabulary and grammar instruction which have not yet attracted much empirical inquiry, or which invite alternative methods of inquiry to what researchers have tried so far.

Valuable steps to distil pedagogical recommendations from research findings have of course been taken before, but for a long time authors of books addressing the needs and interests of L2 practitioners had to rely to a considerable degree on descriptive work regarding second language acquisition, which charts L2 development (often in immersion settings) and the factors that influence it. In addition, recommendations for teaching accrued from theories of learning proposed in educational psychology and from laboratory-type experimental work in the field of cognitive psychology rather than experiments conducted with L2 learners in their classroom settings. However, the past few decades have seen a proliferation of empirical classroom-based work on the merits of instructional interventions for (certain facets of) L2 learning. Not only have several new journals devoted to this line of inquiry been founded in recent years (e.g., *Innovation in Language Learning and Teaching*, *Instructed Second Language Acquisition*, *Language Teaching for Young Learners* and *Journal on Task-Based Language Teaching and Learning*), but longer-established journals have substantially increased their annual volume (e.g., *Language Teaching*

Research, TESOL Quarterly, System and *The Modern Language Journal*). The time therefore seems ripe for a review of this growing collection of studies that specifically examines the effectiveness of instructional interventions as a source of information from which recommendations for language teachers may be drawn. At the same time, it will be worth considering this body of research with a questioning attitude, acknowledging the limitations of the studies and pointing to areas in need of further exploration. It is in this regard that this book is intended to be a resource for researchers as well as teachers.

Dealing with Vocabulary *and* Grammar in One Book?

As the title suggests, this book examines instructional approaches to words, phrases and patterns. Put differently, it encompasses issues of vocabulary and grammar teaching. Readers may wonder if this scope is not too ambitious, and if vocabulary and grammar are not distinct components of language, whose learning and teaching must involve very different mechanisms and thus invite separate treatment. It is indeed not unusual for language learners and teachers to view language as being made up of 2 distinct components—some sort of grammar manual on the one hand and some sort of dictionary on the other (Taylor, 2010). In such a view, the grammar provides a finite and fixed set of sentence templates and a set of "rules" that words should abide by, while the dictionary provides the large repertoire of words to be slotted into the templates in their appropriate form as dictated by the grammar rules. The position taken in the present book, however, is that vocabulary and grammar are inseparable, and that an alternative view to the grammar-plus-dictionary conception of language needs to be adopted.

That vocabulary and grammar cannot be divorced from one another can be illustrated in several ways. One is to consider what knowing a word involves. Knowledge of a word clearly includes more than knowing its (phonological/orthographic) form and its meaning; it also includes its phraseological behaviour (e.g., that *make* rather than *do* is the verb that goes with *an effort*; that *decide* is followed by *to* + infinitive rather than an –ing form) and its morpho-syntactic behaviour (e.g., that *advice* is not pluralized by adding –s; that *sneeze* is not normally used as a transitive verb—one does not normally say that somebody has sneezed *something*). Conversely, even though grammar patterns are often labelled rules, mastering these includes knowing what words the given rules apply to and what words (so-called exceptions) they do not apply to. Put differently, the application of grammar rules depends on word characteristics as much as word use depends on grammar rules. Or, as Lewis (1993) put it, instead of viewing language as lexicalized grammar, we could also view it as grammaticalized lexis. Grammar and vocabulary are 2 sides of the same coin.

One could nonetheless argue that mastering grammar patterns involves a greater amount of "system learning" than does mastering vocabulary and that building vocabulary knowledge involves a greater amount of "item learning".

This not a clear-cut distinction, however. For example, vocabulary exhibits patterns of derivational morphology, such as the creation of adjectives by adding the suffix –ful to nouns (e.g., *doubtful, playful, stressful*). Appreciating the existence of this recurring pattern is clearly a case of system learning, but it is just as much a feature of the lexicon. Learning derivational patterns does not suffice because one needs to learn which words they apply to (e.g., *friendly*, not *friendful; hazardous*, not *hazardful*). System learning involves item learning, and vice versa.

Upholding a clear-cut distinction between vocabulary and grammar is difficult also because a typical grammar book contains sections on so-called function words (also called grammatical or closed-class words): articles (*the, a, an*), pronouns (*she, who, him, mine*), auxiliary verbs (*have, do, will, may*), conjunctions (*but, unless, that, while*) and so on. As these are obviously words, they are also included in dictionaries, and so recognized also as members of the vocabulary club. It might nonetheless be argued that vocabulary is different from grammar because it is so-called content words (or open-class words), such as nouns and adjectives, that should be considered the more prominent members of the vocabulary club. As suggested by the label content words, these are considered different from grammar patterns and from said function words, because they more clearly convey meaning. According to popular perception, grammar provides structural frames, and it is the words chosen to fill the frames that communicate meaning. However, also this is too simplistic, because many grammatical forms *do* carry meaning, even though it is often meaning of an abstract nature. For example, the –s ending in *books* carries meaning (i.e., there is more than one book). The –ed ending in *She danced* carries meaning (i.e., the dancing happened in the past). The definite article *the* in *Would you like the red one?* carries meaning (i.e., there is only one red item among the available options). The word order in the previous example carries meaning (i.e., it indicates a question). Sentence patterns more generally carry meaning. That is why one can try to guess the meaning of the following sentences, even though they contain made-up content words: *Helen clackoped the strimpot into the bramster; My wife dibroidered me a strafferick this morning; Shirley sprighted her hair bimbulore*. So, while it is undeniable that lexical items stand out as conveyors of meaning, grammar patterns are meaningful, too, even though their meaning will typically be abstract. It is worth noting in this context that also content words display considerable variation in degrees of concreteness or specificity of meaning (e.g., *pear* has a more concrete meaning than *fate; sprint* is more specific than *run*). Many words have both concrete and abstract meanings (e.g., *on* in *on the table* vs. *on purpose; have* in *I don't have a smart phone* vs. *I haven't slept well*). If vocabulary and grammar were different nations, then many items would have dual citizenship.

There is a long tradition in applied linguistics circles to distinguish between meaning-focused and form-focused instruction (e.g., Doughty & Williams, 1998), where the latter refers to a focus on grammar. This terminology is potentially misleading as it disregards the fact that many grammatical forms are meaningful in their own right—if they were not, their existence would probably be pointless. In this book, I will instead distinguish between activities with a primary focus on the communicative content of discourse (or *content-focused activities*, for short) and activities with a primary focus on the linguistic means to convey content (or *language-focused activities*, for short), where both broad types can be applied to vocabulary as well as grammar.

Perhaps grammar is different from vocabulary in the sense that it is more rigid, more fixed or more rule-like than vocabulary? When considering the notion of linguistic accuracy, this is indeed often associated with "grammaticality". A good command of grammar is popularly associated with "correct" use of the language. Such associations, as far as English is concerned, hark back as far as the 18th century when the first prescriptive grammar manuals were published. One of those early grammarians, Robert Lowth (1762) (quoted in Freeborn, 2006, p. 396), put it as follows:

> The principal design of a grammar of any language is to teach us to express ourselves with propriety in that language, and to be able to judge of every phrase and form of construction, whether it be right or not. The plain way of doing this, is to lay down rules, and to illustrate them by examples. But besides showing what is right, the matter may be further explained by pointing out what is wrong.

What such a normative conception of grammar ignores is that grammar fulfils communicative functions and is adaptable to fulfil those functions. Like vocabulary, grammar constitutes a set of options available to the user of a given language to package messages. For example, a teenager may prefer to tell his parents that *the screen of his new phone got broken* (using passive voice) rather than *I broke the screen of my new phone* (using active voice). It is of course undeniable that one option will often be more conventional than another. For example, the verb *mean* is more commonly used in simple tenses (e.g., *I meant to say that I was sorry*) than in progressive ones (e.g., *I was meaning to say that I was sorry*). Still, it is ultimately the language users themselves who decide how to deploy the available resources of their language to package a message in a way that best fits the intended meaning. For example, it is not so difficult to imagine a context where a speaker is having a hard time trying to express an apology and uttering *what I am meaning to say is that I'm sorry* (even though old prescriptive grammar manuals may tell learners of English that *mean* is a verb that is not to be used in this way). These options for deploying grammar to meet communicative needs are not dissimilar from the options available in the lexicon, where lexical choices (e.g., between saying *he's fat* vs. *he's chubby*) also depend on context and communicative intent. A certain lexical option may seem the default just like a certain grammar pattern may be, but this does not exclude irregularities. For example, it is undoubtedly more conventional to talk about a *mug of coffee* than a *bucket of coffee*, but it is not difficult to imagine a scenario where the latter fits a person's intended meaning—jokingly referring to an unusually large mug.

There is yet another reason why the dictionary-plus-grammar view of language is difficult to maintain. Dictionaries have traditionally (in the case of English at least since the efforts to develop a dictionary by Samuel Johnson in the 18th century) treated *words* as the building blocks that make up a language's lexicon. However, since the 1990s there has been growing recognition that languages also have extensive stocks of fixed and semi-fixed expressions comprised of 2 or more words (e.g., Nattinger & DeCarrico, 1992). Diverse terms have been used in the literature to refer to multiword expressions of various kinds, including such labels as formulaic sequences, phrasal expressions, lexical phrases, multiword units, lexical bundles, prefabs, idioms, collocations and chunks. In this book, I will use *phrases* as the umbrella term. Like single words, phrases perform a multitude of functions. They may be referential (e.g., *mow the lawn*) or expressive (e.g., *What the heck!*). They may signpost discourse organization (e.g., *On the other hand*), be part of interactional routines (e.g., *How's it going?*), express an evaluation (e.g., *Good as gold*), help speakers to maintain their speech flow (e.g., *You know what I mean*) and so on. While estimates vary, a substantial proportion (over 50%, according to Erman and Warren, 2000) of natural discourse is made up of phrases or, to put it differently, is *idiomatic* (Sinclair, 1991). Phrases thus serve as building blocks of language alongside single words, and research has demonstrated that L2 learners stand to gain a lot from acquiring a large repertoire of lexical units beyond single words (e.g., Bestgen, 2017; Kremmel et al., 2017; Tavakoli & Uchihara, 2020). Importantly for the sake of the argument being made here, neither the teaching of single words nor the teaching of grammar rules alone will serve learners well when it comes to mastering the phraseology of language. This is, firstly, because the meaning of many phrases (e.g., *cut corners* and *by and large*) transcends that of the meaning of their lexical constituents, and so having learned the single words that make them up does not suffice to understand them. Secondly, many phrases are morpho-syntactically peculiar, and so applying the "grammar rules" one may have studied does not at all guarantee accurate renderings of such phrases. For example, *corners* is always plural in the phrase *cut corners*, while *doubt* is always singular in the phrase *there is no doubt about it*. The verb *cut* is usually followed by an object, but not so in the phrase *cut and run*. The noun *ear* is normally preceded by a determiner in its singular form, and it can normally be pluralized (e.g., *my left ear, floppy ears*), but not so in the phrase *play it by ear*. And so on. This again demonstrates that vocabulary learning is more than learning single words and that grammar learning involves a substantial amount of item learning—knowing when to apply the pattern and when *not* to apply it.

For all these reasons, then, a dichotomous dictionary-plus-grammar conception of language is too simplistic. An alternative conception is to view language as *a large inventory of form-meaning relations*, where the forms vary in size from morphemes and single words to phrases and syntactic patterns, and where the meanings range from concrete (e.g., *apple, blow your nose*) to abstract (e.g., *fate, on purpose, plurality, past*). This is by no means a new idea. It is a view of language that has become increasingly established in the discipline of Linguistics, where it is part and parcel of such theories as *Cognitive Grammar* (e.g., Langacker, 1990) and *Construction Grammar* (e.g., Goldberg, 2006). What this alternative view entails is that words, phrases and patterns have more in common than how vocabulary and grammar are often portrayed in L2 study materials and teaching manuals: all linguistic units, great and small, have in common that they are form-meaning relations.

Returning to the question of whether dealing with words, phrases and patterns in one book is ambitious, the answer is: yes, it is certainly ambitious, but one cannot properly deal with vocabulary without frequent excursions into the realm of grammar and one cannot properly deal with grammar without frequent excursions into the realm of vocabulary. At the same time, this broad scope of the book does not deny that the challenges which words, phrases and grammar patterns pose for L2 learners differ in certain respects and may as a result require different instructional interventions. In fact, adopting this broad scope invites discussion of whether (and why) similar instructional interventions yield different learning outcomes depending on whether they are applied to words, phrases or grammar patterns.

Outside the Scope of This Book

It is important to note that, while the scope of this book is broad in the sense discussed above, it is narrow in many other ways. One is that it does not deal directly with work on skills development, such as instructional methods for practising listening, speaking, reading and writing strategies, or interventions designed specifically to enhance learners' pragmatic and cross-cultural awareness. It deals exclusively with instructional methods for helping learners to expand and deepen their knowledge of lexical items (including phrases) and grammar patterns. While this knowledge naturally serves the purpose of communication, becoming a truly proficient language user requires additional competencies, which are not addressed in this book.

Another way in which the book's scope is confined is that, when we talk about L2 learners here, this refers to school-age children and adults, not to pre-school children. The book is primarily intended to be of use to teachers of a second or foreign language as a subject at school (including post-secondary education) and to researchers interested in this type of L2 settings.

There are additional limits to the scope of this book. While surveying the rapidly expanding collection of empirical research about L2 teaching, the instructional setting I had in mind was that of a classroom where a teacher interacts with a group of students. As a result of this, I will say little about research on individual differences, such as differences in students' aptitude for language learning (Granena, 2019) and their working memory capacity (Wen & Li, 2019). While teachers should certainly be aware that such individual differences exist among their students, it is not easy to see how they could, for instance, use their students' results on a working-memory-span test to inform their teaching when they are working with a *group* of students and thus need to accommodate a range of individual differences. Another limitation is that I will only occasionally (e.g., in chapters 4 and 5) address the relative effects of specific corrective feedback strategies. State-of-the-art reviews of that topic are already available (Hyland & Hyland, 2019; Nassaji & Kartchava, 2017).

Finally, it is important to note that, in order to keep the task of synthesizing the large collection of classroom studies concerning vocabulary and grammar teaching manageable, I will review exclusively studies with a comparative dimension, that is, studies which compare the outcome of an intervention to that of a comparison or control condition. Available as well are numerous studies which describe a single type of intervention, but which do not evaluate its outcome through a comparison with other procedures. My assumption is that teachers are more interested in the question which of 2 or more available instructional procedures work the best than in the question whether a given teaching intervention has any effect in the first place. Teachers likely presume that doing something is better than doing nothing at all— why else would they have chosen the teaching profession? Due to this focus on empirical studies that compare learning outcomes from different teaching options, some promising perspectives on L2 learning (e.g., *Sociocultural Theory*; Lantolf & Poehner, 2014; van Compernolle, 2019) are unfortunately under-represented in this book. Underrepresented as well is the fast-developing and exciting strand of psycholinguistics research which examines how learners process language during various activities, but which is less focused on the learning outcomes from those activities (e.g., Godfroid et al., 2020). In this book, I focus on what learning gains can be expected from various types of instruction and classroom activities.

How This Book is Organized

Before discussing various instructional interventions, it is necessary to evaluate whether such interventions with a focus on specific words, phrases and patterns are really needed in the first place. After all, learners might acquire certain words, phrases and patterns also without any instructional steps by a teacher or course designer. If so, devoting precious class time to the teaching in one way or another of such items or patterns is arguably not time well spent. Instead, this time could be freed up to focus on other target items or patterns that do not stand a good chance of being acquired naturally, or, at least as importantly, to activities intended to foster communicative skills, such as practice in the use of listening strategies, practice to develop speaking fluency, and activities to enhance learners' pragmatic and cultural awareness. In the next chapter, I therefore consider the complex interplay of factors likely to influence the chances of incidental acquisition, that is, learners' uptake of words, phrases and grammar patterns from mere exposure to and use of the language.

I then turn to the panoply of options available to teachers and materials designers if they wish to stimulate students' acquisition of selected words, phrases or patterns in one way or another. We distinguish between 2 broad approaches. One broad approach, reviewed in Part II of the book, is to create opportunities for acquisition while the learners' focus remains primarily on the content of what is being communicated. Any learning of new words, phrases or grammar patterns in this approach is still a by-product or side-effect, as it were, of the learner's engagement with the content of a message, not the result of intentionally studying the linguistic packaging of the message. Many applied linguists champion this approach over the deliberate study of and explicit instruction about the language code, for various reasons. One reason is that by eschewing explicit work on the language code, priority can be given to classroom activities that engage students in the use of language for communication, which arguably fosters communicative competence directly and can at the same time provide opportunities for expanding and refining one's repertoire of means of expression. Related to the latter is the observation that children acquire most of the vocabulary and the grammar of their mother tongue incidentally. They do so by listening to their caregivers and by trying to express their own messages rather than by studying sets of words or grammar rules. If this is the recipe that makes children proficient users of their mother tongue, then (young) adult learners of a second language should benefit from using a similar recipe, so the argument goes. An example of this stance is Stephen Krashen's *Natural Approach* (e.g., Krashen & Terrell, 1983), according to which second language acquisition—like first language acquisition—builds on comprehensible input (a proposal known as the *Input Hypothesis*). The deliberate study of L2 vocabulary and grammar should be eschewed according to this proposal because it cannot equip learners with the implicit language knowledge that characterizes L1 speakers. This is sometimes referred to as the "no-interface" view—the view that explicit language knowledge is fundamentally different from implicit knowledge and does not contribute to the development of the latter. Krashen's publications have been immensely influential, and so a lot of research has been devoted to ways of fostering L2 acquisition without explicit explanations about the language code and without instructions for students to engage in deliberate language-focused study. At the same time, it is possible to modify textual input for learners with a view to increasing the chances of incidental acquisition of words, phrases and patterns without shifting learners' attention too much from text content to the language code. Three prominent types of text modification that I will discuss in chapter 3 are (a) the "seeding" or "flooding" of texts with instances of the words, phrases or patterns that one wishes learners will pick up, (b) the use of typographic means to make those items or patterns more visually salient for the learners, and (c) the addition of glosses or annotations to clarify meanings.

While Krashen considered comprehensible input the most vital condition for language learning, others have pointed out that learners also need to express themselves and interact with others to expand and fine-tune their language resources. These views have become known as the *Output Hypothesis* (e.g., Swain,

1995) and the *Interaction Hypothesis* (e.g., Long, 1996). Essentially, learners need to try and express themselves in the target language so that they become aware of the lacunae in their L2 resources, and they need to interact with others to receive some sort of feedback (e.g., requests for clarification) that help them re-evaluate the wording they used to convey a given message. These are the kinds of opportunities for language acquisition that occur naturalistically for children when they learn their mother tongue and for L2 learners in immersion contexts, for example, where they need to communicate with L1 users on a regular basis. Again, learning in these circumstances can happen in the absence of explicit instruction or deliberate language study. Following the above premise that incidental or naturalistic learning is the more direct route to communicative competence, many applied linguists have investigated how opportunities for naturalistic learning through interaction can be created in the language class-room, and how the design and sequencing of communicative tasks influence the pace of learning. Such endeavours, associated with *Task-Based Language Teaching* (e.g., Ellis, 2018; Long, 2015; Willis & Willis, 2007), are discussed in chapter 4. The same chapter also evaluates text-based output activities, where it is hoped that learners will pick up relevant words, phrases or patterns from texts if the contents of these texts fuel subsequent output activities. Because these activities are usually framed as content focused (e.g., "retell the story you have just read/listened to") without explicitly asking students to study the precise wording of the input text, they are included among the diverse options for promoting learning without an explicit language focus.

In Part III of the book I will turn to this other broad approach—a deliberate focus on the language code. Proponents of this approach argue that for the many students around the world who are learning a foreign language in a classroom, courses made up almost exclusively of activities that imitate naturalistic opportu-nities for learning words, phrases and grammar patterns will generate a pace of language learning that is too slow. The conditions for acquiring a second or for-eign language are quite different from the conditions under which children pick up their mother tongue, and advocates of explicit instruction will argue that deliberate language-focused study is needed to accelerate L2 learning and to equip learners with aspects of knowledge which they are very unlikely to acquire from content-focused communication alone. Whether all explicit instructional methods and deliberate study procedures are truly much more efficient than the incidental pathways for learning will inevitably depend on the soundness of these methods and the quality of their implementation. Evaluating this will be a recurring theme in the book.

While proponents of explicit instruction do not dispute that the explicit or "declarative" language knowledge it fosters will differ in nature from the implicit knowledge that L1 speakers have of their language, they also point out that, with a lot of practice, learners may manage to "automatize" their explicit knowledge, such that the fluency with which they can deploy it will approximate that of L1 users in behavioural terms (e.g., DeKeyser, 2015; Elgort, 2011). This view stands in stark contrast to the "no-interface" view that I mentioned earlier in connection with Krashen's *Natural Approach*. The difference between L1 users and highly competent L2 users who learned, for instance, a given grammar rule initially through explicit instruction may ultimately just be that the L1 users cannot explain the grammar rule (unless they are given plenty of time to reflect on it, perhaps) while the L2 users can (if they remember the explanation they were given about it). I will start the third part of the book by discussing interventions that are primarily meant to foster new declarative or explicit language knowledge. Some of these interventions offer learners explanations about the items or patterns directly, while others encourage learners to use their inferencing skills and promote so-called discovery learning. The former is also known as deductive learning and the latter as guided inductive learning. There is a general belief (e.g., Bjork, 1994) that learning activities that are challenging and thus require cognitive effort leave the strongest memories. If so, inferencing and discovery learning should be considered the better option. This cannot be taken at face value, however, because (as illustrated in chapter 5) many factors can undermine the efficiency of inductive learning.

According to *Skill Acquisition Theory* (Anderson, 1993, 2000; DeKeyser, 2015), acquiring declarative knowledge is but a first step in the learning process if the aim is to be able to use this knowledge smoothly. In this view, practice is needed to transfer declarative knowledge (knowledge of *what*) into procedural knowledge (knowledge of *how*) and eventually into automatic knowledge. This is the main topic of chapter 6. A recurring question there will concern the alignment of practice with the purpose it is meant to serve. For example, ample receptive practice will almost certainly foster receptive skills, but will it also foster productive skills well? In a similar vein, repeatedly doing exercises that imitate discrete-item tests (e.g., multiple-choice tests) may be useful preparation for taking such tests, but does it also prepare learners for communicative interaction? How well a language item or pattern is retained in learners' memory will also depend on how it is presented to them and what further information is given about it. Chapter 7 examines what steps teachers and materials writers can take to make new words, phrases and patterns more memorable. It will be shown that teachers' elaborations about words, phrases and patterns can sometimes make a big difference to how well their students remember them.

Part IV of the book takes stock of what the available body of research has demonstrated so far, and charts avenues for further pedagogy-oriented research. One of the observations is that there is a surprising dearth of empirical research about the effectiveness of how mainstream L2 textbooks deal with vocabulary and grammar. Some procedures that are abundant in L2 textbooks have not yet attracted much scrutiny. Conversely, some procedures that have been the focus of dozens of research studies are virtually absent from L2 textbooks. This illustrates that there is still a disconnect between what researchers find worth investigating and what could make a more direct impact on how teachers and textbook writers practise their craft.

Each of the approaches discussed in the book finds support in one or more theories or schools of thought about language and about language learning that have been influential in our discipline. However, the organization of this book is determined first and foremost by the nature of the instructional interventions or classroom activities rather than the schools of thought they may be affiliated to. It is assumed here that readers of this book wonder more about whether a given classroom activity or a given instructional procedure "works" than whether the activity or procedure bears the stamp of approval of a certain school of thought. It is nonetheless hoped that mentioning the theoretical underpinnings will stimulate readers' reflections on their own conceptions and beliefs regarding language learning and will potentially raise their awareness of alternative conceptions.

Although it may seem to contradict the arguments made above that it is hard to draw a line between vocabulary and grammar, I will in some of the chapters devote separate sections to how an instructional approach has been applied to words, phrases and patterns. This is to keep the length of the sections manageable, while still allowing to illustrate parallels as well as differences in the research endeavours and findings concerning diverse targets for learning. The sections on words will deal specifically with content words (e.g., nouns, adjectives and most verbs) rather than function words (e.g., articles, pronouns and auxiliary verbs). The sections on phrases will consider work on multiword items of various kinds. They will review studies on the learning and teaching of idioms (i.e., expressions whose meaning does not follow straightforwardly from the basic meaning of the constituent words; e.g., *go out on a limb*), collocations (i.e., word partnerships; e.g., *commit + suicide*) and phrasal verbs (e.g., *break down*). The sections on grammar patterns will be concerned with what is typically covered in a grammar book: (a) inflectional morphology (e.g., –ed suffix to signal past time reference; –s suffix to signal plurality), (b) syntax (e.g., inversion of subject and main verb in interrogative sentences; difference in word order between active and passive voice) and (c) function words (e.g., pronouns, articles and auxiliary verbs). Each section will describe the kind of pedagogical intervention under examination, present the rationale behind it and review relevant research studies. I will review studies in enough detail to illustrate and evaluate the type of research procedures and instruments used and, importantly, to put the findings into perspective and suggest avenues for further inquiry.

Further Reflection

How Do You Define Grammar?

The phenomenon of language is complex. We inevitably use metaphors or analogies as we try to conceptualize the nature of language and language learning. For example, when I ask my students of Applied Linguistics to define "grammar", they tend to propose diverse metaphors, including the following: the rules of language, the structure of language, the skeleton of language, the trunk of a tree, the foundation of language, the glue that binds words together, the mechanics of language, a toolbox to assemble sentences and a manual to put words together. Each of these metaphors entails certain beliefs. For example, thinking of grammar as a collection of rules reflects a rather prescriptive stance and a belief that grammar is fixed—and yet grammar is of course amenable to change—if it were not, then contemporary English would resemble Old English. Some of the metaphors depict grammar as more fundamental than vocabulary (e.g., without the trunk, there can be no branches, and you first lay the foundation before you construct a building)—and yet few will deny that content words are more direct means of communication than grammar is. Other metaphors suggest that grammar just provides a way of stringing together the meaningful elements of language (i.e., words), and yet grammar patterns themselves convey meaning. Awareness of the metaphors or analogies you use to conceptualize language can be helpful, because each metaphor has its own "logic" and may influence your reasoning (Boers, 1997; Gentner & Bowdle, 2008). For example, if you were to think of language as a building, and of grammar as the foundation of that building, then this conception of language may fuel a belief that grammar should be given priority in a language course—which is questionable. Sharing and evaluating one's metaphors about language and language teaching can be useful reflective practice (Farrell, 2016, p. 20; Thornbury, 1991).

How Does Your L2 Textbook Portray Vocabulary and Grammar?

Examine how vocabulary and grammar are presented in a contemporary L2 textbook. Does the book reflect the popular grammar–lexis dichotomy by devoting separate sections to each? Is grammar presented as a resource to express meaning or merely as a collection of forms? Do sections on vocabulary include attention to word grammar? Do they include attention to multiword expressions and the phraseological behaviour of words? Do grammar-focused exercises take account of the fact that strictly following the proposed grammar "rules" does not guarantee success because the rules do not apply to all words in the same way? Does the book have a companion "workbook"? If so, what is this "work" mostly about? If the textbook has a companion "teacher's book", do the authors mention any theoretical or empirical support for their approaches to vocabulary and grammar?

What Research Journals Are You Familiar with? How Do You Stay Informed?

The following are (in alphabetical order) a handful of the numerous international peer-reviewed journals that publish empirical studies comparing the effectiveness of different instructional approaches, including approaches to vocabulary and grammar: *Applied Linguistics, Foreign Language Annals, International Review of Applied Linguistics, ITL International Journal of Applied Linguistics, Language Awareness, Language Learning, Language Teaching Research, Studies in Second Language Acquisition, System, TESOL Quarterly* and *The Modern Language Journal.* Are you familiar with any of these journals? Does the institution where you teach, study or conduct research provide free access to them? Or do you use alternative ways of staying informed about the research findings in our discipline, such as attending professional development workshops and reading more accessible periodicals? It is well documented that, although language teachers tend to express a positive predisposition towards research in general, they find research articles too daunting to read, and they often feel sceptical about the practical implications of the research publications they come across (Borg, 2009; Marsden & Kasprowicz, 2017; Nassaji, 2012). Does this also ring true for you?

References

Anderson, J. R. (1993). *Rules of the mind.* Lawrence Erlbaum Associates.

Anderson, J. R. (2000). *Learning and memory: An integrated approach* (2nd ed.). Wiley.

Bestgen, Y. (2017). Beyond single-word measures: L2 writing assessment, lexical richness and formulaic competence. *System*, 69, 65–78. https://doi.org/10.1016/j.system.2017.08.004

Bjork, R. A. (1994). Memory and metamemory considerations in the training of human beings. In J. Metcalfe & A. Shimamura (Eds.), *Metacognition: Knowing about knowing* (pp. 185–205). Massachusetts Institute of Technology Press.

Boers, F. (1997). No pain, no gain in a free-market rhetoric: A test for cognitive semantics? *Metaphor and Symbol*, 12, 231–241. https://doi.org/10.1207/s15327868ms1204_2

Borg, S. (2009). English language teachers' conceptions of research. *Applied Linguistics*, 30, 355–358. https://doi.org/10.1093/applin/amp007

DeKeyser, R. M. (2015). Skill acquisition theory. In B. VanPatten & J. Williams (Eds.), *Theories in second language acquisition: An introduction* (2nd ed., pp. 94–112). Routledge.

Doughty, C., & Williams, J. (Eds.). (1998). *Focus on form in classroom second language acquisition.* Cambridge University Press.

Elgort, I. (2011). Deliberate learning and vocabulary acquisition in a second language. *Language Learning*, 61, 367–413. https://doi.org/10.1111/j.1467-9922.2010.00613.x

Ellis, R. (2018). *Reflections on task-based language teaching.* Multilingual Matters. De Gruyter. https://doi.org/10.21832/9781788920148

Erman, B., & Warren, B. (2000). The idiom principle and the open choice principle. *Text*, 20, 29–62. https://doi.org/10.1515/text.1.2000.20.1.29

Farrell, T. S. C. (2016). *From trainee to teacher: Reflective practice for novice teachers.* Equinox.

Freeborn, D. (2006). *From Old English to Standard English: A course book in language variation across time*(3rd ed.). Palgrave Macmillan.

Gentner, D., & Bowdle, B. (2008). Metaphor as structure-mapping. In R. Gibbs (Ed.), *The Cambridge handbook of metaphor and thought* (pp. 109–128). Cambridge University Press.

Godfroid, A., Winke, P., & Conklin, K. (Eds.) (2020). *Special issue: Eye tracking. Second Language Research*, 36, 243–370.

Goldberg, A. (2006). *Constructions at work: The nature of generalization in language.* Oxford University Press.

Granena, G. (2019). Language aptitudes in second language acquisition. In J. W. Schwieter & A. Benati (Eds.), *The Cambridge handbook of language learning* (pp. 390–408). Cambridge University Press. https://doi.org/10.1017/9781108333603.017

Hyland, K., & Hyland, F. (Eds.) (2019). *Feedback in second language writing: Contexts and issues* (2nd ed.). Cambridge University Press.

Krashen, S. D., & Terrell, T. D. (1983). *The Natural Approach: Language acquisition in the classroom.* Alemany Press.

Kremmel, B., Brunfaut, T., & Alderson, J. C. (2017). Exploring the role of phraseological knowledge in foreign language reading. *Applied Linguistics*, 38, 848–870. https://doi.org/10.1093/applin/amv070

Langacker, R. W. (1990). *Foundations of Cognitive Grammar, volume 2: Descriptive applications.* Stanford University Press.

Lantolf, J. P., & Poehner, M. E. (2014). *Sociocultural theory and the pedagogical imperative in L2 education. Vygotskian praxis and the theory/practice divide.* Routledge.

Lewis, M. (1993). *The Lexical Approach: The state of ELT and a way forward.* Language Teaching Publications.

Long, M. H. (1996). The role of the linguistic environment in second language acquisition. In W. Ritchie & T. Bhatia (Eds.), *Handbook of second language acquisition* (pp. 413–468). Academic Press.

Long, M. H. (2015). *Second language acquisition and task-based language teaching.* Wiley-Blackwell.

Marsden, E., & Kasprowicz, R. (2017). Foreign language educators' exposure to research: Reported experiences, exposure via citations, and a proposal for action. *The Modern Language Journal*, 101, 613–642. https://doi.org/10.1111/modl.12426

Nassaji, H. (2012). The relationship between SLA research and language pedagogy: Teachers' perspectives. *Language Teaching Research*, 16, 337–365. https://doi.org/10.1177/1362168812436903

Nassaji, H., & Kartchava, E. (2017). *Corrective feedback in second language teaching and learning.* Routledge.

Nattinger, J., & DeCarrico, J. (1992). *Lexical phrases and language teaching.* Oxford University Press.

Sinclair, J. (1991). *Corpus, concordance, collocation.* Oxford University Press.

Swain, M. (1995). Three functions of output in second language learning. In G. Cook & G. Seidhofer (Eds.), *Principles and practices in applied linguistics: Studies in honour of H. G. Widdowson* (pp. 125–144). Oxford University Press.

Tavakoli, P., & Uchihara, T. (2020). To what extent are multiword sequences associated with oral fluency? *Language Learning*, 70, 506–547. https://doi.org/10.1111/lang.12384

Taylor, J. (2010). Language in the mind. In S. De Knop, F. Boers, & A. De Rycker (Eds.), *Fostering language teaching efficiency through Cognitive Linguistics* (pp. 27–58). De Gruyter Mouton.

Thornbury, S. (1991). Metaphors we work by: EFL and its metaphors. *ELT Journal*, 45, 193–200. https://doi.org/10.1093/elt/45.3.193

van Compernolle, R. A. (2019). The qualitative science of Vygotskian Sociocultural psychology and L2 development. In J. W. Schwieter & A. Benati (Eds.), *The Cambridge handbook of language learning* (pp. 62–83). Cambridge University Press. https://doi.org/10.1017/9781108333603.004

Wen, Z., & Li, S. (2019). Working memory in L2 learning and processing. In J. W. Schwieter & A. Benati (Eds.), *The Cambridge handbook of language learning* (pp. 365–389). Cambridge University Press. https://doi.org/10.1017/9781108333603.016

Willis D., & Willis, J. (2007). *Doing task-based teaching.* Oxford University Press.

2.

ESTIMATING THE CHANCES OF INCIDENTAL ACQUISITION

Introduction

There are various definitions of incidental language learning (Hulstijn, 2003). I consider incidental language acquisition as the acquisition of items or patterns of language over the course of an activity where the learner is primarily engaged with the content of a message, not its linguistic packaging. In this view, incidental language acquisition is a side benefit, so to speak, of language use for communicative purposes rather than the outcome of a conscious effort to study the language code. The word primarily in the above description is necessary because learners do shift their attention occasionally to items or features of the target language even if they are primarily engaged with communicative content. They may be puzzled by a new word or expression (e.g., Godfroid & Schmidtke, 2013), they may realize that their own choice of wording is not optimal when an interlocutor asks for clarification (e.g., Pica, 1994), they may wonder about the spelling of a word they are writing in an email message, be surprised that a certain word is pronounced differently than expected and so on.

Because learners may spontaneously turn their attention temporarily to the language code proper even though their primary concern lies with the content of what is communicated, researchers have found it hard to operationalize incidental acquisition. After all, it is hard to determine to what extent learners are focusing exclusively on content rather than features of language during a communicative activity. What is more feasible is to distinguish circumstances where a language focus may occur spontaneously from circumstances where a teacher overtly directs students' attention to the language code. For example, informing learners that a language-focused test will follow an activity is almost certain to stimulate engagement with language proper (and many researchers in fact use test announcement as the criterion for distinguishing intentional from incidental learning). Presenting discrete language items or patterns as material to be studied or practised is another way of focusing learners' attention on these items or patterns. Explicit explanations of a grammar pattern, pointing out contrasts between L1 and L2 patterns, and asking students to infer the meaning of certain words or phrases are other examples of steps that create a conscious focus on the language code. The absence versus presence of such overt stimuli for learners to study the language code is how incidental and intentional learning will be distinguished in this book.

Even so, the distinction can get blurred. Take, for example, the use of glosses added in the margin of a text to explain the meanings of unfamiliar words. This is clearly expected to temporarily direct a learner's attention to these words. However, the learner may consider the glosses merely as assistance with the reading task at hand, not as a source of information that will be relevant *beyond its immediate usefulness* for said reading task. It is the awareness that remembering the information is worth the trouble because it is likely to bring benefits at a later point in time—be it for the purpose of obtaining good grades in an exam or, preferably, for the purpose of becoming a more competent L2 user—that turns a learning opportunity into an episode of intentional learning.

The fact that language acquisition can occur without deliberate efforts to study the language code is undisputed. Children acquire their mother tongue mostly without explicit instruction or deliberate study. Children of immigrants usually pick up the language of their host community successfully as well and often manage to do so with limited curricular assistance. Exchange students will also tend to improve their mastery of the language spoken in the host community by being immersed in it. Even adult learners whose contact with the target language is much less direct and less frequent may pick up L2 words and phrases they encounter in TV sitcoms, movies, advertisements, news articles and so on. It goes without saying that the amount of exposure to helpful samples of the target language will matter. Learners who are immersed in the second language community are obviously at an advantage in this respect in comparison to the millions of children, teenagers and adults around the world whose exposure to a target language is largely confined to language classrooms. Still, incidental learning opportunities also occur inside language classrooms. A well-balanced language learning program includes numerous activities in which the students engage primarily with communicative content, not just language-focused activities (Nation, 2007).

It is useful to estimate the chances that certain words, phrases or patterns will be acquired incidentally (inside or outside the language classroom) by a given group of learners, for 2 broad reasons. One is that, if certain elements or features of the target language are likely to be picked up incidentally, then it may not be necessary to invest much precious time in doing language-focused work on them. If so, time could be freed up for other activities, such as activities of a more communicative nature or activities with a focus on language elements or features that the students do need more assistance with. The second reason is that understanding the obstacles to incidental acquisition can inform interventions to remove those obstacles. If we know why particular words, phrases or patterns resist acquisition, it may become possible to design suitable instructional procedures to deal with this.

Regardless of whether the learning challenge concerns words, phrases or patterns, there are at least 8 factors that, together, are likely to influence the chances of incidental acquisition.

Eight Factors Likely to Influence the Chances of Incidental Acquisition

Frequency of Encounters

Items or features that are encountered repeatedly by a given group of learners are more likely (all else being equal) to be picked up than items or features which occur with low frequency in the samples of language the learners are exposed to. Evidence that frequency influences the processing and acquisition of diverse facets of language has been reviewed, for example, by Ellis (2002). Its influence on L2 learning has been demonstrated particularly often regarding vocabulary (Uchihara et al., 2019). How many times a word or an expression needs to be encountered by a learner for measurable learning to happen will inevitably depend on many things. For one, it depends on what aspect of knowledge is measured. It may take relatively few encounters with a word for learners to recognize it when it is met again, but it typically takes many more encounters for them to work out and remember its meaning (e.g., Elgort & Warren, 2014; Godfroid et al., 2018; Mohamed, 2018; Pellicer-Sánchez, 2016; Pellicer-Sánchez & Schmitt, 2010; Pujadas & Muñoz, 2019; Serrano & Huang, 2018). The pace of acquisition is also likely to depend on the modality of the input. More encounters with a word seem required in the case of aural input than in the case of written input (Hatami, 2017; van Zeeland & Schmitt, 2013; Vidal, 2011), unless the aural input is accompanied by written script (e.g., Malone, 2018; Teng, 2018), in which case the written modality can help learners to segment the speech stream and to connect the phonological forms to the written forms of words. Faster learning of word meanings can also be expected from reading texts accompanied by illustrations (e.g., Horst et al., 1998) or when new words, such as technical terms, are paraphrased within the text (e.g., Hulme et al., 2019). Audiovisual materials such as TV programs and movies may provide visual support that can help viewers infer word meanings as well, but even so, encountering a new word just a couple of times in a video seldom suffices for learners to be able to figure out and recall its meaning (Peters et al., 2016; Peters & Webb, 2018). Again, fewer encounters seem necessary if captions (i.e., the written form of the words) are added to audiovisual materials (Cintrón-Valentin et al., 2019; Montero Perez et al., 2013, 2014; Peters, 2019).

Incidental acquisition of a word is an incremental process, where various facets of knowledge develop gradually over time through repeated encounters with the word. In the case of highly frequent words, repeated encounters are by definition very likely. The 2,000 most frequent words of English generally make up between 86% and 89% of English discourse (Nation, 2006; Schmitt & Schmitt, 2014). These words are bound to be met time and again. Beyond these high-frequency words, however, the same word is much less likely to occur several times in a single sample of authentic discourse, and so extensive exposure to the target language will be required for a learner to meet it repeatedly. The time interval between encounters is likely to matter, because a vague memory left by one encounter may dissipate by the time the item is met again, thereby offsetting the process of incremental acquisition. Determining the role of frequency is further complicated by the question of what counts as repetition. Researchers may consider encounters with various derivational forms of a given word (e.g., *argue, arguably, argument; argumentative*) as repetitions, each presenting the learner with an opportunity to acquire the same "word family" (Bauer & Nation, 1993). This presumes that the different derivational forms are experienced by the learner as representing the same lexical item. It is likely, however, that establishing a form-meaning relation will require more encounters with a word if its form is variable (Reynolds, 2015). In addition, most lexical items have more than one meaning (i.e., they are polysemous), and so repeated encounters with a word in its various senses may be required for a learner to acquire its full semantic range. This is a topic I will return to further below as part of the discussion of intralingual factors that may hinder acquisition.

It was mentioned above that, beyond the highest-frequency bands, one and the same word is not very likely to occur multiple times in an authentic stretch of discourse. This inevitably also holds true for multiword items (or phrases). A combination of words cannot be more frequent than each of the individual words that make up the combination, after all. For example, *slippery* and *slope* occur around 3,300 and 7,900 times in the *Corpus of Contemporary American English* (COCA) (Davies, n.d.), but their combination (*slippery slope*) occurs only around 700 times (according to my corpus query in October 2019). Learners would therefore need extensive exposure to the target language to re-encounter the same phrases (unless the phrase belongs to a small set of exceptionally common ones, such as *you know* in conversational discourse and *for example* in a book such as the one you are reading). The benefits of re-encounters may again be weakened if there is too long a time lag between them. For example, the phrase *time and again* has occurred only once so far in this book and will occur only once more, in the closing chapter.

It is highly likely that also the acquisition of grammar patterns is influenced by their frequency in the samples of language which learners are exposed to. For example, the plural morpheme –s (e.g., *bottles*) is more frequent than the comparative morpheme –er (e.g., *larger*) and may for that reason be expected to be acquired faster (but see below). Similarly, the simple past tense (e.g., *I washed her hair*) is more frequent in narratives than the past continuous tense (e.g., *I was washing her hair*). Again, however, the variability among instances of the given pattern may complicate things. For instance, while part of learning the English past tense concerns the –ed ending, there are of course many verbs (so-called strong verbs) that signal past tense differently (e.g., *spoke, came, slept, ate, told, thought*). Moreover, it is typically the highly frequent verbs which behave in these "irregular" ways. The 15 most frequent verbs in COCA are all strong verbs (see https://www.wordfrequency.info/free.asp), and strong verbs appear more frequently than regular ones in teacher talk as well (Collins et al., 2009). This means that, although learners may be exposed to an appreciable quantity of past tense instances in general, many of these will *not* exhibit the –ed morpheme.

While frequency of encounters is but one of several factors likely to influence the pace of incidental acquisition, the notion that it plays a role is no longer disputed. It is not surprising, then, that several applied linguists have examined the benefits of increasing the number of instances of certain words, phrases or patterns in the samples of language that learners are exposed to. This is one of the lines of research that will be reviewed in chapter 3.

Noticeability

Items or features that are perceptually salient stand a better chance of being noticed than items or features with low perceptual salience. For example, the –ed ending signalling past tense in English regular verbs (e.g., *She walked to school*) is hardly audible in natural speech. This offers an additional explanation for why this feature tends to be acquired relatively late (Collins et al., 2009). In comparison, the –ing ending that signals the progressive aspect (e.g., *I was walking to school*) can be heard better, and so this feature stands a slightly better chance of being picked up. Input modality may matter here as well, since elements or features that are almost imperceptible in speech may be more noticeable in written text. Moreover, when reading a text, a learner may return to a previous passage and process it again, which is not often an option in the case of listening. Novelty attracts attention, too. Eye-tracking experiments have demonstrated that unfamiliar words are looked at longer during reading than familiar words, and longer fixation times are positively associated with learning at least the form of words (e.g., Godfroid et al., 2013; Mohamed, 2018). When the same words are encountered repeatedly, the amount of attention given to them gradually decreases (Elgort et al, 2017; Pellicer-Sánchez, 2016), which reflects the learner's growing familiarity with them. As already mentioned, this growing familiarity with the form of a word does unfortunately not guarantee that learners also acquire its meaning. In a study on vocabulary acquisition from reading a whole book, Elgort and Warren (2014) found that some learners still had not picked up the meaning of certain words after as many as 80 encounters.

The flipside of the coin is that highly familiar forms attract comparatively little attention. This helps to explain why learners often use unconventional word combinations, such as *do an effort* and *make an accident* (Laufer & Waldman, 2011; Nesselhauf, 2003), because highly familiar verbs like *do, make* and *have* are often overlooked by learners, and so their presence in collocations (or word partnerships) such as *make an effort* and *have an accident* will go unnoticed. There is now a broad consensus that giving attention to a language item or feature is a crucial first step in the acquisition process (Schmidt, 2001). Items or patterns with high perceptual salience naturally attract more attention. Applied linguists have therefore investigated ways of making items or patterns more noticeable for language learners by making them stand out in reading texts through typographic means such as underlining, bold font, italics or colour. This is a strand of research that will also be reviewed in chapter 3.

Comprehension of the Context

Learners may notice items if these are relatively salient, and they may gradually become familiar with the form of the items thanks to repeated encounters. Whether learners will figure out the meaning or communicative function of said items depends to a large extent on how well they can extract clues from the context in which the items are met. If the context itself is insufficiently understood, then it obviously cannot help the learner infer the meaning of an unfamiliar item that occurs in it. Context comprehension hinges on many things, including how much of the target language has already been acquired. For instance, vocabulary researchers (e.g., Hu & Nation, 2000; Laufer & Ravenhorst-Kalovski, 2010) have demonstrated that adequate text comprehension generally requires receptive knowledge (i.e., comprehension) of at least 95% of the words. Put differently, when more than 5 out of 100 words of a text are unknown, it usually becomes hard to grasp the content of the text, and so it inevitably also becomes hard to use one's understanding of text content to infer the meaning of the unknown words. To improve the chances that a learner will be able to figure out the meaning of new words from the context, the lexical profile of the input text should be matched to the learner's proficiency level. This is in fact part of the rationale for using so-called graded readers, that is, texts that have been modified with a view to making them easier for language learners at a certain level of proficiency. If low-frequency words are replaced by higher-frequency synonyms, fewer words will be unfamiliar and their meaning will stand a better chance of being inferred correctly (Nation & Deweerdt, 2001; Waring & Takaki, 2003).

Context comprehension is also influenced by topic familiarity. A reader may know all the words that make up a given text but may still find the text hard to follow if it is about a specialized topic which he or she knows very little about. If then also some of the words are unfamiliar, inferring their meaning is particularly hard (Pulido, 2004). Because topic familiarity aids text comprehension and so

can we bring in more comic style texts?

indirectly also language acquisition, it can be useful to read and/or listen to several texts on the same topic (provided the learners are interested in the topic; Lee & Pulido, 2017). This has been referred to as narrow reading (Krashen, 1981) and, in the case of other modalities, narrow listening (Krashen, 1996) and narrow viewing (Rodgers & Webb, 2011). Exposure to materials about the same subject matter also increases the likelihood that the same topic-related words are met repeatedly (e.g., Chang, 2019; Kang, 2015). It is worth noting that context is a broader notion than co-*text*. In the case of comic strips, illustrated stories, manuals with diagrams, and other documents containing pictorial support, the visuals are likely to assist comprehension where text alone does not suffice (Mayer, 2009). This also applies to audiovisual input such as TV programs and movies, especially in the case of programs such as documentaries where words often refer directly to things and events shown on the screen (e.g., Mayer et al., 2014; Mohd Jelani & Boers, 2018; Pellicer-Sánchez et al., 2020 Peters, 2019; Rodgers, 2018).

The above considerations relate mostly to unidirectional communication, but L2 learners may of course also engage in bidirectional communication in the target language, such as face-to-face interaction. If they experience a comprehension problem, they will at least have the option to seek clarification from their interlocutor—if they do not feel too shy to do so (Foster & Ohta, 2005). Some of the research on the benefits of interaction for language learning will be discussed in chapter 4.

Perceived Relevance

Elements which learners perceive to be important for comprehending or conveying a given message (e.g., words that are crucial to understand or tell a story) stand a better chance of receiving attention than elements considered to contribute little meaning or to be non-essential (e.g., Elgort & Warren, 2014). Content words (e.g., *play* and *tennis*) are not only more perceptually salient than function words (e.g., the indefinite article *a*) and inflectional morphemes (e.g., the –ed ending in *played*), but they also tend to give more direct access to the meaning or content of messages. As we naturally process messages first and foremost for their content rather than their linguistic packaging (VanPatten, 2015), we tend to focus more on content words than on inflectional morphology or function words. Research has indeed demonstrated that content words generally receive more attention during reading than inflectional morphemes, especially when the content words make the inflectional morphemes redundant for adequate interpretation of the message (Ellis & Sagarra, 2010, 2011). For example, in the sentence *Yesterday we played a fun board game* the adverb *Yesterday* makes the past tense morpheme in the verb (i.e., *played*) redundant because the adverb suffices to interpret when the activity happened. Similarly, the presence of plural quantifiers (e.g., *three, a few, a lot of*) makes the plural –s morpheme (e.g., *I've bought six bottles of white wine*) redundant. Only when no lexical clues to this effect are available do grammatical clues become essential for interpretation. Usually, however, lexical or situational clues *are* available somewhere in the context, and this helps to explain why the incidental acquisition of many grammar features is a very slow process, despite their high frequency. Learners can fortunately be trained to pay more attention to inflectional morphology (Cintrón-Valentín & Ellis, 2015). One way of doing this is by asking them to interpret sentences *without* lexical elements that "overshadow" the grammar feature to be acquired. Interventions of this kind will be reviewed in chapter five.

Relevance does not only refer to how important a given language item or feature is perceived to be for the communication at hand. It also relates to whether learners consider a given item or feature a worthwhile addition to their own language resources beyond the immediate circumstance. Elements which a learner recognizes as potentially useful for expressing messages in future (i.e., beyond their *immediate* relevance) stand a better chance of attracting a study effort than ones which the learner finds superfluous. For example, if learners know how to say *very angry*, they may not feel the need to also learn *furious*. If learners can say *I didn't know you were in hospital; sorry I didn't visit*, they may not feel the need to learn the complicated counter-factual past conditional construction *If I'd known you were in hospital, I would have visited you*. This is one of the factors (in addition to frequency effects and other factors) that can help to explain why, after an initial steep growth, the development of a learner's repertoire may seem to plateau out, after reaching a level where they feel they manage to communicate what they need to communicate.

Formal Complexity

Items or patterns that are formally complex may be relatively noticeable, but they will often take longer to be integrated accurately in a learner's productive repertoire. For example, the words *serendipitous* and *phlegmatic* may well attract more attention in a text than the shorter words *lucky* and *calm*, but their considerable length will make their form harder to recall. *Don't tell lies* is slightly more complex than *Don't lie*, and *Steer clear of him* is more complex than *Avoid him*. Length is not all that matters, however. Phonological (and orthographic) properties also play a part. For example, alliteration in *slippery slope* and rhyme in *steer clear* could make these phrases more learnable in comparison to phrases of similar length which do not exhibit these kinds of sound repetition—all else being equal (e.g., Boers et al., 2014). Grammar patterns vary in their degrees of formal complexity as well. A certain grammar pattern may simply be too far beyond a learner's current stage of L2 development, and so the learner is not yet "ready" to acquire it. For example, it typically takes several stages for learners to master question formation in English (e.g., Pienemann et al., 1988), from a stage where they may simply use rising intonation (e.g., *You live here long?*) over stages where they manage to use subject-verb inversion with single verbs (e.g., *Is this your house?*) up to the stage where they accurately use subject-verb inversion with auxiliary verbs

(*How long have you been living here?*). Similarly, it is hard to imagine learners accurately producing an *if*-clause of the type *If only he'd worn a helmet at the construction site*, if they have not yet started producing simpler ones such as *If you need help*.

Concreteness of Meaning and Other Semantic Variables

Concrete meanings are easier to acquire than abstract meanings (all else being equal). The meaning of lexical items whose referents are physical, tangible things (e.g., *table*) thus tends to be easier to remember than the meaning of lexical items denoting abstract concepts (e.g., *fate*). Closely related to concreteness is image-ability, that is, the likelihood that a lexical item will call up a mental image of its referent. For example, the verb *sprint* is more likely to call up a precise image of an action than, say, *allocate*. Although both *table* and its hypernym (a broader, more generic term) *furniture* refer to concrete objects, the former probably evokes a mental picture more readily. Both concreteness and imageability facilitate L2 word learning (e.g., de Groot & Keijzer, 2000; Mestres-Missé et al., 2014; Tonzar et al., 2009). Imageability also has the potential to make idioms easier to remember (e.g., Steinel et al., 2007) because, even though idioms such as *pull the strings* have an abstract meaning ('have full control'), they can nonetheless call up an image of the concrete context from which their use is derived (e.g., the image of a puppeteer pulling the strings attached to his puppets). Ways of unlocking this mnemonic potential will be discussed in chapter 7. Another variable that influences the acquisition of lexical items is learners' emotional response to them. Words felt to be pleasing (e.g., *kiss*) or displeasing (e.g., *leech*) and that trigger an emotion (Kuperman et al., 2014) are more memorable than neutral words (Ayçiçeği & Harris, 2004).

When it comes to the meanings of grammar patterns (e.g., plurality, past time reference, perfective aspect, hypotheticality), it is obvious that these are neither concrete nor emotionally arousing. This is yet another factor that helps to explain why many grammar patterns are acquired so slowly. That said, it might be possible to distinguish between degrees of abstractness even in the area of grammar. For instance, an imperative (e.g., *Come here*) seems intuitively less abstract than a counterfactual conditional clause (e.g., *If only I could find a better paid job*). Some grammatical meanings may be less abstract than others because they are more closely linked to perception. For example, plurality often refers to physical things of which there is more than one, whereas the perfective aspect (e.g., *I've finished*) seems to have no direct link to physical experience. However, these different degrees of abstractness must remain speculation because, while concreteness ratings are available for many words (Brysbaert et al., 2014), to my knowledge similar ratings are not available for grammar patterns. Instructional procedures to make the meaning of certain grammar patterns imageable will also be reviewed in chapter 7.

Interlingual Congruency and Confusability

This factor concerns similarities and differences between the learners' mother tongue (or other languages they are familiar with) and the items or patterns to be learned in the target language. It includes the facilitative effect of cognates (i.e., words in the target language which phonologically and semantically resemble words and phrases in the L1), but also the negative effect of deceptive cognates (or "false friends"). For example, French learners of English will easily understand *bracelet, comedy* and *development*, thanks to close equivalents in French (although these differ at the level of pronunciation, most notably word stress), but these same learners may be confused by *eventually* (because French *éventuellement* means 'possibly' rather than 'in the end'). The extent to which vocabulary learning can benefit from cognateness naturally depends on how closely related the 2 languages are, on the number of loan words available, and if the latter are still recognizable as loanwords (Rogers et al., 2015).

At the level of phraseology, L1 transfer is also very common, and may again be facilitative in the case of translation equivalents (Wolter & Gyllstad, 2011) but leading to "malformed" L2 collocations such as *make damage* and *say the truth* when the L1 counterpart phrases are *not* congruent with L2 (Laufer & Waldman, 2011; Nesselhauf, 2003). The likelihood of transfer will again depend on how closely related the 2 languages are. For example, Dutch and German learners of English have an advantage when it comes to acquiring English phrasal verbs (e.g., *give up*) because a similar class of phrases exists in their L1. This does not mean that Dutch or German learners get a free ride when it comes to English phrasal verbs, because these include false friends as well (e.g., the Dutch counterpart of *find out* means 'to invent', not 'to discover'). Nonetheless, for many other learners, acquiring phrasal verbs is more challenging because their L1s have no structural counterparts. Such learners may then tend to avoid using L2 phrasal verbs (Liao & Fukuya, 2004; Siyanova & Schmitt, 2007).

Positive transfer can also be expected when the target language exhibits syntactic and inflectional patterns that have counterparts in the learners' L1. On the downside, acquisition of L2 patterns will be slow if the learners' L1 is very different (e.g., Jiang et al., 2011). Contrary to a long-standing belief (e.g., Krashen, 1987; Wode, 1976) that grammar acquisition follows a universal order (e.g., that in English plural –s is acquired before the use of articles, and that the latter are acquired before the regular past tense), recent research (e.g., Murakami & Alexopoulou, 2016) has shown that the order in which learners master facets of L2 grammar is influenced by whether their L1 has similar form-function pairings. For example, learners whose L1 makes no use of articles (e.g., Japanese, Korean, Russian and Turkish) are slow at mastering articles in English in comparison to learners whose L1 does have articles (e.g., German, Spanish and French). At a more general level, learners whose L1 makes little use of inflectional morphology are at a disadvantage if the target language makes abundant use of it. I already mentioned above that language users give priority to lexical clues over inflectional morphology to interpret sentences. Research shows this holds true especially for L2 learners whose L1 (e.g., Mandarin) makes little use of inflectional morphology (Sagarra & Ellis, 2013). However, even if acquisition is facilitated by similarities at this general level of language typology, problems are still likely to arise at the item level. For example, like English, French uses –s endings to signal plurality (at least in writing), but several cognate words (e.g. *transport, information*) that are pluralized this way in French are not pluralized this way in English.

Intralingual Consistency and Confusability

This factor concerns regularities and irregularities *within* the target language itself that may facilitate or hinder acquisition. Recall that I consider language as a vast collection of form-meaning (or form-function) relations of various sorts. However, one form (be it a morpheme, a word, a phrase or a syntactic pattern) may correspond to more than one meaning (or function). If a given word, phrase or pattern always occurs with the same meaning or function, this will make it easier for the learner to determine its form-meaning relation (Ellis, 2008). Unfortunately, unique form-meaning relations are by no means the default in natural language. For instance, the noun *intelligence* can refer to cognitive abilities but also to information of military value. The verb *run* refers to different actions in *running a marathon, running a bath, running a business, running risks* and *running out of gas*. In clear cases of polysemy (i.e., when it is easy to see how one meaning of a word is related to or derived from another), learners may experience the different uses of a word as similar enough for these uses to represent essentially a single form-meaning pairing (Bogaards, 2001). The relatedness of the diverse meanings of a lexical item is not always obvious, however. For example, the word *board* may be met in the sense of *whiteboard, noticeboard, chess board, chopping board, diving board* and *ironing board*, in which case a learner might recognize the similarity among the referents. But this is less likely when the learner then also encounters *board* in the sense of *schoolboard* or *board of directors*. According to a recent analysis of vocabulary test data collected from a large group of learners of English, polysemy is indeed a factor that can hinder learning (Hashimoto & Egbert, 2019), possibly because learners tend to ascribe a familiar meaning to words they meet, ignoring contextual clues indicating that the words actually denote something else (Bensoussan & Laufer, 1984). It is worth mentioning in this regard that empirical studies of frequency effects in incidental vocabulary acquisition have typically examined learners' uptake of words that exhibit one single meaning in the materials given to the learners. In the case of polysemes, it is likely that more encounters with a word are needed for learners to work out its various form-meaning correspondences.

Also phrases often have more than one meaning. Even if a learner recognizes the lexical composition of a phrase after several exposures, it may require considerably more encounters for the learner to determine its meanings. A subclass of lexical phrases already mentioned earlier which illustrates this problem of polysemy is that of phrasal verbs (e.g., Garnier & Schmitt, 2015, 2016), where a single verb-particle (i.e., verb-preposition or verb-adverb) combination usually expresses diverse meanings (e.g., *make up a story, make up one's face, make up a bed, make up after an argument, make up the difference, make up for something*).

That a single form can have various functions is also a common phenomenon in grammar. For example, the –ed ending occurs in the past tense (*I walked*), in verb forms which do not actually denote past time reference (*If you walked to work every day, you'd be in better shape*) and in modifiers (*a heated debate*). The –s ending can signal plurality (*oranges*), possession (*Jack's oranges*) and 3rd person singular in the simple present tense (*Jack eats an orange every day*). The *be* + *–ing* pattern often refers to the here and now (*I'm preparing dinner now*) but can also refer to the future (*Who's preparing dinner tomorrow?*). Such inconsistencies of form-function connections are bound to make language acquisition very challenging (Ellis & Collins, 2009).

To make things worse, identifying the function or meaning of a form is often made extra intricate by inconsistencies in its manifestation. For example, not all nouns are pluralized by adding –s (*children, sheep*), not all verbs take an –ed ending to signal past time reference (*cut, froze*), not all verbs feature 3rd person singular –s (*she can swim well*) and so on. After learners have managed to establish the meaning or function of a given item or pattern, the next challenge if they wish to incorporate it in their own productive L2 resources is to delineate its usage restrictions— knowing where it is *not* used. Working this out only from exposure to samples of the target language is far from self-evident, since these samples exemplify how items and patterns are used, not how they are *not* used. Put differently, exposure to a language provides "positive evidence" of how the language is used, but it does not as such provide "negative evidence". Developing intuitions about this requires abundant exposure—which is natural in L1 acquisition but missing in many L2 learning contexts.

The above considerations were made under the assumption that learners accurately identify new forms and then attempt to determine their meaning or function. That this cannot be taken for granted has been pointed out by Laufer (1997) regarding L2 vocabulary. Learners all too readily mistake a new word they encounter for one they already know if the 2 look or sound alike, such as *adapt* and *adopt*, *comprehensive* and *comprehensible*, *prosecute* and *persecute*, *interesting* and *interested*, *price* and *prize*, *precede* and *proceed*, *principle* and *principal*, *scared* and *scarred*, and *statue* and *statute*. This is likely to extend to grammar patterns, too. For instance, it is not difficult to imagine how learners may fail to distinguish *used to* + *gerund* (*e.g. I'm used to getting up early*) from *used to* + *infinitive* (*e.g., I used to get up early*).

A complex picture

The recurring caveat "all else being equal" in the above discussion is important, because all 8 described factors interact, and so a facilitative effect of one can be countered by another. For example, the articles in English are clearly high-frequency items (*the* is the most frequent word in English and *a* comes in fifth place), and yet it takes many learners a very long time to master them (if they ever do). Factors such as their lack of perceptual salience, their abstract meaning, apparent inconsistencies in their usage (uncountable nouns are not preceded by an article) and, for many learners, a lack of congruency with the L1 may all help to account for this. A well-known example of a grammar pattern in English that is typically mastered late despite its relatively high frequency in discourse is the 3rd person –s ending with singular subjects in the present tense (*Our son sleeps in on Sundays*). The lack of perceived relevance may be one of the factors in this case: This –s ending is semantically redundant since the subject of the sentence (*Our son*) is stated explicitly. This is different in a language such as Spanish, where the subject is often omitted, and so verb endings need to be attended to in order to avoid ambiguity. Verbs such as *have, make* and *be* are also high-frequency items, and learners may therefore be expected to acquire them relatively fast, but mistakes such as **I have 12 years* and **I've done a mistake* show that their high frequency does not make them immune to L1 interference at the level of phraseology.

Considering just the above 8 factors produces a very complex picture, and yet several things have been left unmentioned. One is that knowledge of a given item or pattern is not an all-or-nothing concept, since a learner may have acquired knowledge of some of its facets but not all, may understand it but not use it accurately, or may use it accurately in planned speech but not in spontaneous speech. A learner may have become perfectly aware, for example, that the meaning of a certain deceptive cognate word in L2 is different from its L1 counterpart, and yet confuse the 2 once again when speaking under time pressure. In a similar vein, learners may be perfectly aware of plural –s in English, carefully monitor its use in formal writing tasks, and yet omit it during spontaneous conversation. Estimating whether a given word, phrase or pattern stands a good chance of being acquired purely incidentally (i.e., without a targeted instructional intervention or a deliberate study effort) thus includes the question *how well* it is likely to be acquired. Estimating the chances of incidental acquisition gets even more intricate than suggested so far, because it also needs to take into account the learning context (such as how much exposure to the target language the particular group of learners has inside and outside the language classroom, and what kind of discourse this typically involves) as well as the learners' individual characteristics (such as their motivation and aptitude for language learning).

While the list of 8 factors described above is by no means comprehensive, it suggests that the ideal candidates for incidental acquisition are concrete-meaning words that occur frequently in comprehensible input and that are experienced by the learner as relevant. Additional bonuses include cognate status, phonological/orthographic regularity, monosemy (i.e., having one distinct meaning) and absence of deceptive lookalikes. The fewer of these conditions are met, the slimmer the chances of incidental acquisition and thus the more necessary some sort of instructional intervention will be. Considering the number of potential obstacles to incidental acquisition discussed above, it is probably safe to say that with regard to most words, phrases and patterns, a total reliance on opportunities for incidental acquisition would produce a pace of learning which many L2 learners around the world would find frustratingly slow. That, of course, is why it is worth investigating the effectiveness of instructional interventions—the subject of this book. Several of the studies reviewed in the book assess the effectiveness of one or the other instructional intervention by comparing its outcomes to the learning gains from a condition without any specific intervention apart from exposing participants to the target language. A recurring observation will be that the rate of learning under the latter tends to be marginal, which supports the assertion made just above that for many items and patterns purely incidental acquisition is likely to be experienced as unsatisfactory by many educators and learners alike.

Further Reflection

What Can We Learn from How L1 Acquisition Happens?

Consider how some of the above factors may play a part in children's L1 acquisition. In what ways are the circumstances for children's L1 acquisition more favorable than those of post-childhood L2 learners? Could this comparison be informative in any way for L2 pedagogy?

The same factors as mentioned above can help to explain why certain grammar patterns tend to be acquired relatively early and others only later in L1 development. For example, most children growing up in an English language environment will acquire progressive tense –ing forms (e.g., *playing*) before they do past tense –ed forms (e.g., *played*). They also acquire the plural –s ending (e.g., *toys*) before the possessive (or genitive) 's' (e.g., *Tom's toys*). The 3rd person singular –s ending (e.g., *Tom plays with his toys*) tends to be acquired late. Also, children will first produce the past tense forms of some strong verbs (e.g., *ate, came, gave, got, took, went*) and only later master the regular –ed past tense ending (e.g., *arrived, laughed, rushed, shared, wished*). What interplay of factors (related to the properties of the language features themselves and related to their frequency distributions in the language that a child is exposed to) could account for such typical sequences of L1 development? Another question is whether these sequences are necessarily paralleled in L2 learning, especially in instructed L2 contexts.

Repetition: Same or Different?

One way of ensuring that certain language items or patterns are encountered repeatedly is to read the same article or story again, watch the same sitcom episode again, watch the same film again and so on. This is different from re-encountering the items or patterns across various text passages, sitcom episodes and films. What may be the advantages and disadvantages of these 2 types of repetition? Factors to consider include the likelihood of noticing (the amount of attention given to the given items or patterns) and the opportunities for establishing form-meaning connections.

References

Ayçiçeği, A., & Harris, C. (2004). Bilinguals' recall and recognition of emotion words. *Cognition and Emotion*, 8, 977–987. https://doi.org/10.1080/02699930341000301

Bauer, L., & Nation, I. S. P. (1993). Word families. *International Journal of Lexicography*, 6, 253–279. https://doi.org/10.1093/ijl/6.4.253

Bensoussan, M., & Laufer, B. (1984). Lexical guessing in context in EFL reading comprehension. *Journal of Research in Reading*, 7, 15–32. https://doi.org/10.1111/j.1467-9817.1984.tb00252.x

Boers, F., Lindstromberg, S., & Webb, S. (2014). Further evidence of the comparative memorability of alliterative expressions in second language learning. *RELC Journal*, 45, 85–99. https://doi.org/10.1177/0033688214522714

Bogaards, P. (2001). Lexical units and the learning of foreign language vocabulary. *Studies in Second Language Acquisition*, 23, 321–343. https://doi.org/10.1017/S0272263101003011

Brysbaert, M., Warriner, A. B., & Kuperman, V. (2014). Concreteness ratings for 40,000 generally known English word lemmas. *Behavior Research Methods*, 46, 904–911. https://doi.org/10.3758/s13428-013-0403-5

Chang, A. C.-S. (2019). Effects of narrow reading and listening on L2 vocabulary learning: Multiple dimensions. *Studies in Second Language Acquisition*, 41, 769–794. https://doi.org/10.1017/S0272263119000032

Cintrón-Valentín, M., & Ellis, N. C., (2015). Exploring the interface: Explicit focus-on-form instruction and learned attentional biases in L2 Latin. *Studies in Second Language Acquisition*, 37, 197–235. https://doi.org/10.1017/S0272263115000029

Cintrón-Valentin, M., García-Amaya, L., & Ellis, N. C. (2019). Captioning and grammar learning in the L2 Spanish classroom. *The Language Learning Journal*, 47, 439–459. https://doi.org/10.1080/09571736.2019.1615978

Collins, L., Trofimovich, P., White, J., Cardoso, W., & Horst, M. (2009). Some input on the easy/difficult grammar question: An empirical study. *The Modern Language Journal*, 93, 336–353. https://doi.org/10.1111/j.1540-4781.2009.00894.x

Davies, M. (n.d.). Corpus of contemporary American English. https://www.english-corpora.org/coca/

de Groot, A. M. B., & Keijzer, R. (2000). What is hard to learn is easy to forget: The roles of word concreteness, cognate status, and word frequency in foreign language vocabulary learning and forgetting. *Language Learning*, 50, 1–56. https://doi.org/10.1111/0023-8333.00110

Elgort, I., Brysbaert, M., Stevens, M, & Van Assche, E. (2017). Contextual word learning during reading in a second language: An eye-movement study. *Studies in Second Language Acquisition*, 40, 341–366. https://doi.org/10.1017/S0272263117000109

Elgort, I., & Warren, P. (2014). L2 vocabulary learning from reading: Explicit and tacit lexical knowledge and the role of learner and item variables. *Language Learning*, 64, 365–414. https://doi.org/10.1111/lang.12052

Ellis, N. C. (2002). Frequency effects in language processing: A review with implications for theories of implicit and explicit language acquisition. *Studies in Second Language Acquisition*, 24, 143–188. https://doi.org/10.1017.S0272263102002024

Ellis, N. C. (2008). Usage-based and form-focused language acquisition: The associative learning of constructions, learned-attention, and the limited L2 end state. In P. Robinson & N. C. Ellis (Eds.), *Handbook of Cognitive Linguistics and second language acquisition* (pp. 372–405). Routledge.

Ellis, N. C., & Collins, L. (2009). Input and second language acquisition: The roles of frequency, form, and function: Introduction to the special issue. *Modern Language Journal*, 93, 329–335. https://doi.org/10.1111/j.1540-4781.2009.00893.x

Ellis N. C., & Sagarra, N. (2010). The bounds of adult language acquisition: Blocking and learned attention. *Studies in Second Language Acquisition*, 32, 553–580. https://doi.org/10.1017/S0272263110000264

Ellis, N. C., & Sagarra, N. (2011). Learned attention in adult language acquisition: A replication and generalization study and meta-analysis. *Studies in Second Language Acquisition*, 33, 589–624. https://doi.org/10.1017/S0272263111000325

Foster, P., & Ohta, A. S. (2005). Negotiation for meaning and peer assistance in second language classrooms interaction. *Applied Linguistics*, 26, 402–430. https://doi.org/10.1093/applin/ami014

Garnier, M., & Schmitt, N. (2015). The PHaVE List: A pedagogical list of phrasal verbs and their most frequent meaning senses. *Language Teaching Research*, 19, 645–666. https://doi.org/10.1177/1362168814559798

Garnier, M., & Schmitt, N. (2016). Picking up polysemous phrasal verbs: How many do learners know and what facilitates this knowledge? *System*, 59, 29–44. https://doi.org/10.1016/j.system.2016.04.004

Godfroid, A., Ahn, J., Choi, I., Ballard, L., Cui, Y., Johnston, S., Lee, S., Sarkar, A., & Yoon, H.-J. (2018). Incidental vocabulary learning in a natural reading context: An eye-tracking study. *Bilingualism: Language and Cognition*, 21, 563–584. https://doi.org/10.1017/S1366728917000219

Godfroid, A., Boers, F., & Housen, A. (2013). An eye for words: Gauging the role of attention in L2 vocabulary acquisition by means of eye tracking. *Studies in Second Language Acquisition*, 35, 483–517. https://doi.org/10.1017/S0272263113000119

Godfroid, A., & Schmidtke, J. (2013). What do eye-movements tell us about awareness? A triangulation of eye-movement data, verbal reports and vocabulary learning scores. In J. M. Bergsleithner, S. N. Frota, & J. K. Yoshioka (Eds.), *Noticing and second language acquisition: Studies in honour of Richard Schmidt* (pp. 183–205). University of Hawai'i.

Hashimoto, B. J., & Egbert, J. (2019). More than frequency? Exploring predictors of word difficulty for second language learners. *Language Learning*, 69, 839–872. https://doi.org/10.1111/lang.12353

Hatami, S. (2017). The differential impact of reading and listening on L2 incidental acquisition of different dimensions of word knowledge. *Reading in a Foreign Language*, 29, 61–85. http://nflrc.hawaii.edu/rfl/April2017/articles/hatami.pdf

Horst, M., Cobb, T., & Meara, P. (1998). Beyond A Clockwork Orange: Acquiring second language vocabulary through reading. *Reading in a Foreign Language*, 11, 207–223.

Hu, H.-C. M., & Nation, P. (2000). Unknown vocabulary density and reading comprehension. *Reading in a Foreign Language*, 13, 403–430.

Hulme, R. C., Barsky, D., & Rodd, J. M. (2019). Incidental learning and long-term retention of new word meanings from stories: The effect of number of exposures. *Language Learning*, 69, 18–43. https://doi.org/10.1111/lang.12313

Hulstijn, J. H. (2003). Incidental and intentional learning. In C. Doughty & M. Long (Eds.), *The handbook of second language acquisition* (pp. 349–381). Blackwell Publishing.

Jiang, N., Novokshanova, E., Masuda, K., & Wang, X. (2011). Morphological congruency and the acquisition of L2 morphemes. *Language Learning*, 61, 940–967. https://doi.org/10.1111/j.1467-9922.2010.00627.x

Kang, E. Y. (2015). Promoting L2 vocabulary learning through narrow reading. *RELC Journal*, 46, 165–179. https://doi.org/10.1177/0033688215586236

Krashen, S. D. (1981). The case for narrow reading. *TESOL Newsl*, 12, 23.

Krashen, S. D. (1987). *Principles and practice in second language acquisition*. Prentice-Hall.

Krashen, S. D. (1996). The case for narrow listening. *System*, 24, 97–100. https://doi.org/10.1016/0346-251X(95)00054-N

Kuperman, V., Estes, Z., Brysbaert, M., & Warriner, A. (2014). Emotion and language: Valence and arousal affect word recognition. *Journal of Experimental Psychology: General*, 143, 1065–1081. https://doi.org/10.1037/a0035669

Laufer, B. (1997). The lexical plight in second language reading: Words you don't know, words you think you know and words you can't guess. In J. Coady & T. Huckin (Eds.), *Second language vocabulary acquisition: A rationale for pedagogy* (pp. 20–34). Cambridge University Press.

Laufer, B., & Ravenhorst-Kalovski, G. C. (2010). Lexical threshold revisited: Lexical text coverage, learners' vocabulary size and reading comprehension. *Reading in a Foreign Language*, 22, 15–30. https://nflrc.hawaii.edu/rfl/April2010/articles/laufer.pdf

Laufer, B., & Waldman, T. (2011). Verb-noun collocations in second language writing: A corpus analysis of learners' English. *Language Learning*, 61, 647–672. https://doi.org/10.1111/j.1467-9922.2010.00621.x

Lee, S., & Pulido, D. (2017). The impact of topic interest, L2 proficiency, and gender on EFL incidental vocabulary acquisition through reading. *Language Teaching Research*, 21, 118–135. https://doi.org/10.1177/1362168816637381

Liao, Y., & Fukuya, Y. J. (2004). Avoidance of phrasal verbs: The case of Chinese learners of English. *Language Learning*, 54, 193–226. https://doi.org/10.1111/j.1467-9922.2004.00254.x

Malone, J. (2018). Incidental vocabulary learning in SLA: Effects of frequency, aural enhancement, and working memory. *Studies in Second Language Acquisition*, 40, 651–675. https://doi.org/10.1017/S0272263117000341

Mayer, R. E. (2009). *Multimedia learning* (2nd ed.). Cambridge University Press.

Mayer, R. E., Lee, H., & Peebles, A. (2014). Multimedia learning in a second language: A cognitive load perspective. *Applied Cognitive Psychology*, 28, 653–660. https://doi.org/10.1002/acp.3050

Mestres-Missé, A., Münte, T. F., & Rodriguez-Fornells, A. (2014). Mapping concrete and abstract meanings to new words using verbal contexts. *Second Language Research*, 30, 191–223. https://doi.org/10.1177/0267658313512668

Mohamed, A. A. (2018). Exposure frequency in L2 reading. *Studies in Second Language Acquisition*, 40, 269–293. https://doi.org/10.1017/S0272263117000092

Mohd Jelani, N. A., & Boers, F. (2018). Examining incidental vocabulary acquisition from captioned video: Does test modality matter? *ITL International Journal of Applied Linguistics*, 169, 169–190. https://doi.org/10.1075/itl.00011.jel

Montero Perez, M., Peters, E., Clarebout, G., & Desmet, P. (2014). Effects of captioning on video comprehension and incidental vocabulary learning. *Language Learning & Technology*, 18, 118–141. http://dx.doi.org/10125/44357

Montero Perez, M., Van Den Noortgate, W., & Desmet, P. (2013). Captioned video for L2 listening and vocabulary learning: A meta-analysis. *System*, 41, 720–739. https://doi.org/10.1016/j.system.2013.07.013

Murakami, A., & Alexopoulou, T. (2016). L1 influence on the acquisition order of English grammatical morphemes: A learner corpus study. *Studies in Second Language Acquisition*, 38, 365–401. https://doi.org/10.1017/S0272263115000352

Nation, I. S. P. (2006). How large a vocabulary is needed for reading and listening? *The Canadian Modern Language Review*, 63, 59–82. https://doi.org/10.3138/cmlr.63.1.59

Nation, I. S. P. (2007). The Four Strands. *International Journal of Innovation in Language Learning and Teaching*, 1, 2–13. https://doi.org/10.2167/illt039.0

Nation, I. S. P., & Deweerdt, J.-P. (2001). A defence of simplification. *Prospect*, 16, 55–67.

Nesselhauf, N. (2003). The use of collocations by advanced learners of English and some implications for teaching. *Applied Linguistics*, 24, 223–242. https://doi.org/10.1093/applin/24.2.223

Pellicer-Sánchez, A. (2016). Incidental L2 vocabulary acquisition *from* and *while* reading. *Studies in Second Language Acquisition*, 38, 97–130. https://doi.org/10.1017/S0272263115000224

Pellicer-Sánchez, A., & Schmitt, N. (2010), Incidental vocabulary acquisition from an authentic novel: Do things fall apart? *Reading in a Foreign Language*, 22, 31–55. https://nflrc.hawaii.edu/rfl/April2010/articles/pellicersanchez.pdf

Pellicer-Sánchez, A., Tragant, E., Conklin, K, Rodgers, M., Serrano, R., & Llanes, A. (2020). Young learners' processing of multimodal input and its impact on reading comprehension: An eye-tracking study. *Studies in Second Language Acquisition*, 42, 577–598. https://doi.org/10.1017/S0272263120000091

Peters, E. (2019). The effect of imagery and on-screen text on foreign language vocabulary learning from audiovisual input. *TESOL Quarterly*, 53, 1008–1032. https://doi.org/10.1002/tesq.531

Peters, E., Heynen, E., & Puimège, E. (2016). Learning vocabulary through audiovisual input: The differential effect of L1 subtitles and captions. *System*, 63, 134–148. https://doi.org/10.1016/j.system.2016.10.002

Peters, E., & Webb, S. (2018). Incidental vocabulary acquisition through viewing L2 television and factors that affect learning. *Studies in Second Language Acquisition*, 40, 551–577. https://doi.org/10.1017/S0272263117000407

Pica, T. (1994). Research on negotiation: What does it reveal about second-language learning conditions, processes, and outcomes? *Language Learning*, 44, 493–527. https://doi.org/10.1111/j.1467-1770.1994.tb01115.x

Pienemann, M., Johnston, M., & Brindley, G. (1988). Constructing an acquisition-based procedure for second language assessment. *Studies in Second Language Acquisition*, 10, 217–243. https://doi.org/10.1017/S0272263100007324

Pujadas, G., & Muñoz, C. (2019). Extensive viewing of captioned and subtitled TV series: A study of L2 vocabulary learning by adolescents. *The Language Learning Journal*, 47, 479–496. https://doi.org/10.1080/09571736.2019.1616806

Pulido, D. (2004). The relationship between text comprehension and second language incidental vocabulary acquisition: A matter of topic familiarity? *Language Learning*, 54, 469–523. https://doi.org/10.1111/j.0023-8333.2004.00263.x

Reynolds, B. L. (2015). The effects of word form variation and frequency on second language incidental vocabulary acquisition through reading. *Applied Linguistics Review*, 6, 467–497. https://doi.org/10.1515/applirev-2015-0021

Rodgers, M. P. H. (2018). The images in television programs and the potential for learning unknown words: The relationship between on-screen imagery and vocabulary. *ITL International Journal of Applied Linguistics*, 169, 191–211. https://doi.org/10.1075/itl.00012.rod

Rodgers, M. P. H., & Webb, S. (2011). Narrow viewing: The vocabulary in related television programs. *TESOL Quarterly*, 45, 689–717. https://doi.org/10.5054/tq.2011.268062

Rogers, J., Webb, S., & Nakata, T. (2015). Do the cognacy characteristics of loanwords make them more easily learned than noncognates? *Language Teaching Research*, 19, 9–27. https://doi.org/10.1177/1362168814541752

Sagarra, N., & Ellis, N. C. (2013). From seeing adverbs to seeing verbal morphology: Language experience and adult acquisition of L2 tense. *Studies in Second Language Acquisition*, 35, 261–290. https://doi.org/10.1017/S0272263112000885

Schmidt, R. W. (2001). Attention. In P. Robinson (Ed.), *Cognition and second language instruction* (pp. 3–32). Cambridge University Press.

Schmitt, N., & Schmitt, D. (2014). A reassessment of frequency and vocabulary size in L2 vocabulary teaching. *Language Teaching*, 47, 484–503. https://doi.org/10.1017/S0261444812000018

Serrano, R., & Huang, H-Y. (2018). Learning vocabulary through assisted repeated reading: How much time should there be between repetitions of the same text? *TESOL Quarterly*, 52, 971–994. https://doi.org/10.1002/tesq.445

Siyanova, A., & Schmitt, N. (2007). Native and non-native use of multi-word vs.one-word verbs. *International Review of Applied Linguistics in Language Teaching*, 45, 119–139. https://doi.org/10.1515/IRAL.2007.005

Steinel, M. P., Hulstijn, J. H., & Steinel, W. (2007). Second language idiom learning in a paired-associate paradigm: Effects of direction of learning, direction of testing, idiom imageability, and idiom transparency. *Studies in Second Language Acquisition*, 29, 449–484. https://doi.org/10.1017/S0272263107070271

Teng, F. (2018). Incidental vocabulary acquisition from reading-only and reading-while-listening: A multi-dimensional approach. *Innovation in Language Learning and Teaching*, 12, 274–288. https://doi.org/10.1080/17501229.2016.1203328

Tonzar, C., Lotto, L., & Job, R. (2009). L2 vocabulary acquisition in children: Effects of learning method and cognate status. *Language Learning*, 59, 623–646. https://doi.org/10.1111/j.1467-9922.2009.00519.x

Uchihara, T., Webb, S., & Yanagisawa, A. (2019). The effects of repetition on incidental vocabulary learning: A meta-analysis of correlational studies, *Language Learning*, 69, 559–599. https://doi.org/10.1111/lang.12343

VanPatten, B. (2015). Foundations of processing instruction. *International Review of Applied Linguistics in Language Teaching*, 53, 91–109. https://doi.org/10.1515/iral-2015-0005

van Zeeland, H., & Schmitt, N. (2013). Incidental vocabulary acquisition through L2 listening: A dimensions approach. *System*, 41, 609–624. https://doi.org/10.1016/j.system.2013.07.012

Vidal, K. (2011). A comparison of the effects of reading and listening on incidental vocabulary acquisition. *Language Learning*, 61, 219–258. https://doi.org/10.1111/j.1467-9922.2010.00593.x

Waring R., & Takaki, M. (2003). At what rate do learners learn and retain new vocabulary from reading a graded reader? *Reading in a Foreign Language*, 15, 130–163. http://nflrc.hawaii.edu/rfl/October2003/waring/waring.html

Wode, H. (1976). Developmental sequences in naturalistic L2 acquisition. *Working Papers on Bilingualism*, 1, 1–13.

Wolter, B., & Gyllstad, H. (2011). Collocational links in the L2 mental lexicon and the influence of L1 intralexical knowledge. *Applied Linguistics*, 32, 430–449. https://doi.org/10.1093/applin/amr011

PART II

IMPROVING THE CHANCES OF INCIDENTAL ACQUISITION

3.

ENHANCING TEXTUAL INPUT

Introduction

This chapter examines ways of improving the likelihood that learners pick up language items or patterns from texts while they are primarily focusing on text content. Textual materials can be created or modified to increase the number of encounters with certain items or a certain pattern, make said items or pattern more noticeable, and make it easier for learners to find their meaning. Usually the input materials are reading texts (e.g., Rott, 1999) or multimodal materials that include reading input (e.g., Montero Perez et al., 2018). Recall from chapter 2 that language acquisition from listening to texts without written support tends to be more challenging (e.g., Vidal, 2011).

The way the effect of a given text modification (such as increasing the number of occurrences of a word) on acquisition is typically investigated in this line of research is as follows. The researchers first choose a text containing lexical items or a grammar pattern unlikely to be familiar to a given population of learners, or they themselves compose a text in which they embed the items or pattern. Then different versions of the text are created, varying in the way the learners will be exposed to the items or pattern of interest (such as the number of times they occur and in what contexts). These different versions are then read by different groups belonging to the same broader population of students. The students are asked to read the text for comprehension, and they may be told a quiz *about content* will follow. This is done because this strand of research is interested in incidental acquisition, that is, acquisition as a side benefit from communicative language use rather than deliberate language-focused study. A surprise post-reading test (or posttest, for short) about the language items or grammar pattern of interest is subsequently administered to determine if the manipulation of the text has made a difference. Unless the researcher is sure the students have no knowledge of the target items or pattern before the reading activity, a pre-reading test (or pretest, for short) is administered beforehand, so a more reliable calculation can be made of how much knowledge the students gained through the reading activity. A potential problem with pretesting is that it may alert the students to the true purpose of the experiment and raise their awareness of the presence of certain language items or patterns in the text if they remember being quizzed about these before the reading activity. Taking a pretest may thus alter the learners' engagement with the text. This is worth bearing in mind, in case the learning gains reported in the collection of studies reviewed in the following pages are not generalizable to circumstances where learners' curiosity has not been aroused by a pretest.

In many of the studies I will be reviewing, more than one type of posttest was administered, but lack of space prevents detailing all of them. Instead, I will focus on findings from the types of posttest used most commonly across the studies as this will allow for clearer comparisons. For example, in the below section on the acquisition of words from modified textual input, I will prioritize findings from tests where students were asked to provide (e.g., through translation into their L1) the meaning of words they had met in the text. This is understandably a very common type of test in vocabulary research because establishing a connection between word form and word meaning is the most crucial step in word learning (Schmitt, 2008). It is also worth mentioning from the start that in this review the focus is on learning gains observed in tests that were administered shortly after the reading activities (e.g., in the same lesson). This is because not all studies include additional, delayed testing (testing again one week later, for example), thus making comparisons of longer-term effects across experiments difficult. It suffices to mention that, when delayed tests were administered, these almost invariably showed much poorer outcomes, due to attrition (i.e., forgetting over time) in the absence of further engagement with the language items or patterns after the initial learning opportunity.

Words

As discussed in chapter 2, one of the variables known to influence the pace of incidental acquisition of words from reading is their frequency in the texts (Horst et al., 1998; Waring & Takaki, 2003). The chances of uptake can thus be improved by presenting learners with reading materials that expose them to selected lexical items multiple times. Rott (1999), for example, created a series of short paragraphs for students of German. Each paragraph contained the same 6 words which the students were not yet familiar with. Some students read only 2 of the paragraphs and were thus exposed to the words only twice; another group read 4 of the paragraphs, and a third group read 6, thus encountering each target word 6 times. Unsurprisingly, it was the latter group that performed best on a posttest inviting them to supply the meaning of the words—with a success rate of close to 50% immediately after reading the sixth paragraph. To put this success rate into perspective, it is worth mentioning that each of the paragraphs was written in such a way that the meaning of the words was easy to guess. In 2 comparable studies but without such special efforts to create highly supportive contexts, the success rates were considerably poorer: 29% after as many as 10 encounters in Webb (2007) and 15% after 7 encounters in Chen and Truscott (2010). Still, there is no doubt that exposure frequency is in general positively associated with uptake (Uchihara et al., 2019). It is perhaps worth reiterating that investigations of frequency effects such as the above examine rates of acquisition of lexical items whose form–meaning connections are consistent in the input materials (i.e., one form, one meaning). As argued in chapter 2, more encounters with the same form may be required for a learner to determine form–meaning correspondences if these differ across encounters—as in the case of polysemy. It is also worth noting that the target words in experiments such as these are typically ones with a concrete meaning, and, as mentioned in chapter 2, concreteness makes learning easier. In short, the learning gains observed in these experiments are probably not generalizable to vocabulary at large.

Deliberately inserting multiple instances of an item or a pattern in a text (often referred to metaphorically as "flooding" or "seeding" a text with those instances) must require a considerable amount of time and resourcefulness as well. A much less demanding kind of text modification is to make words that are already present in an existing text more visually salient, for example by highlighting them, underlining them, or using a different font (e.g., boldface). Making items in a text stand out this way is called typographic enhancement (or visual enhancement). The rationale for typographic enhancement is that, for items or patterns to be acquired, they first need to be noticed (Schmidt, 2001; Sharwood-Smith, 1993). Kim (2006) is a study which included reading conditions where unfamiliar words occurred just once in a text but were either printed in bold font or left untouched. In a posttest where the students were asked if they recognized the words, those who had seen the words in bold font outperformed the others by 9%, which suggests that the typographic enhancement had indeed drawn their attention. When it came to a test which asked them to match the words with their meanings, however, both groups of students did equally poorly (less than 4% success rate). That no effect of enhancement emerged on the form–meaning matching test is unsurprising because, while bold font can make an item stand out, it does not clarify its meaning. Typographic enhancement can also be applied to captioned audiovisual input. Montero Perez et al. (2014) had Flemish students watch video clips in French with normal captions or with captions in which lexical items were high-lighted. The posttest results showed no difference in the students' ability to recognize these items or to supply their meaning. The short time available to read captions on screen before they disappear can help to explain why the visual enhancement made no difference.

So, flooding a text with instances of the same words does not necessarily bring about impressive learning gains, and using typographic means to channel more of L2 readers' attention to a single instance of a new word does not appear to have a big impact either. A solution might therefore be to apply the 2 kinds of text modification in conjunction—flooding and typographic enhancement combined. Sánchez-Gutiérrez et al. (2019) tried this in an experiment with learners of Spanish but found a significant effect only for flooding, not for typographic enhancement. Cintrón-Valentín et al. (2019), on the other hand, did find evidence of an additive effect for vocabulary uptake of typographic enhancement in combination with flooding compared to flooding alone. I will review several more studies which combined flooding and visual enhancement further below when we turn to grammar patterns as the targets for learning.

Repeated encounters with a word will only help learners to acquire its *meaning* if helpful contextual clues are available. For example, Webb (2008) exposed students to unfamiliar word forms (they were in fact made-up words, or pseudo-words, in lieu of existing words) in 3 very short passages (one or two sentences long). The first passage contained helpful contextual clues for the students to work out the meaning of the words, but the second and third passage differed. For one group of students, these were additional supportive contexts, whereas for another group they were not. Unsurprisingly, the former group was better able to supply the meaning of the words in a posttest administered shortly after the reading activity. The success rate was nonetheless very modest (13%). Teng (2019) also presented learners with unfamiliar words (this time real, but low-frequency words) embedded in very short passages that differed in their degree of contextual support for meaning guessing. After seeing the words 10 times in the more supportive contexts, the students managed to supply the correct meaning of about half of them. After seeing the same words 10 times in the less supportive contexts, they supplied correct meanings for only one third. While supportive contexts clearly help, the fact remains that meaning-inferencing is not error-free even if contextual clues are available (Bensoussan & Laufer, 1984; Laufer & Sim, 1985; Na & Nation, 1985; Nassaji, 2003; van Zeeland, 2014), and it requires multiple encounters with the item for learners to remember and fine-tune their interpretation.

A type of text modification which can assist adequate interpretation of an unknown word more directly is the insertion within the reading passage of a so-called *appositive*, inserting a synonym or clarification straight after the word (as illustrated just now regarding the word appositive). This was done as part of a study by Watanabe (1997), where typographically enhanced words in a short text were followed immediately by this type of clarification (e.g., *Each year infants die in their cribs, babies' beds,* ...). The students were asked to supply the meanings of the words before and after the reading activity. Rather surprisingly, the posttest scores were only 8.5% better than the pretest scores. A possible explanation is that the students did not realize that the phrases which followed the new words were meant as clarifications. When some of the students were asked to interpret the words *during* the reading activity, they performed very poorly, indicating they were not using the clues provided. Part of the experiment by Kim (2006), which I introduced above, also tested the effect of appositives. To help students recognize their purpose, these were explicitly presented as clarifications (…, *which means* …), and yet, the success rate on a meaning-recall test remained poor (9%). It needs to be mentioned that in Kim's experiment there were as many as 26 words to be learned. Even if the students remembered the clarifications given in the text, it must have been challenging to remember precisely which of the newly met words they related to.

In most of the above experiments, the target words (i.e., the words selected by the researchers as candidates for learning and thus to test knowledge of) were typically flagged by bold font or other typographic means in the texts. This is common practice also when explanatory glosses are added to a text. A typical implementation of glossing is to highlight certain words in the body of the text and to provide explanations in the margin, close to the text line where the highlighted word occurs. The explanations can be given in the form of L1 translations (if translation equivalents are available) or in the form of brief L2 definitions (provided these are formulated in a way that is easy for the learners to understand). Although some studies found little difference between the effectiveness of the 2 modes (e.g., Ko, 2012; Yoshii, 2006), a meta-analysis of the effects of glossing (Yanagisawa et al., 2020) suggests L1 translations tend to have the greater effect. According to eye-tracking research, L1 glosses also take less time to process (Kang et al., 2020). When new words are encountered during listening, explanations of their meaning in L1 also appear at least as effective as explanations in the target language (Hennebry et al., 2013; Lee & Levine, 2020; Tian & Macaro, 2012; Zhang & Graham, 2020), and they typically require less time. A third option is to elucidate word meaning by means of pictures, but I will say more about this option further below.

The usefulness of providing marginal glosses was investigated by Hulstijn et al. (1996), who gave students of French a 3-page story to read either with marginal glosses (L1 translations) clarifying unfamiliar words or without glosses. Some of the target words occurred once in the text while others occurred 3 times. The glosses were found to have a positive effect on the students' ability to supply the meaning of the target words after the reading activity: 16% for words that occurred once in the text and 26% for words that occurred 3 times, compared to 4% and 7.5% after reading the text version without glosses. A similar research design was applied by Teng (2020). Students read 15 texts distributed over time, each containing one target word in bold font. Depending on the text version, students encountered the bolded target word once, 3 times, or 7 times. In half of the text versions the word was accompanied by a marginal gloss (L1 translation). The results were analogous to those of Hulstijn et al. (1996): the provision of marginal glosses was found to benefit students' recall of the words' meanings, and repeated encounters had a positive effect as well. After 7 encounters with a target word, there was a 47% likelihood of correct meaning recall if the word was glossed in the margin of the text (compared to 31% after 7 encounters without a gloss). The success rate after just a single encounter with a glossed word was much lower (16.5%). Several additional studies have found that learners are not very likely to remember a glossed word's meaning after encountering it just once. For instance, Jung (2016) reported a score of 37% on a 4-option multiple-choice test, which is only 12% better than the 25% success rate expected under blind guessing. Similar unimpressive learning gains were reported by Ko (2012), but that study was different because the explanatory notes were given at the bottom of the text, and a retrospective questionnaire revealed that many students had ignored them. Annotations at the bottom of a text instead of in the margin (closer to where the words occur in the text) indeed seem less effective. In a study by Cheng and Good (2009), for instance, they brought about an improvement by only 6.5% in the posttest relative to the pretest. Placing the clarifications closer to the unfamiliar words is more helpful (Yanagisawa et al., 2020). Zhang and Webb (2019) even inserted L1 translations in the actual reading text immediately after each target word. The improvement from pretest to posttest was 26%, compared to 10% when students read the text without the translations. It is important to realize that, while my use of percentage figures in this section can help to compare the learning gains in the various experiments, these percentage figures are often based on small sets of target words. For example, Zhang and Webb's (2019) experiment involved 12 target words, and so the students who read the glossed text learned the meaning of on average 2 words more than their peers who read the unmodified text. When the test was administered again one week later the difference shrank to just one word on average. The fact that we are dealing here with small sets of target words is worth bearing in mind lest the percentage figures leave too positive an impression of the learning outcomes. Although these outcomes undeniably indicate that the various text modifications examined here can positively influence vocabulary uptake, it is also undeniable that, for substantial gains in overall vocabulary knowledge to accumulate from this kind of input, learners would need to engage with very large amounts of it.

In the above studies, the words which occurred more than once in the texts were glossed only on their first occurrence. The students may have revisited the gloss when they came across subsequent instances of the word, but it is unknown if that is what the students did. If readers take in an explanation more than once, then this could entrench the information a little deeper in their memory. Rott (2007) examined whether reiterating the marginal gloss for a word repeatedly has this expected effect. Four instances of unknown words were inserted in short texts for students of German. In one version these were accompanied by a gloss on all 4 occasions, and in another version only the first instance was glossed (the other instances were nonetheless made salient by means of bold font). The students' ability to recall the meaning of the words after reading the short texts was found to be better when the glosses had been repeated. It needs to be noted that this repetition of glosses meant that these texts, which were only about 350 words long, had no fewer than 20 glosses (roughly one gloss per 18 words). One must wonder if this abundance of material in the text margin is not likely to tip the balance from a primary focus on text content to deliberate language study (see Cheng & Good, 2009; Huang & Lin, 2014; Watanabe, 1997; and Yoshii, 2006, for more experiments on glossing where the students probably experienced the activities as vocabulary-focused work rather than reading comprehension). Researchers may design materials with a view to investigating incidental acquisition, but whether the actual study participants experience the materials in the way that they were intended is of course not guaranteed. The distinction between incidental and intentional learning can easily get blurred in practice.

As more and more people read text on computer screens, there has been increasing interest in the use of hyperlinks for learners to look up word meanings (Abraham, 2008). As in printed texts, words can be highlighted on screen to indicate that an annotation is available for them. Different from printed texts, however, it is usually up to the reader to mouse-click on a word to call up its gloss in a pop-up window. Since computer software can record if and how often a learner calls up a gloss for a word, this presents a valuable opportunity for researchers to verify whether learners in fact use the information that is at their disposal, because this cannot at all be taken for granted (De Ridder, 2002; Laufer & Hill, 2000; Yoshii, 2013). This holds true even for glosses that are provided in the margin of a text and which therefore require no action from the learner apart from simply looking at them. One eye-tracking experiment found that learners ignored on average 1 in 5 marginal glosses consisting of L2 clarifications (Boers, Warren, Grimshaw, et al., 2017). If glosses attract less attention than is hoped by materials designers who take the trouble of providing them, then this could in part help to explain why incidental vocabulary acquisition from reading glossed texts has in general been unimpressive. After all, one cannot expect an effect of glosses if learners do not even look at them. In an experiment that illustrates this (Montero Perez et al., 2018), students of French watched short video clips twice with either normal captions or captions where keywords were marked as having hyperlinks. The students who watched the clips with the latter type of captions could pause the video and mouse-click on the words to see their translation. Computer software created a log of each student's mouse-clicking data. This revealed that, on average, the students ignored 3.5 of the 18 available glosses and called up only 2.5 of the glosses again during the second viewing of the clips. As expected, it was when learners paused the video to read a gloss that the meaning of the glossed word stood the best chance of being recalled later, especially if learners inspected the same gloss more than once. This raises the question what steps can be taken to direct learners to glosses during reading activities. Teachers could of course straightforwardly tell their students that they should check out every available gloss to ensure good text comprehension (e.g., Khezrlou et al., 2017; Rassaei, 2018). Another option is to create text-comprehension questions the answers to which require engagement with the glossed words. This was done as part of an experiment by Peters et al. (2009), who had students of German read a text on computer screen and answer content-related questions which required comprehension of some words but not others. Put differently, some of the words were more relevant for the task at hand than others (recall from chapter 2 that perceived relevance is one of the factors likely to influence acquisition). Students could mouse-click on words to request clarifications. As expected, the meanings of task-relevant words were looked up far more often than the meaning of words which were not crucial for answering the content-related questions. Also as expected, the former word meanings were far better recalled (45% success rate) than the latter (10.5%) in a posttest.

It could also be argued that taking in the information provided by a gloss requires too little effort to leave strong memories. Perhaps asking learners to look up word meanings in dictionaries themselves might be better, because finding the right information in a dictionary takes more effort. The effort invested in evaluating which dictionary sub-entry corresponds to the contextual use of a word is in theory bene-ficial for learning (Laufer & Hulstijn, 2001). This possibility was actually explored as part of Hulstijn et al.'s (1996) study, which I already mentioned above. Instead of marginal glosses, some of the learners in this experiment were given dictionaries to look up unfamiliar words encountered in the text. Unfortunately, it turned out that few students made use of the dictionaries, probably because dictionary lookups were felt to interrupt the flow of reading. Overall, the learning gains for this group of students were understandably small. Many learners are indeed reluctant to interrupt a reading activity to look up unknown words in a dictionary (Luppescu & Day, 1993). In our modern age, however, online dictionaries are available, and learners may find consulting these easier and less time-consuming (Hill & Laufer, 2003). Nonetheless, in cases of polysemy (and homonymy) a learner will still need to decide which meaning listed in a dictionary fits the reading context, a challenge absent from tailor-made glosses created to assist learners' comprehension of a word in its specific con-text. It is well documented that learners occasionally fail to extract the information from dictionaries that matches the use of a word in context, regardless of whether it concerns a print or online dictionary (e.g., Chen, 2010). The clarity and organization of dictionary entries probably matter more in this regard than whether the learner navigates a print or an electronic version (e.g., Chen, 2011; Dziemianko, 2011).

There have been additional suggestions for prompting engagement with unfami-liar words in a text. Hulstijn (1992), for example, explored the potential of multiple-choice glosses, which oblige readers to determine which of the proposed meanings in the gloss best matches the word's use in the given context. One conclusion was that the number of options in such multiple-choice glosses should be kept small lest learners pick the wrong meaning. Following up on this, Watanabe (1997) included glosses where 2 meanings for the same word were proposed (e.g., *cribs = (1) babies' beds; (2) small beds*), and it was up to the learners to determine which of the 2 fit the context best. Unfortunately, the 2 options in these glosses were often semantically similar and were thus probably both perceived by the learners as plausible matches for the reading context. Since there was no further evidence in the text for students to confirm or rectify their interpretations, it is not surprising that their posttest scores did not trump those of the students who had been provided with regular, single-meaning glosses. The next question, then, is whether immediate confirmation or correction leads to a better outcome. Nagata (1999) investigated this with students of Japanese who were asked to read a text on computer accompanied in the margin by either a single translation or a choice between 2 translations. In the latter case, the students were explicitly asked to make a choice, after which they were informed if their choice was correct or not. This time, the multiple-choice glosses led to better meaning recall (67%) in a posttest immediately after the reading activity than the regular glosses did (54%). Even the latter success rate is quite high in comparison to the rates observed in many of the studies reviewed earlier. However, it needs to be mentioned that the reading text was just 260 words long (which corresponds to about half the length of the present paragraph) and that the students were given 40 minutes to do the activity. This is more than enough time to not only read the text but to start memorizing the glossed words. It is unlikely that the students experienced the marginal glosses merely as assistance with reading comprehension, because there were no fewer than 26 glosses (i.e., one gloss per 10 words on average), and so these occupied virtually as much space on the computer screen as the actual reading text. Besides, the students were given a pretest shortly before the reading activity on the words that were subsequently met as glossed items in the text, which probably alerted them to the vocabulary focus of the activity. This illustrates again that, when robust word learning gains occasionally emerge from experiments with modified texts (also see Rott et al., 2002), this is probably due to the students' deliberate engagement with the language code. A few more studies that made use of glosses, but which *overtly* engaged students in deliberate vocabulary-focused learning, will be mentioned in chapter 5.

I mentioned above that a partial explanation for the modest learning outcomes observed in some of the studies is that glosses may attract insufficient attention. A possible remedy not yet discussed here is to make the glosses more appealing. For example, while the above-mentioned eye-tracking study by Boers, Warren, Grimshaw, et al. (2017) revealed that marginal glosses consisting of verbal definitions were ignored by their participants 20% of the time, glosses containing a picture were ignored far less often (7%). This indicates that pictures attract attention where words alone may fail to do so. Several studies have compared vocabulary uptake from reading activities assisted by different kinds of glosses (see Mohsen & Balakumar, 2011 and Yun, 2011 for meta-analyses). With a few exceptions (e.g., Acha, 2009; Boers, Warren, He, et al., 2017), the results point to the benefits of multimodal glosses, although the nature of the posttest may matter. For example, using a picture as a test prompt will give an advantage to learners who have seen the picture during the reading activity over those who have only seen a translation, and vice versa (e.g., Kost et al., 1999). The informativeness of the glosses matters as well. Yoshii and

Flaitz (2002) and Yoshii (2006) seem to have used textual definitions which under-specified word meaning (e.g., *dash* = *move very quickly*), whereas the combination with a picture in the multimodal gloss provided a more precise meaning (e.g., a picture of a running figure, thus specifying the manner of motion expressed by the verb *dash*). Since the learners received full scores in the posttest only if they supplied the precise meaning of the glossed words (e.g., *dash* = *run very quickly*), it is not surprising that those who had seen the multimodal glosses outperformed their peers who had only seen the underspecified definitions. Had the textual glosses provided the definition that was awarded the maximum score in the posttest, the outcome of this experiment might have been different. Besides studies where textual and pictorial information were co-presented in a single marginal gloss, other studies (e.g., Akbulut, 2007; Jones & Plass, 2002) have examined the benefits of providing textual and pictorial glosses sequentially when learners read texts on a computer screen and can mouse-click on words to call up clarifications. For some of the learners in these experiments only one gloss was available per word, but for others 2 glosses could be called up per word—one textual clarification and the other a picture (occasionally also a video clip or a recording of the word's pronunciation). Posttests typically show better results when 2 glosses were available, which is then considered evidence of the mnemonic benefits of multimodality. An alternative account, though, is that the availability of 2 glosses prompts learners to check the meaning of the words twice instead of just once, and this has a positive effect on learning (Montero Perez et al., 2018; Peters et al., 2009; Ramezanali et al., 2020).

Many authors invoke *Dual Coding Theory* (Paivio, 1986, 1991, 2010) to explain the proclaimed mnemonic benefits of multimodal glosses. According to this theory, words that are associated with a mental image of their referents are easier to remember than words which only have a propositional representation in the mental lexicon. In other words, concrete meanings are easier to remember than abstract meanings, because concrete meanings are imageable whereas abstract meanings are not. Adding pictures to glosses should thus be beneficial as it exploits the imageability of word meanings, so the reasoning goes. However, it is not entirely clear how this line of reasoning helps to explain the findings from above-mentioned experiments on multimodal glossing, because the words glossed with pictures in these experiments had concrete meanings anyhow and were therefore imageable also without the provision of pictures. To give an example, if the word *apple* evokes a mental picture of its referent, then there seems to be little ground for believing that learning its French translation *pomme* makes its referent any less imageable. Put differently, why would a picture of an apple be needed to create a mental image of an apple, if that mental picture is readily called up also by the translation? It is probably when referents are introduced that learners are not yet familiar with, such as objects or actions that are culture-specific or otherwise novel to the learners, that visuals are helpful (Mayer & Anderson, 1992; Mayer & Gallini, 1990). That said, the fact remains that the addition of visuals has often been found to make glosses more effective, for one or more of the reasons just discussed. A potentially interesting avenue for research could be to investigate how the choice of gloss type influences learning when the same word is encountered several times in a text. One study of this kind (Warren et al., 2018), where unfamiliar words occurred twice more in a story after they had been glossed in the margin on their first occurrence, rather unexpectedly found better posttest results when the glosses provided *only a picture* than when they provided both a definition and a picture. It is conceivable that the picture alone left learners with some uncertainty as to the precise meaning of the words, and this may have stimulated further processing of the words when they were re-encountered because the learners needed to fine-tune their interpretation. For example, one of the words denoted a sleeveless jacket, but a picture of a sleeveless jacket as such does not stipulate that the absence of sleeves must be a defining feature of the object. That the absence of sleeves indeed mattered became clear later in the story, when the bare-armed protagonist of the story was described to be clambering through thorny bushes.

There may thus be several ways of engaging learners in more effortful processing of the information provided by a gloss. A final example here is Boers (2000), an experiment where university students specializing in commerce and economics read a text containing metaphorically used items such as *hurdles* (in the sense of diffi-culties to be overcome), *wean off* (as in *weaning an industry off state support*) and *weed out* (as in *weeding out corruption*). Although these items occurred in the text in these abstract meanings, they also have literal meanings (*hurdles* are the barriers that ath-letes jump over in track sports such as steeplechase, *weaning off* means gradually stop breastfeeding one's baby, and *weeding* refers to pulling out unwanted plants in one's garden). Half of the students read the text with marginal glosses which only gave these literal meanings; the other half received glosses paraphrasing the abstract uses from the text (e.g., *hurdles* = difficulties; *weaning off* = making independent; *weeding out* = removing). Three days later, the students were given a new text but with blanks for them to recall and insert the words and expressions that were glossed in the earlier text. The students who had received only the literal meanings were more successful at this gap-fill exercise, even though the target items were again used in their abstract senses. A possible explanation for this is that these students needed to put some effort into working out the connection between the literal meaning given in the gloss and the contextual, metaphorical use of the items. The literal meanings may also have made the items easier to remember. This is where *Dual Coding Theory* offers a plausible account—linking abstract word uses to their literal origins increases their imageability. I will say more about this possibility in chapter 7.

Phrases

When it comes to phrases, a recurring focus in the research has been on L2 learners' acquisition of the conventional combinations of words (or word part-nerships) in the target language, referred to in the literature as *collocations* (see, e.g.,

Boers and Webb, 2018, for an overview of this strand of research). For example, in English the combination *slim chance* is conventional while *narrow chance* is not; *keep an eye on someone* is conventional while *hold an eye on someone* is not; *deeply in love with someone* is conventional while *profoundly in love* is not. Even though 2 words are near-synonymous, substituting one for the other often results in word combinations that are considered odd (Nesselhauf, 2003). L2 learners cannot safely transfer combinations that are conventional in their L1 to produce L2 phrases, because they may not be conventional in L2. For example, the French counterpart of English *have a dream* is 'make a dream', and the Dutch counterpart of *make an effort* is 'do an effort'. Learning collocation (i.e., learning which words tend to seek each other's company) is of course but one of the challenges in developing knowledge of L2 phraseology. Another challenge lies with comprehension, because many phrases have meanings that are not easily inferable from their constituent words. These are called *idioms* (e.g., *call the shots, keep tabs on someone, see red, in a nutshell*). However, because in the strand of research to be reviewed here it is collocations (rather than idioms) that have most often been of interest, it is this facet of vocabulary knowledge that I will focus on for now.

Several of the text-modification techniques meant to increase the likelihood that learners pick up words from textual input have in recent years also been explored in connection with phrases. One such text modification is to increase the number of encounters with the same phrase. For example, Webb et al. (2013) incorporated 18 verb–noun phrases (e.g., *raise questions*) into short stories. The texts were accompanied by an audio-recording of the stories for the learners to silently read along with. Learners read 1 of 4 versions of the texts, which differed in the number of instances of each target phrase (once, 5, 10, and 15 times). As expected, repetition positively influenced learning, and after 10 and 15 encounters the average scores in a recall test where the learners were presented with the verbs of the phrases and invited to recall their associated nouns (e.g., *raise* ____) were 28% and 56%, respectively. It needs to be mentioned that these repeated encounters with the same phrases occurred in a relatively short time span (30 to 35 minutes' worth of reading). Seeding short stories with such an abundance of instances of the same phrases must have required considerable time and effort on the part of the research team. Teachers who themselves wish to modify texts in this way may find a more moderate amount of seeding better feasible. Unfortunately, moderate seeding reduces the impact dramatically. After reading the story versions in Webb et al. (2013) that exposed them to 5 instances of the same phrase, the students obtained a score of just 11% in the above-mentioned test, that is, less than 2 out of 18 test items. (See Pellicer-Sánchez, 2017, for a similar experiment.)

Compared to inserting multiple instances of the same phrases in a text, visually enhancing phrases already present in the original version of a text is much easier to implement, and research suggests that making phrases stand out in a text can reduce the need for multiple encounters. Boers, Demecheleer, et al. (2017), for example, presented learners with texts that were only manipulated by underlining phrases. The learners were found more likely in a post-reading test to recognize these phrases, even though they occurred only once. Recognizing phrases that one has seen before is of course just a preliminary step in knowledge development. Evidence of productive knowledge would be more informative. Such evidence was garnered by Choi (2017). Participants were asked to read a text containing 14 phrases in either an enhanced or unenhanced version while their eye movements were tracked. The latter was done to ascertain that the typographic enhancement (boldface) effectively drew the students' attention to the phrases (see below, for more studies of this kind). The eye-movement data confirmed that the phrases in the enhanced version of the text attracted more and longer fixations than the same phrases in the unenhanced version of the text. Two weeks later, a productive recall test (L1 to L2 translation) was administered. The students who had read the enhanced text recalled on average 3 target phrases (21%) which they did not yet know prior to the reading activity, while their peers who had read the unenhanced version recalled on average just 1.5 (10.5%). A learning gain of 3 phrases may seem marginal, but this was a challenging test, especially as it was administered with a delay. Interestingly, the learners who read the enhanced version of the text were less able to remember segments of the text which had been left untouched than their peers who had read the version without any enhancement. Students probably interpret typographic enhancement as an effort on the part of the teacher/materials designer to flag the important elements of a text, and so it is not so surprising that students will then focus less on what is left unenhanced. Typographic enhancement of phrases has also become possible in the case of audiovisual input, thanks to captioning software. Majuddin et al. (2019) had students of English watch an episode of an American sitcom with either normal captions or captions in which 18 phrases (e.g., *I beg to differ*) were enhanced (underlined and in bold font). Each of these target phrases occurred only once. In a productive recall test administered shortly after watching the video, the students who had seen the enhanced captions recalled on average 4 phrases (22%) they did not previously know, while the students who had seen the normal captions recalled on average 3 (17%). A possibility for improving learning gains is to play the same video twice, so students can become familiar with its content during the first viewing and can then attend better to the language code during the second viewing. This logically also doubles the number of encounters with the lexical items. In Majuddin et al. (2019), some groups of students watched the same sitcom episode twice, again either with normal or enhanced captions. As expected, the repeated viewing positively influenced learning, with the enhanced captions bringing about the best result: on average close to 7 phrases (39%) learned, compared to about 5 (28%) in the normal captions condition. However, on a test about the content of the video, the group which had been exposed to the enhanced captions performed more poorly than their peers who had been exposed to the normal captions. It thus appears that typographic enhancement can create a trade-off in students' allocation of their attentional resources: while they pay more attention to *how* things are said, they pay less attention to *what* is said.

A few studies have combined the 2 text-modification techniques—flooding the text with instances of the target phrases plus making them salient through typographic enhancement. Szudarski and Carter (2016) had students read several texts in which target phrases (verb-noun collocations, such as *take a shortcut*, and adjective-noun collocations, such as *deep aversion*) occurred either 6 or 12 times each. In one version of the texts these were underlined; in another they were not. In a test where the nouns were given and the students were required to provide their associated verbs or adjectives, the best results were, as expected, observed for the condition where the underlined phrases had been met as often as 12 times. The researchers also included a test on the meaning of the phrases, but this revealed no effect of either repetition or enhancement—in fact the meaning of most phrases remained obscure to the learners. As said before, typographic enhancement can make items stand out in a text, but this cannot ensure that the items will also be understood if no informative contextual clues are available. In Sonbul and Schmitt (2013) and Toomer and Elgort (2019), comprehension of the target phrases was facilitated through inclusion of definitions in the texts (akin to the use of so-called appositives mentioned earlier). The target phrases in these experiments were 15 medical terms (e.g., *stone heart*) occurring several times in specialized reading texts, either enhanced (in red and bold font) or unenhanced. One of the posttests presented the learners with the second word and the meaning of the phrases as cues for them to recall the associated first word. After 3 encounters with the enhanced phrases in Sonbul and Schmitt (2013) the success rate on this test was 52%. This compared to 35% after 3 encounters with the unenhanced phrases. The positive effect of typographic enhancement was confirmed in Toomer and Elgort's (2019) replication study: after 9 encounters with the enhanced phrases, the success rate was 75%, as compared to 64% after the same number of encounters with the unenhanced phrases. Overall, a combination of flooding texts with instances of the same phrases and making these perceptually salient thus appears to have the greatest positive effect, at least as far as acquisition of the lexical composition of the phrases is concerned. It needs to be said again, however, that while researchers can invest time in the creation of texts with an artificially high number of repetitions of the same items, this may not be a realistic option for teachers. Textbook writers might be resourceful enough to apply these techniques (albeit in moderation, lest the text becomes too contrived), but then the next question concerns the matter of selection or prioritization. After all, there are thousands of potentially useful phrases. Corpus frequency may be a good proxy to estimate the usefulness of a phrase, but frequency can only be one of several criteria for selection (Martinez & Schmitt, 2012), because learners need more help with some phrases than others.

In sum, typographic enhancement appears relatively effective as a means of pointing out phrases to learners (where the learners might otherwise not realize a given word string is in fact a conventional lexical unit) and at pointing out their lexical composition (which is especially useful when L1 counterparts are different).

In this sense, there may in fact be a stronger rationale for applying typographic enhancement to phrases than to single words. Owing to the nature of the script of many languages where words are separated from one another by blank spaces, single words are likely to be recognized as distinct units anyhow. The enhancement then serves the purpose of signalling that a given word merits special attention for one reason or another. In the case of multiword items, however, learners may fail to recognize these as constituting distinct semantic units were it not for the enhancement—provided the learners sense this is what the enhancement is intended for. As said, in neither case does enhancement alone help learners to also acquire the meaning of the phrases. It is therefore semantically transparent phrases that are most directly learnable through enhancement alone, while phrases containing words that the learner does not yet know or phrases whose meaning does not follow straightforwardly from that of the constituent words (i.e., idioms) will require additional steps.

In addition to the experiments reviewed here, there have been other studies involving typographic enhancement of phrases, but these will be reviewed later in the book (in chapter 5) because they belong to the realm of language-focused learning, while for now we are looking at activities (such as reading for comprehension) intended to be primarily content-focused.

Patterns

Research about ways of promoting uptake of grammar patterns from textual input has also predominantly focused on the effects of textual enhancement, where this is typically implemented as a combination of flooding a text with instances of a selected target pattern and typographically enhancing these instances (e.g., through using boldface, underlining, italics or colour highlighting). That it is the cumulative effect of flooding and typographic enhancement which has been examined in this line of inquiry is worth emphasizing. As I mentioned previously, if teachers choose to modify a text themselves with a view to directing their students' attention, they may find the task of flooding the text with instances of target items or patterns daunting and time-consuming. Highlighting instances already present in the original text is probably the more realistic option for most teachers. If so, it follows that, unless teachers use texts that have already been modified for them by materials writers, it is the grammar patterns which naturally occur repeatedly in a text that may lend themselves best to this intervention, because the presence of just 1 or 2 instances is unlikely to suffice for learners to discern a recurring pattern. That the experiments on the benefits of typographic enhancement reviewed below used textual input that was also intentionally flooded with instances of a selected grammar pattern is worth bearing in mind, lest the considerable number of such experiments leave the impression that this is an intervention that is straightforwardly applicable to a wider range of target patterns than it actually is.

As in the studies reviewed in the preceding sections, the research design that is commonly used here is to test learners' knowledge of a selected grammar pattern before and after they read one or more texts in which the pattern is or is not typographically made salient. A useful example of such a study is Lee (2007). Korean students of English read 3 texts which were flooded with instances of passive-voice sentences. One group of students read versions of the texts where the instances were bolded, while another group read versions without any typographic enhancement of these instances. The students' knowledge of the form of the passive voice was tested before and after the reading activities by means of an error-spotting task, also known as a grammaticality judgement test: The students were presented with 10 sentences containing errors (e.g., *They were exciting about the unexpected results of the soccer game; He was offer the job but did not accept it; Snow boarding considered as the most exciting winter sport among teens*), and they were to correct these if they detected an error. The students who were given the text versions with typographically enhanced instances of the passive voice were found to improve their test scores more than the students who were given the versions without enhancement. The latter group in fact showed hardly any improvement. This demonstrates that typographic enhancement can indeed make a difference also in the case of grammar patterns. It needs to be mentioned, though, that the learning gains were not spectacular: an average improvement from pretest to posttest of about 2.5 out of 10 test items. It is important to note as well that the test used here measures only knowledge of the formal characteristics of the passive voice. It does not assess whether the learners also understand the communicative function of this grammar pattern. In other words, students in this experiment may have improved their knowledge of the formal properties of passive sentences somewhat, but this does not mean they also learned what purpose the passive voice serves. Lee (2007) also tested the students' ability to recall text content after reading the texts with or without typographic enhancement. Reminiscent of what was mentioned previously in connection with some of the studies on typographic enhancement of phrases (e.g., Choi, 2017), the enhancement appeared to have attracted students' attention at the cost of the unenhanced parts of the text, thus negatively affecting their recall of text content.

Lee and Huang (2008) reviewed a collection of 16 studies on the effectiveness of textual enhancement for grammar acquisition available at the time and concluded that the effect tends to be small. Several more experimental studies on textual enhancement have appeared since Lee and Huang (2008), but the overall conclusion remains unchanged: when a positive effect on grammar learning is attested, it is typically on the small side. In a study by Labrozzi (2016), for example, learners of Spanish read a text in which present and past tense markers were typographically enhanced. The pretest and the posttests required the learners to translate present and past tense verbs into their L1—thus testing their ability to distinguish between the 2 form-meaning pairings. The learners who had been given enhanced text versions improved their scores from pretest to posttest by on average just about 2.5 out of 20 test items. This was nonetheless a better outcome than that of a comparison group who had read an unenhanced version because that group showed hardly any improvement. Some studies have in fact failed to demonstrate any advantage for enhanced texts over unenhanced ones. For example, in an experiment by Meguro (2017), Japanese students of English read 3 texts in which tag questions (e.g., *[…], don't you?*) were either enhanced or not enhanced. Multiple-choice tests requiring the students to choose the correct form of tag questions revealed no benefits of enhancement. The improvement from pretest to posttest was negligible (on average just about one out of 18 test items). No effect of typographic enhancement was observed in a study by Della Putta (2016) about Italian grammar either. Even though the students had been exposed to 50 enhanced instances of a grammar pattern across 5 lessons, their average score on a grammaticality judgement test (a test where they had to decide if a sentence was correct or not) remained below 60%—not much better than chance—and similar scores were obtained after reading texts where the pattern had *not* been visually enhanced.

One possible explanation for the limited impact that typographic enhancement seems to have on grammar learning is that it might not attract as much attention as is assumed. Several of the more recent experimental studies in this strand have examined this possibility. Jahan and Kormos (2015), in a study where the future reference markers *going to* and *will* were enhanced in texts, asked the students after the reading activity if they had noticed this. Close to 80% of them reported they had. While this confirms the attention-drawing potential of enhancement, it nonetheless indicates that it may also go unnoticed by at least some learners. Incidentally, although the majority of the students in this experiment reported noticing the enhanced target elements, the effect of this turned out negligible. Their improvement from a pretest to a posttest which required them to choose between *going to* and *will* in a sentence-completion task was, on average, just one out of 10 items. The difference between *going to* and *will* to express future reference may be too hard to infer from textual input alone, regardless of whether these forms are made visually salient. Other studies have made use of eye-tracking as a way of capturing what readers pay attention to as they are reading. We already mentioned such studies when we discussed uptake of words and phrases from reading. The same methodology is being applied increasingly often in the realm of research on grammar learning. For example, Winke (2013) replicated Lee's (2007) experiment targeting English passive voice, but in addition to pre-testing and posttesting she recorded the students' eye-movements during reading. The latter data confirmed that typographically enhanced text elements attract more and longer fixations. On the downside, this replication study did *not* furnish evidence that the enhancement benefited students' learning of the grammar pattern under examination: the students who read the enhanced text did not improve their ability to correct passive voice errors any more than did those who read the unenhanced version. Both groups improved their scores from the pretest to the posttest by, on average, just about one out of 10 test items. A possible explanation for the different outcomes in Winke (2013) and Lee (2007), proposed by Winke herself, is that the learner-participants in her study had not received any prior instruction about the passive voice, whereas the participants in Lee's experiment had received explicit instruction at some earlier time in their English courses. Perhaps typographic enhancement is less helpful as a means of introducing new patterns than it is to illustrate or remind learners of patterns that were explicitly introduced earlier. This is a possibility I will return to further below.

Two other eye-tracking experiments (Issa & Morgan-Short, 2019; Issa et al., 2015), however, which also involved learners who had not yet received explicit instruction on the target pattern—the use of the Spanish direct object pronouns *lo* and *la* in sentences such as *lo besa* (she kisses him) and *la besa* (he kisses her)—did yield some evidence that typographic enhancement not only attracts attention but also benefits learning. Intriguingly, though, in Issa et al. (2015) no correlation was found between the learners' eye fixations on the instances of said grammar pattern and how much they improved on the test. The findings by Winke (2013) and Issa et al. (2015) are a useful reminder that, while attention is crucial for learning, the amount of attention given to a target item or pattern in a text is clearly not the only factor that influences the likelihood of learning. The *quality* of the cognitive operations performed as one gives attention to a language element or feature and how the information is processed further must play a vital part as well. What also matters is what information a learner is required to look for during a reading task. For example, in one of the experiments about Spanish direct object pronouns *lo* and *la*, the participants were given tasks which directed their attention to different language elements than the direct object pronouns. If the learners did not perceive these pronouns to be particularly relevant for the tasks at hand, it is not surprising they did not learn them well. It also needs to be noted that Issa et al.'s (2015) and Issa and Morgan-Short's (2019) experiments do not fit optimally in the present chapter, because, unlike the other experiments reviewed here so far, they used decontextualized sentences as stimuli rather than texts in the more conventional sense of the word. The same comment applies to a study by Lee and Révész (2018). In this study, Korean students of English were presented with very short audio-recorded narrative passages which first introduced a character (e.g., *my grandmother*) and then switched to the use of the pronoun (e.g., *she*) to refer to this antecedent (the noun introduced before) in the remainder of the passage. The students were asked to match sentences to pictures (e.g., what the grandmother was described to be doing). The target for learning here was the distinction between the English pronouns *he, she* and *they* (which is something L1 Korean learners find difficult). For half of the students, the antecedent noun phrase and the subsequent instances of the pronoun were highlighted in the sentences. The eye-tracking data showed that this had an attention-catching effect, but this effect was much clearer for the antecedents (i.e., the nouns: e.g., *my grandmother*) than the pronouns. The finding that the pronouns attracted comparatively little attention is not surprising—once the reader understood from the antecedent noun phrase (e.g., *my grandmother*) who the passage was about, there was little need to pay attention to the personal pronoun (e.g., *she*) since its referent stayed the same in the text passage. More surprising, then, is the finding that the group of students who had read the enhanced versions of the passages nonetheless made greater improvement from a pretest to a posttest about pronoun choice than the group who had read the unenhanced versions. However, similar to Issa et al. (2015), no compelling evidence emerged that it was those students who had fixated on the target elements the most who made the greatest improvement on the test. An experimental study which did show the expected positive relation between fixations on instances of a given pattern and the likelihood of the pattern being learned was conducted by Indrarathne and Kormos (2017). Apart from examining the effect of enhancement, their study also included a more explicit instructional intervention, but for now I will review only what Indrarathne and Kormos's (2017) experiment reveals about the benefits of enhancement. The learners in this experiment were students of English in Sri Lanka, and the target pattern was the causative *have* construction (e.g., *They had their house painted*), which these learners had little or no prior knowledge of. The students in the reading conditions of interest for now read 3 text passages containing a total of 21 instances of this construction. Some of the students read a version of the texts in which the instances were bolded, while others read a version without typographic enhancement. Changes in their knowledge of the pattern were gauged by means of a sentence-rewriting task which invited use of causative *have* and a grammaticality judgement test. The group of students who read the enhanced text passages showed more improvement from pretest to posttest than those who read the unenhanced versions. The amount of improvement was again small, however. The students who had read the enhanced versions improved their scores on average by less than one item out of 6 and just 1.5 out of 10 in the sentence-rewriting and the grammaticality judgement test, respectively. Those who had read the unenhanced versions hardly improved their scores at all.

The recurring finding is thus that *when* typographic enhancement is found to have a positive influence on grammar learning over and above flooding a text with instances of the target pattern, this is relative to a reading condition whose effect on grammar learning is negligible.

Worse, some studies on typographic enhancement show neither an effect on attention nor an effect on learning. In an experiment with learners of Spanish by Loewen and Inceoglu (2016), where the enhancement (different colour fonts) was intended to direct attention to 2 past tense forms, the learners did not fixate on these forms much more often or for much longer in comparison to a group who read the same text without enhancement. There may be an explanation for this unexpected result, however. The input text used here was a very short version (about 200 words) of a familiar story (*Little Red Riding Hood*), and the students were given as much time as they liked to read it. On average, they spent 15 minutes on it, which is arguably long enough to closely study such a short text instead of just reading it with an interest in the story line. Moreover, the students had just been telling the story in Spanish themselves, prompted by a series of pictures. As the story content was thus already familiar to them, they could devote their attention to the wording and grammar used in the model text so as to compare it to how they themselves had tried to tell the story (see chapter 4 for similar procedures). This use of textual input is therefore rather different from other experiments on textual enhancement, where it was expected that learners would engage with the content of texts rather than treat the texts as language-study material. If both groups of learners in Loewen and Inceoglu (2016) read the short text in a studious manner regardless of enhancement, then this could explain why the comparison of the 2 groups' eye-tracking data produced no strong evidence of its influence on reading behaviour. Given that the enhancement did not appear to significantly influence reading behaviour, it is not surprising either that the amount of learning of the target patterns (i.e., the 2 Spanish past tenses) did not differ between students who read the enhanced version and those who read the unenhanced version of the text. The improvements from a pretest to a posttest which required the students to turn the infinitive form of verbs into their appropriate past tense form nonetheless turned out very small (by on average just 1.2 out of 18 test items), which at first sight is surprising. However, to perform well on this test, learners needed to know not only the formal characteristics of the 2 tenses but also when to use which. An analogy may be drawn here with the English simple past tense (*gave*) and the present perfect tense (*have given*). Knowing how to conjugate a verb in accordance with a tense is one thing, but knowing when to use one tense rather than the other (i.e., distinguishing the 2 form-meaning pairings) is quite another. Similar to what was mentioned earlier in connection to Jahan and Kormos's (2015) experiment targeting the use of *will* and *going to*, it must be very difficult for learners to infer the precise meaning and use of such patterns just from seeing a number of instances in a short text. Also, without going into detail here, one of the challenges learners of Spanish face is to determine which verbs are compatible with one but not the other tense. Many of the verbs in the tests used in Loewen and Inceoglu (2016) did not occur in the story which the students were asked to read. So, even if the highlighted instances of the tense forms in the story raised the learners' awareness of the existence of 2 distinct ways of referring to the past in Spanish, this will not have helped them choose the appropriate tense form when confronted with novel verbs in the test if they did not yet know which of the 2 tenses these verbs were compatible with. This illustrates again that system learning and item learning are inseparable.

Considerations such as this also raise the question whether the types of test that have been used in studies on the benefits of typographic enhancement for grammar learning thus far are optimally suitable to detect evidence of the kind of learning that can realistically be expected from exposure to texts alone. Typographic enhancement may direct learners' attention to the presence of a certain linguistic form in a text, but that, as such, does not guarantee that the learner will also understand the meaning or function of that form, unless contextual information were to make this clear enough or clarifications were provided in the form of annotations or glosses. While common in the realm of vocabulary research, the latter option remains underexplored when it comes to grammar (but see Jung, 2016, for an exception). If typographic enhancement alone cannot clarify meaning, then it follows that it is tests of *form* knowledge that are best suited to capture the kind of learning that can reasonably be expected from this type of text modification. But even the tests gauging learners' uptake of formal features may not have been optimal. For example, a grammaticality judgement test requires test takers to distinguish between what *is* appropriate and what is *not* appropriate in the target language. However, the input texts which learners read in these studies can only provide examples of what *is* done in that language. Put differently, they provide positive evidence but no negative evidence (informing learners that something is *not* right). In order to develop an intuition for what is *un*conventional in a language, one first needs to develop a sense of what *is* conventional. In the absence of explicit instruction, developing this intuition must require numerous encounters of instances to the point that a deviation from a recurring pattern is indeed perceived as a deviation.

Another problem already mentioned previously is that, even if learners manage to discern a pattern from a series of its instances in an enhanced text, this does not by itself inform the learners about its usage restrictions (Han et al., 2008). For example, one might typographically enhance all the –ed endings of regular past tense verbs in a text to help learners notice this inflectional morpheme. Unfortunately, learners may then over-use the pattern (e.g., *drived; *lended). Similarly, one might flood a text with relative clauses starting with *who* (e.g., *my daughter, who is a talented singer, …*), but this may not prevent learners from over-extending the use of this pronoun (e.g., **the city Dresden, who was destroyed in the war, …*). One might of course try flooding the text with multiple instances of different relative pronouns (*who, which, that* and *whose*) and for the sake of comprehensiveness even include both defining and non-defining relative clauses (i.e., with or without commas to separate the relative clause from the main clause). The English relative clause system is very complex, however, and it would require a great many instances for language learners to work it out, even if these learners were endowed with exceptional analytical skills. The same can be said about the system of tag questions (*…haven't you? …did he?*), which was the subject of Meguro's (2017) study, which I mentioned above, and so it is no wonder that so little learning was observed in that study. Instead, it is probably the comparatively simple patterns (i.e., with minimal variability in appearance and demonstrating unique form-function pairings) that lend themselves relatively well to textual enhancement as an intervention on its own.

It remains puzzling that several of the studies reviewed above failed to find a positive association between the amount of attention (as gauged by means of eye-tracking) that learners gave to the typographically enhanced elements in a text and their grammar learning. It is difficult to tell from the behavioural data collected in these studies how the learner-participants experienced the presence of typographic enhancement (bold font, etc.), but it is nonetheless worth asking whether they always realized what the enhancement was meant to draw their attention to. It is even conceivable that in some cases, when complete noun phrases or clauses were enhanced, as was done for the causative *have* construction in Indrarathme and Kormos's (2017) experiment, learners assumed this was meant to draw their attention to important text content. In other cases, when enhancement was meant to draw learners' attention to the inter-dependency of different elements (e.g., antecedent noun – pronoun), learners may not have realized this. The distance between such elements in a text may play a part here. For example, in *She has five cats*, it is probably easy for learners to guess that both the quantifier and the suffix –s in *cats* are underlined to illustrate plurality. Not all such inter-dependencies are adjacent, however. For example, in *If I'd known you were coming to visit me, I would have prepared your favourite meal*, it may not be self-evident to learners that the 2 underlined parts should be processed in association with one another. Although eye-tracking may show that certain elements in a text receive more attention if they are typographically enhanced, it does not necessarily follow that the learner recognizes that it is the *combination* of these different elements that matters. One might consider deploying additional text-modification techniques, such as adding bidirectional arrows between related elements in the text or using different enhancement types (e.g., boldface vs. underlining; different colour codes) to indicate distinct phenomena, but this then raises the question how far these modifications can be stretched before they become too distracting. A related question is how much of a text can be typographically enhanced before the enhancement defeats its purpose of making selected elements perceptually salient. After all, the more elements are enhanced, the less each of the enhanced elements will stand out relative to the rest of the text. An additional practical limitation to typographic enhancement is that it is difficult to enhance the *absence* of a feature. For example, one might want to draw learners' attention to the absence of the definite article in a certain noun phrase (e.g., *France*, not *the France*) or the absence of plural –s (e.g., *sheep*, not *sheeps*), but one can hardly use a different font to highlight what is *not* there in the first place. Della Putta (2016), whose experiment I briefly mentioned above, in fact tried to indicate the absence of a certain element by drawing arrows under the word sequences where it was absent, but this turned out to be ineffective. Another practical issue (already mentioned before) is that, unless the pattern of interest naturally occurs frequently enough in an authentic text for learners to determine its regularities, materials writers will need to modify existing texts or create texts flooded artificially with instances of the pattern that they wish to typographically enhance. This is indeed what was done by the researchers who conducted the studies reviewed in this section, but it is debatable whether teachers are in a position to invest the time it requires. In reality, then, there may not be many grammar patterns that lend themselves straightforwardly to this intervention. Digitally extracting a collection of examples of a grammar pattern (or of lexical items, for that matter) from an online language corpus (i.e., a large collection of texts) could be an alternative, but that is a topic I will discuss in chapter 5.

It is useful to reiterate that the present section has reviewed the use of textual enhancement as a way of promoting learners' uptake of language features and elements without distracting them from the content of the texts—that is, the primary focus was meant to be on text content, not language study. The fundamental problem, however, is that it is very difficult to attend to the content of a message and its linguistic packaging at the same time (Skehan, 1998). There is arguably a contradiction in the rationale for textual enhancement: On the one hand, enhancement is intended to shift learners' attention to language features which will otherwise go unnoticed during content-focused reading; on the other hand, it is hoped that enhancement is so *un*intrusive that it does *not* divert attention away from content. Typographic enhancement could of course also be incorporated in a *sequence* of activities, where the learners at some stage do engage more directly with the linguistic packaging of the message. One simple option is to have learners read a text twice (Han et al., 2008), first with a focus on content and then again with a focus on a language feature which could be typographically enhanced in the second reading of the text but left untouched in the first. As the content of the text will be familiar when the text is read the second time, the learner should be better able to attend to language features without compromising text comprehension. A further step could be to leave some of the instances of the selected pattern untouched and to ask the students themselves to identify them (see chapter 5 about "discovery learning")—but this would then shift the focus overtly from text content to the language code. Typographic enhancement can indeed also be used in conjunction with explicit language-focused instruction. This was in fact done in the aforementioned experiment by Indrarathne and Kormos (2017) with one of their groups of participants. This group was given explanations about the causative *have* construction (e.g., *I had my watch repaired*) before they read texts with typographically enhanced instances of this construction. As could be expected, the learning gains attested for this group were much better—more than 3 times as high on the sentence-reconstruction test—than those of the group who had merely read the enhanced texts. This clearly indicates that investing a little bit of time in giving explicit explanations is worth doing.

In fact, one may even ask the question whether explicit instructions about a grammar pattern might not make the typographic enhancement of its instances superfluous. In Cintrón-Valentín et al. (2019), for example, students of Spanish first received explicit instruction about grammar patterns and then watched captioned video clips in which the instances of the patterns were either enhanced or left in their regular font. Enhancement was *not* found to make a difference. It is possible that the explicit instruction sufficed to raise the students' awareness of the instances of the grammar patterns even in the absence of typographic enhancement. An eye-tracking experiment could help to test this possibility. On the other hand, it is also possible that the learning gains were simply due to the explicit teaching, and that watching the video clips added little, regardless of whether they included enhancement. The benefits of pre-teaching were also illustrated in a study by Pujadas and Muñoz (2019), albeit regarding vocabulary: teaching students a set of target words before having them watch captioned videos including instances of the words led to learning gains that were twice as large as the gains from watching the captioned videos alone. The practice of explicitly teaching words, phrases or grammar patterns clearly belongs to the realm of language-focused approaches, however, and so will be discussed later in the book. The point I wanted to make here is that, even if modified textual input alone is not very effective, it may still be a useful part of a larger ensemble of learning activities—a point I will elaborate on in chapter 8.

Further Reflection

What Text Modifications Are Used in Your L2 Textbook?

Examine a contemporary L2 textbook for the text-modification features discussed in this chapter. What kind of language elements are they applied to? Do the techniques used by the textbook authors(s) resemble what was done in the research studies reviewed in this chapter? Are the (modified) texts used only for content-focused activities or are they also used at some point to explicitly draw learners' attention to examples of certain words, phrases or grammar features?

Are Grammar Explanations Also "Texts"?

Examine the sections in a contemporary L2 textbook that give explanations about grammar. Do these include the use of typographic enhancement (boldface, underlining, highlighting)? If so, what purpose might this serve? After all, these sections overtly direct learners' attention to the language code anyhow, and so might the enhancement not be superfluous in this case?

What Purposes Do Pictures Serve?

Pictures (or visual illustrations more generally) were mentioned in the section about word learning as a way of making glosses more appealing and as a way of clarifying meanings where textual descriptions might fail. These are not the only purposes for which pictures are used in L2 textbooks. Examine a contemporary L2 textbook for the use of visuals. Are the visuals often used to clarify meaning, are they used as prompts to elicit language from the students, or are they just included to make the pages more appealing? When pictures are used to clarify meaning, would you consider them truly helpful?

References

Abraham, L. B. (2008). Computer-mediated glosses in second language reading comprehension and vocabulary learning: A meta-analysis. *Computer Assisted Language Learning*, 21, 199–226. https://doi.org/10.1080/09588220802090246

Acha, J. (2009). The effectiveness of multimedia programmes in children's vocabulary learning. *British Journal of Educational Technology*, 40, 23–31. https://doi.org/10.1111/j.1467-8535.2007.00800.x

Akbulut, Y. (2007). Effects of multimedia annotations on incidental vocabulary learning and reading comprehension of advanced learners of English as a foreign language. *Instructional Science*, 35, 499–517.https://doi.org/10.1007/s11251-007-9016-7

Bensoussan, M., & Laufer, B. (1984). Lexical guessing in context in EFL reading comprehension. *Journal of Research in Reading*, 7, 15–32. https://doi.org/10.1111/j.1467-9817.1984.tb00252.x

Boers, F. (2000). Enhancing metaphoric awareness in specialised reading. *English for Specific Purposes*, 19, 137–147. https://doi.org/10.1016/S0889-4906(98)00017-9

Boers, F., Demecheleer, M., He, L., Deconinck, J., Stengers, H., & Eyckmans, J. (2017). Typographic enhancement of multiword units in second language text. *International Journal of Applied Linguistics*, 27, 448–469. https://doi.org/10.1111/ijal.12141

Boers, F., Warren, P., Grimshaw, G., & Siyanova-Chanturia, A. (2017). On the benefits of multimodal annotations for vocabulary uptake from reading. *Computer Assisted Language Learning*, 30, 709–725. https://doi.org/10.1080/09588221.2017.1356335

Boers, F., Warren, P., He, L., & Deconinck, J. (2017). Does adding pictures to glosses enhance vocabulary uptake from reading? *System*, 66, 113–129. https://doi.org/10.1016/j.system.2017.03.017

Boers, F., & Webb, S. (2018). Teaching and learning collocation in adult second and foreign language learning. *Language Teaching*, 51, 77–89. https://doi.org/10.1017/S0261444817000301

Chen, C., & Truscott, J. (2010). The effects of repetition and L1 lexicalization on incidental vocabulary acquisition. *Applied Linguistics*, 31, 693–713. https://doi.org/10.1093/applin/amq031

Chen, Y. (2010). Dictionary use and EFL Learning. A contrastive study of pocket electronic dictionaries and paper dictionaries. *International Journal of Lexicography*, 23, 275–306. https://doi.org/10.1093/ijl/ecq013

Chen, Y. (2011). Studies on bilingualized dictionaries: The user perspective. *International Journal of Lexicography*, 24, 161–197. https://doi.org/10.1093/ijl/ecr002

Cheng, Y.-H., & Good, R. L. (2009). L1 glosses: Effects on EFL learners' reading comprehension and vocabulary retention. *Reading in a Foreign Language*, 21, 119–142. https://files.eric.ed.gov/fulltext/EJ859583.pdf

Cintrón-Valentín, M., García-Amaya, L., & Ellis, N. C. (2019). Captioning and grammar learning in the L2 Spanish classroom. *The Language Learning Journal*, 47, 439–459. https://doi.org/10.1080/09571736.2019.1615978

Choi, S. (2017). Processing and learning of enhanced English collocations: An eye-movement study. *Language Teaching Research*, 21, 403–426. https://doi.org/10.1177/1362168816653271

Della Putta, P. (2016). The effects of textual enhancement on the acquisition of two nonparallel grammatical features by Spanish-speaking learners of Italian. *Studies in Second Language Acquisition*, 38, 217–238. https://doi.org/10.1017/S0272263116000073

De Ridder, I. (2002). Visible or invisible links: Does the highlighting of hyperlinks affect incidental vocabulary learning, text comprehension, and the reading process? *Language Learning & Technology*, 6, 123–146. http://dx.doi.org/10125/2514

Dziemianko, A. (2011). User-friendliness of noun and verb coding systems in pedagogical dictionaries of English: A case of Polish learners. *International Journal of Lexicography*, 24, 50–78. https://doi.org/10.1093/ijl/ecq037

Han, Z., Park, E. S., & Combs, C. (2008). Textual enhancement of input: Issues and possibilities. *Applied Linguistics*, 29, 597–618. https://doi.org/10.1093/applin/amn010

Hennebry, M., Rogers, V., Macaro, E., & Murphy, V. (2013). Direct teaching of vocabulary after listening: Is it worth the effort and what method is best? *Language Learning Journal*, 45, 282–300. https://doi.org/10.1080/09571736.2013.849751

Hill, M., & Laufer, B. (2003). Type of task, time-on-task and electronic dictionaries in incidental vocabulary acquisition. *International Review of Applied Linguistics*, 41, 87–106. https://doi.org/10.1515/iral.2003.007

Horst, M., Cobb, T., & Meara, P. (1998). Beyond A Clockwork Orange: Acquiring second language vocabulary through reading. *Reading in a Foreign Language*, 11, 207–223. https://nflrc.hawaii.edu/rfl/PastIssues/rfl112horst.pdf

Huang, L.-L., & Lin, C.-C. (2014). Three approaches to glossing and their effects on vocabulary learning. *System*, 44, 127–136. https://doi.org/10.1016/j.system.2014.03.006

Hulstijn, J. H. (1992). Retention of inferred and given word meanings: Experiments in incidental vocabulary learning. In P. J. L. Arnaud & H. Bejoint (Eds.), *Vocabulary and applied linguistics* (pp. 113–125). Palgrave Macmillan.

Hulstijn, J. H., Hollander, M., & Greidanus, T. (1996). Incidental vocabulary learning by advanced foreign language students: The influence of marginal glosses, dictionary use, and reoccurrence of unknown words. *The Modern Language Journal*, 80, 327–339. https://doi.org/10.2307/329439

Indrarathne, B., & Kormos, J. (2017). Attentional processing of input in explicit and implicit learning conditions: An eye-tracking study. *Studies in Second Language Acquisition*, 39, 401–430. https://doi.org/10.1017/S027226311600019X

Issa, B., & Morgan-Short, K. (2019). Effects of external and internal attentional manipulations on second language grammar development: An eye-tracking study. *Studies in Second Language Acquisition*, 41, 389–417. https://doi.org/10.1017/S027226311800013X

Issa, B., Morgan-Short, K., Villegas, B., & Raney, G. (2015). An eye-tracking study on the role of attention and its relationship with motivation. In L. Roberts, K. McManus, N. Vanek, & D. Trenkic (Eds.), *EUROSLA yearbook 2015* (pp. 114–142). John Benjamins.

Jahan, A., & Kormos, J. (2015). The impact of textual enhancement on EFL learners' grammatical awareness of future plans and intentions. *International Journal of Applied Linguistics*, 25, 46–66. https://doi.org/10.1111/ijal.12049

Jones, L. C., & Plass, J. L. (2002). Supporting listening comprehension and vocabulary acquisition in French with multimedia annotations. *The Modern Language Journal*, 86, 546–561. https://doi.org/10.1111/1540-4781.00160

Jung, J. (2016). Effects of glosses on learning of L2 grammar and vocabulary. *Language Teaching Research*, 20, 92–112. https://doi.org/10.1177/1362168815571151

Kang, H., Kweon, S.-O., & Choi, S. (2020). Using eye-tracking to examine the role of first and second language glosses. *Language Teaching Research*. Online early view. https://doi.org/10.1177/1362168820928567

Khezrlou, S., Ellis, R., & Sadeghi, K. (2017). Effects of computer-assisted glosses on EFL learners' vocabulary acquisition and reading comprehension in three learning conditions. *System*, 65, 104–116. https://doi.org/10.1016/j.system.2017.01.009

Kim, Y. (2006). Effects of input elaboration on vocabulary acquisition through reading by Korean learners of English as a foreign language. *TESOL Quarterly*, 40, 341–373. https://doi.org/10.2307/40264526

Ko, M. H. (2012). Glossing and second language vocabulary learning. *TESOL Quarterly*, 46, 56–79. https://doi.org/10.1002/tesq.3

Kost, C. R., Foss, P., & Lenzini, J. J. (1999). Textual and pictorial glosses: Effectiveness on incidental vocabulary growth when reading in a foreign language. *Foreign Language Annals*, 32, 89–97. https://doi.org/10.1111/j.1944-9720.1999.tb02378.x

Labrozzi, R. M. (2016). The effects of textual enhancement type on L2 form recognition and reading comprehension in Spanish. *Language Teaching Research*, 20, 75–91. https://doi.org/10.1177/1362168814561903

Laufer, B., & Hill, M. (2000). What lexical information do L2 learners select in a CALL dictionary and how does it affect word retention? *Language Learning & Technology*, 3, 58–76. http://llt.msu.edu/vol3num2/laufer-hill/index.html

Laufer, B., & Hulstijn, J. H. (2001). Incidental vocabulary acquisition in a second language: The construct of task-induced involvement. *Applied Linguistics*, 22, 1–26. https://doi.org/10.1093/applin/22.1.1

Laufer, B., & Sim, D. D. (1985). Taking the easy way out: Non-use and misuse of contextual clues in EFL reading comprehension. *English Teaching Forum*, 18, 405–411.

Lee, J. H., & Levine, G. S. (2020). The effect of instructor language choice on second language vocabulary learning and listening comprehension. *Language Teaching Research*, 24, 250–272. https://doi.org/10.1177/1362168818770910

Lee, M., & Révész, A. (2018). Promoting grammatical development through textually enhanced captions: An eye-tracking study. *The Modern Language Journal*, 102, 557–577. https://doi.org/10.1111/modl.12503

Lee, S.-K. (2007). Effects of textual enhancement and topic familiarity on Korean EFL students' reading comprehension and learning of passive form. *Language Learning*, 57, 87–118. https://doi.org/10.1111/j.1467-9922.2007.00400.x

Lee, S.-K., & Huang, H.-K. (2008). Visual input enhancement and grammar learning: A meta-analytic review. *Studies in Second Language Acquisition*, 30, 307–331. https://doi.org/10.1017/S0272263108080479

Loewen, S., & Inceoglu, S. (2016). The effectiveness of visual input enhancement on the noticing and L2 development of the Spanish past tense. *Studies in Second Language Learning and Teaching*, 6, 89–110. https://doi.org/10.14746/ssllt.2016.6.1.5

Luppescu, S., & Day, R. R. (1993). Reading, dictionaries, and vocabulary learning. *Language Learning*, 43, 263–279. https://doi.org/10.1111/j.1467-1770.1992.tb00717.x

Majuddin, E., Siyanova-Chanturia, A., & Boers, F. (2019). The effects of repetition and typographic enhancement on incidental and intentional acquisition of multiword expressions from audio-visual input. Paper presented at EUROSLA 29, Lund University, August 30.

Martinez, R., & Schmitt, N. (2012). A phrasal expressions list. *Applied Linguistics*, 33, 299–320. https://doi.org/10.1093/applin/ams010

Mayer, R. E., & Anderson, R. W. (1992). The instructive animation: Helping students build connections between words and pictures in multimedia learning. *Journal of Educational Psychology*, 84, 444–452. https://doi.org/10.1037/0022-0663.84.4.444

Mayer, R. E., & Gallini, J. K. (1990). When is an illustration worth ten thousand words? *Journal of Educational Psychology*, 82, 715–726. https://doi.org/10.1037/0022-0663.82.4.715

Meguro, Y. (2017). Textual enhancement, grammar learning, reading comprehension, and tag questions. *Language Teaching Research*, 23, 58–77. https://doi.org/10.1177/1362168817714277

Mohsen, M. A., & Balakumar, M. (2011). A review of multimedia glosses and their effects on L2 vocabulary acquisition in CALL literature. *ReCALL*, 23, 135–159. https://doi.org/10.1017/S095834401100005X

Montero Perez, M., Peters, E., Clarebout, G., & Desmet, P. (2014). Effects of captioning on video comprehension and incidental vocabulary learning. *Language Learning & Technology*, 18, 118–141. http://dx.doi.org/10125/44357

Montero Perez, M., Peters, E., & Desmet, P. (2018). Vocabulary learning through viewing video: The effect of two enhancement techniques. *Computer Assisted Language Learning*, 31, 1–26. https://doi.org/10.1080/09588221.2017.1375960

Na, L., & Nation, I. S. P. (1985). Factors affecting guessing vocabulary in context. *RELC Journal*, 16, 33–42. https://doi.org/10.1177/003368828501600103

Nagata, N. (1999). The effectiveness of computer-assisted interactive glosses. *Foreign Language Annals*, 32, 469–479. https://doi.org/10.1111/j.1944-9720.1999.tb00876.x

Nassaji, H. (2003). L2 vocabulary learning from context: Strategies, knowledge sources, and their relationship with success in L2 lexical inferencing. *TESOL Quarterly*, 37, 645–670. https://doi.org/10.2307/3588216

Nesselhauf, N. (2003). The use of collocations by advanced learners of English and some implications for teaching. *Applied Linguistics*, 24, 223–242. https://doi.org/10.1093/applin/24.2.223

Paivio, A. (1986). *Mental representations: A dual coding approach*. Oxford University Press.

Paivio, A. (1991). Dual coding theory: Retrospect and current status. *Canadian Journal of Psychology*, 45, 255–287. https://doi.org/10.1037/h0084295

Paivio, A. (2010). Dual coding theory and the mental lexicon. *The Mental Lexicon*, 5, 205–230. https://doi.org/10.1075/ml.5.2.04pai

Pellicer-Sánchez, A. (2017). Learning L2 collocations incidentally from reading. *Language Teaching Research*, 21, 381–402. https://doi.org/10.1177/1362168815618428

Peters, E., Hulstijn, J. H., Sercu, L., & Lutjeharms, M. (2009). Learning L2 German vocabulary through reading: The effect of three enhancement techniques compared. *Language Learning*, 59, 113–151. https://doi.org/10.1111/j.1467-9922.2009.00502.x

Pujadas, G., & Muñoz, C. (2019). Extensive viewing of captioned and subtitled TV series: A study of L2 vocabulary learning by adolescents. *The Language Learning Journal*, 47, 479–496. https://doi.org/10.1080/09571736.2019.1616806

Ramezanali, N., Uchihara, T., & Faez, F. (2020). Efficacy of multimodal glossing on second language vocabulary learning: A meta-analysis. *TESOL Quarterly*. Online early view. https://doi.org/10.1002/tesq.579

Rassaei, E. (2018). Computer-mediated textual and audio glosses, perceptual style and L2 vocabulary learning. *Language Teaching Research*, 22, 657–675. https://doi.org/10.1177/1362168817690183

Rott, S. (1999). The effect of exposure frequency on intermediate language learners' incidental vocabulary acquisition and retention through reading. *Studies in Second Language Acquisition*, 21, 589–619. https://doi.org/10.1017/S0272263199004039

Rott, S. (2007). The effect of frequency of input-enhancements on word learning and text comprehension. *Language Learning*, 57, 165–199. https://doi.org/10.1111/j.1467-9922.2007.00406.x

Rott, S., Williams, J., & Cameron, R. (2002). The effect of multiple-choice L1 glosses and input-output cycles on lexical acquisition and retention. *Language Teaching Research*, 3, 183–222. https://doi.org/10.1191/1362168802lr108oa

Sánchez-Gutiérrez, C. H., Pérez Serrano, M., & Robles García, P. (2019). The effects of word frequency and typographical enhancement on incidental vocabulary learning in reading. *Journal of Spanish Language Teaching*, 6, 14–31. https://doi.org/10.1080/23247797.2019.1590000

Schmidt, R. W. (2001). Attention. In P. Robinson (Ed.), *Cognition and second language instruction* (pp. 3–32). Cambridge University Press.

Schmitt, N. (2008). Review article: Instructed second language vocabulary learning. *Language Teaching Research*, 12, 329–363. https://doi.org/10.1177/1362168808089921

Sharwood-Smith, M. (1993). Input enhancement in instructed SLA: Theoretical bases. *Studies in Second Language Acquisition*, 15, 165–179. https://doi.org/10.1017/S0272263100011943

Skehan, P. (1998). *A cognitive approach to language learning*. Oxford University Press.

Sonbul, S., & Schmitt, N. (2013). Explicit and implicit lexical knowledge: Acquisition of collocations under different input conditions. *Language Learning*, 63, 121–159. doi:10.1111/j.1467-9922.2012.00730.x

Szudarski, P., & Carter, R. (2016). The role of input flood and input enhancement in EFL learners' acquisition of collocations. *International Journal of Applied Linguistics*, 26, 245–265. https://doi.org/10.1111/ijal.12092

Teng, F. (2019). The effects of context and word exposure frequency on incidental vocabulary acquisition and retention through reading. *The Language Learning Journal*, 47, 145–158. https://doi.org/10.1080/09571736.2016.1244217

Teng, F. (2020). Retention of new words learned incidentally from reading: Word exposure frequency, L1 marginal glosses, and their combination. *Language Teaching Research*, 24, 785–812. https://doi.org/10.1177/1362168819829026

Tian, L., & Macaro, E. (2012). Comparing the effect of teacher codeswitching with English only explanations on the vocabulary acquisition of Chinese university students: A lexical focus-on-form study. *Language Teaching Research*, 16, 367–391. https://doi.org/10.1177/1362168812436909

Toomer, M., & Elgort, I. (2019). The development of implicit and explicit knowledge of collocations: A conceptual replication and extension of Sonbul and Schmitt (2013). *Language Learning*, 69, 405–439. https://doi.org/10.1111/lang.12335

Uchihara, T., Webb, S., & Yanagisawa, A. (2019). The effects of repetition on incidental vocabulary learning: A meta-analysis of correlational studies, *Language Learning*, 69, 559–599. https://doi.org/10.1111/lang.12343

Van Zeeland, H. (2014). Lexical inferencing in first and second language listening. *The Modern Language Journal*, 98, 1006–1021. https://doi.org/10.1111/modl.12152

Vidal, K. (2011). A comparison of the effects of reading and listening on incidental vocabulary acquisition. *Language Learning*, 61, 219–258. https://doi.org/10.1111/j.1467-9922.2010.00593.x

Waring R., & Takaki, M. (2003). At what rate do learners learn and retain new vocabulary from reading a graded reader? *Reading in a Foreign Language*, 15, 130–163. http://nflrc.hawaii.edu/rfl/October2003/waring/waring.pdf

Warren, P., Boers, F., Grimshaw, G., & Siyanova-Chanturia, A. (2018). The effect of gloss type on learners' intake of new words during reading: Evidence from eye-tracking. *Studies in Second Language Acquisition*, 40, 883–906. https://doi.org/10.1017/S0272263118000177

Watanabe, Y. (1997). Input, intake, and retention: Effects of increased processing on incidental learning of foreign language vocabulary. *Studies in Second Language Acquisition*, 19, 287–307. https://doi.org/10.1017/S027226319700301X

Webb, S. (2007). The effects of repetition on vocabulary knowledge. *Applied Linguistics*, 28, 46–65. https://doi.org/10.1093/applin/aml048

Webb, S. (2008). The effects of context on incidental vocabulary learning. *Reading in a Foreign Language*, 20, 232–245. http://nflrc.hawaii.edu/rfl/October2008/webb/webb.pdf

Webb, S., Newton, J., & Chang, A. (2013). Incidental learning of collocation. *Language Learning*, 63, 91–120. doi:10.1111/j.1467-9922.2012.00729.x

Winke, P. (2013). The effects of input enhancement on grammar learning and comprehension: A modified replication of Lee (2007) with eye-movement data. *Studies in Second Language Acquisition*, 35, 323–352. https://doi.org/10.1017/S0272263112000903

Yanagisawa, A., Webb, S., & Uchihara, T. (2020). How do different forms of glossing contribute to L2 vocabulary learning from reading? A meta-regression analysis. *Studies in Second Language Acquisition*, 42, 411–438. https://doi.org/10.1017/S0272263119000688

Yoshii, M. (2006). L1 and L2 glosses: Their effects on incidental vocabulary learning. *Language Learning & Technology*, 10, 85–101. http://llt.msu.edu/vol10num3/yoshii/

Yoshii, M. (2013). Effects of gloss types on vocabulary learning through reading: Comparison of single translation and multiple-choice gloss types. *CALICO Journal*, 30, 203–229. https://journals.equinoxpub.com/CALICO/article/view/22899/18920

Yoshii, M., & Flaitz, J. (2002). Second language incidental vocabulary retention: The effect of text and picture annotation types. *CALICO Journal*, 20, 33–58. https://www.learntechlib.org/p/95532/

Yun, J. (2011). The effects of hypertext glosses on L2 vocabulary acquisition: A meta-analysis. *Computer Assisted Language Learning*, 24, 39–58. https://doi.org/10.1080/09588221.2010.523285

Zhang, P., & Graham, S. (2020). Vocabulary learning through listening: Comparing L2 explanations, teacher codeswitching, contrastive focus-on-form and incidental learning. *Language Teaching Research*, 24, 765–784. https://doi.org/10.1177/1362168819829022

Zhang, Z., & Webb, S. (2019). The effects of reading bilingual books on vocabulary learning. *Reading in a Foreign Language*, 31, 108–139. https://nflrc.hawaii.edu/rfl/April2019/April2019/articles/zhang.pdf

4.

FROM INPUT TO OUTPUT (AND BACK AGAIN)

Introduction

The previous chapter examined opportunities for vocabulary and grammar acquisition from exposure to modified textual input. While exposure to comprehensible input can certainly foster receptive knowledge, it has been argued that it should be complemented by output activities to also foster adequate productive knowledge of learned items and patterns (e.g., DeKeyser & Sokalski, 1996). Apart from the argument that output activities help more directly to develop productive knowledge, another argument for engaging students in L2 output activities is that these can make students aware of lacunae or deficiencies in their L2 repertoires (Swain, 1995). If learners realize during their efforts at communicating in L2 that they cannot yet express a certain idea or if they can tell from their interlocutors' reactions (such as requests for clarification) that the wording they have used is odd or unclear, then this may be an incentive for them to fix the problem. The problem may be fixed on the spot, thanks to feedback from the interlocutor, or it may be fixed later when learners meet the items or patterns that they failed to use adequately and pay them more attention than they would otherwise. This is the essence of Swain's *Output Hypothesis*: Not only do output activities give learners the opportunity to try out newly learned items or patterns and to consolidate this knowledge, it helps them appreciate what is still missing from their L2 repertoire and what aspects of their developing L2 competence (sometimes referred to in the literature as the learners' *interlanguage*) need to be adjusted. I argued in chapter 3 that exposure to model input (including modified texts) can show learners what is done in the target language but cannot directly inform them about what is *not* done. Feedback on learners' *output* is a way of adding the latter (Kartchava, 2019; Nassaji & Kartchava, 2017).

Episodes during interaction where speakers temporarily shift their attention from the content of messages to the language code have been labelled *language-related episodes* by researchers, especially in the literature with roots in the *Interaction Hypothesis* (e.g., Long, 1996; Mackey, 1999, Pica, 1994). Typically, language-related episodes (LREs) occur when there is a need for clarifying a speaker's intended meaning. For example, learners who have been taught British English are likely to be misunderstood in North America if they use the word *boot* instead of *trunk* to refer to the space at the back of their car, but after seeking clarification an American interlocutor will probably understand what is meant and may proffer the American English counterpart ("Oh, you mean the trunk"). This type of LRE is often called *negotiation of meaning* in the literature. As in other negotiations, this may take several turns in a conversation. And as in other negotiations, the outcome is not always satisfactory—sometimes only partial understanding (or no understanding) is reached. LREs can also be about formal features of the language, such as the spelling or pronunciation of a word, its grammatical properties (e.g., that *criteria* is the plural form of *criterion* and that "a criteria" is therefore inaccurate) and so on. This kind of episode has been labelled *negotiation of form*. Distinguishing between negotiation of meaning and negotiation of form is not easy in practice (e.g., Van den Branden, 1997), because misunderstandings are often due to issues with form, such as inaccurate pronunciation. That said, it stands to reason that most communication problems arise due to the inadequate use of language items that carry the most meaning—lexical items. It is thus vocabulary that will be the most likely focus in language-related episodes during naturalistic interaction. After all, inaccurate use of grammar seldom causes communication breakdowns. For instance, the context will usually help to understand whether the speaker is referring to multiple referents rather than a single referent, and so comprehension is not impeded if the plural –s ending is missing from an English noun.

The nature of LREs may be different in a language classroom, however, because students most probably realize the goal (or at least one of the goals) of activities in this setting is to foster proficiency in the target language (Foster & Ohta, 2005). During student–student interaction in the classroom it is therefore more likely that language-related episodes will occur that concern form as well as meaning (Springer & Collins, 2008; Swain & Lapkin, 1998). Besides, output activities in the language classroom are often designed with a view to channelling students' attention to the language code. For example, asking students to collaboratively write a story based on a series of pictures (e.g., Hidalgo & García Mayo, 2019) is likely to prompt discussion about *how* to write the story rather *what* to write, since the story line is already pre-determined by the series of pictures. In addition, opportunities for acquisition are of course different in a language classroom because of the availability of a teacher, whom the students can turn to for assistance and who considers it part of their job to point out language issues which escape the students' attention (Toth, 2008). This does not necessarily mean that teacher-led classroom interaction is always preferable to student–student interaction. Students have fewer output opportunities when the interaction is between the teacher and the whole class than if the students interact in pairs or in small groups. Students probably also take fewer risks when interacting with their language teacher, especially when the whole class is listening. Furthermore, some teachers are weary of long silences and may as a result give their students insufficient time to package their thoughts or insufficient opportunities to adjust their initial replies to questions (Musumeci, 1996). The latter problem should not be generalized, however, as it depends on individual teachers' competences. As aptly put by Toth (2008),

> Rather than categorically eschewing teacher-led discourse as antithetical to the principles of a "learner-centered" curriculum, L2 teacher education programs must, for the sake of learners, do a more adequate job of training teachers to effectively and responsibly conduct whole-class interactions. (p. 274)

As regards the point that during teacher-fronted whole-class interaction students have fewer chances to produce language in comparison to pair work or small groupwork, an interesting observation (Ohta, 2001) is that students who themselves are not directly involved in the interaction nonetheless benefit from listening to the exchanges between the teacher and their classmates. A teacher may prompt a response from the whole class and give only a handful of students the chance to actually provide a response, but this does not prevent the other students from giving thought to what their own response would be, to compare this to their classmates' uttered responses and to subsequently consider the feedback provided by the teacher. Perhaps *thinking* about ways of formulating a message can already bring about some of the benefits associated with output activities. That said, students are likely to have a greater number of conversational turns if they interact in pairs. They may also be prepared to experiment more with their L2 resources in peer–peer interaction than in direct interaction with their teacher. It is therefore not surprising that studies examining the role of interactional output for language development have focused mostly on activities performed as pair work (or so-called *dyadic interaction*), although it must be said that in several of these experiments (e.g., de la Fuente, 2002; Mackey, 1999; Muranoi, 2000) this was not organized as interaction between 2 students but rather as interaction between a student and a native speaker (such as the teacher-researcher). Recurring questions in this line of research concern what aspects of language attract attention in LREs and whether learners recognize that some of the reactions from their interlocutors in fact serve as corrective feedback on language (e.g., Fujii & Mackey, 2009; Mackey, 2006; Mackey et al., 2000; McDonough, 2005; Philp & Iwashita, 2013; Pica et al., 2006). A type of feedback that has attracted a lot of attention in this context is the correct reformulation by the interlocutor of the learner's incorrect utterance—called *recast*. For example, a learner might say "Sorry I'm late; I slept over", and the interlocutor might react by saying "Oh, you overslept, did you?" Recasts are a non-intrusive type of feedback, as the learner is not actually told overtly that there was something odd about their utterance. Recasts do not interrupt the flow of communication, and they are not "face threatening". On the downside, precisely because they are such an implicit way of giving corrective feedback, learners will not always recognize their purpose. Instead, recasts can easily be interpreted as confirmation on the part of an interlocutor that they have understood the message or as interactional moves intended to keep the conversation going.

Even in the context of a language classroom, which, as said, could be expected to heighten learners' alertness to language features, the research findings indicate that grammar features tend to attract little spontaneous attention during interactional output activities. It is vocabulary and features such as pronunciation (if they cause comprehension problems) that tend to attract the most spontaneous attention. It follows that, if interactional output makes learners notice the lacunae in their L2 repertoire, then this will happen more often in connection with vocabulary than grammar. Output activities of course serve more purposes than making learners aware of language deficiencies to be remedied. In the case of grammar patterns whose misuse does not impede communication much, interactional output activities are arguably more useful for the purpose of *consolidating* knowledge than for the purpose of triggering awareness of new patterns (Shintani & Ellis, 2010). When students already have (some) knowledge of a given grammar pattern, then it also becomes feasible for teachers to use *prompts* (e.g., "Sorry, can you say that again?" "Hmm, not drived but...?") as feedback moves, where they invite the students to "repair" their mistakes. Being a more explicit type of feedback, such prompts tend to have a greater immediate impact than recasts on students' language development (e.g., Ammar, 2008; Yang & Lyster, 2010).

In the strand of research reviewed in the present chapter, the philosophy remains that the classroom activities should be primarily focused on content, and that improving one's mastery of the language code is a side benefit of using the language for communicative purposes. It is through the act of communication that students experience the need to add certain new items and patterns to their L2 resources, and this will instil in them a willingness to acquire those items or patterns, so the reasoning goes. This is part of the rationale for *Communicative Language Teaching* (e.g., Brumfit & Johnson, 1979; Littlewood, 1981; Widdowson, 1978) and its spin-off, *Task-Based Language Teaching* (TBLT). Instead of engaging students in decontextualized language practice, proponents of TBLT argue that classroom activities should engage students in language use for similar purposes that they would use language for in real life. Activities of this kind are called *tasks* (Ellis, 2018; Ellis et al., 2019; Long, 2015), and they are distinguished from *exercises*. It is worth noting that the same term—task—is unfortunately also widely used in publications (including L2 textbooks) outside TBLT circles to refer to language-focused exercises, which can be confusing. According to Ellis and Shintani (2013, p. 135), the following characteristics distinguish tasks from exercises:

1.   The focus is on meaning, that is, on the content of messages rather than on the language code.
2.   There is some sort of communication gap between interlocutors, that is, learners exchange information or opinions rather than telling interlocutors—including their teacher—what these interlocutors already know.
3.   The task instructions do *not* stipulate what language elements or patterns the students should use when performing the activity (because that would likely turn the activity into a language-focused exercise).
4.   There is a clear (non-linguistic) purpose (e.g., solving a problem; reaching an agreement about a dilemma) other than practising language (because in the real world, language use is a means to an end, not the end itself).

One way in which doing tasks is expected to foster L2 development is through task repetition.

Learners try a communicative activity and notice (thanks to interactional feedback) problems with their linguistic resources. They are then given the opportunity to reflect on what went wrong and to seek help (e.g., from the teacher) to adjust their L2 resources. They subsequently perform the same task again or perform a task that is similar enough for them to spontaneously deploy the adjusted resources, thereby consolidating the newly acquired knowledge. The feedback and reflection attached to a task before it is repeated (or before a similar task is started) is important if the aim is for the students to add language items to their repertoire or to improve the accuracy of their language use. Immediate repetition of a task without any feedback or other opportunities for language adjustment may help students perform the task faster thanks to a rehearsal effect and because the student does not need to think much about content anymore, but other improvements are much less likely (e.g., Boers, 2014; Bui et al., 2019; Thai & Boers, 2016). It is when tasks are repeated after an interval, with opportunities for learning from some sort of input during this interval, that improvements in dimensions such as accurate language use become more realistic (e.g., Fukuta, 2016; Kim & Tracy-Ventura, 2013). In some versions of TBLT (e.g., Willis & Willis, 2007), students tackle a given task first in pairs or small groups, benefit from their peers' assistance and feedback, and then they report the outcome and how the outcome was arrived at to the whole class, after which they may receive further feedback from the teacher (see Newton & Nguyen, 2019, for an example of this type of sequence). The task performance may even be recorded for the students to listen to afterwards, so they can evaluate what they did well and what could be improved.

Tasks can be designed so that specific lexical items or grammar patterns are highly likely to be experienced by the students as useful or even essential to be able to get the task done. These are sometimes called *focused tasks*. For example, students could be given the following instructions:

In small groups, try to agree on a ranking of the following animals from the most intelligent to the least intelligent species: dogs, pigs, humans, chimpanzees, cats. Then report your ranking to the other groups and explain how your group came to an agreement.

It would be hard for students to express why they consider one species to be more intelligent than another if they had no knowledge at all of comparative patterns (e.g., "X are smarter than Y, because…"; "Z are not as intelligent as Y, because…") or of modal verbs such as *can* ("X can… but Y cannot"; "Z is able to… whereas Y is not able to"). If they have not yet mastered these *task-essential* language features (Loschky & Bley-Vroman, 1993), then trying the task should make them appreciate the communicative relevance of these features and thus increase their readiness to learn from a more proficient group member (if any), from the teacher, or from other sources they may have access to. A little later in the language course, a similar task requiring comparisons can then be given to create an opportunity for the students to transfer the acquired knowledge to a new activity. Apart from agreement tasks such as the above, other common types of tasks include problem-solving tasks (e.g., solving a mystery) and information-gap tasks (where each member of a pair is given partial but complementary information to be exchanged). An activity that is often used in studies of task-based interaction is the "spot-the-differences" task, where students are given pictures or drawings that differ in certain details and where the students' task is to find the differences by asking each other questions (e.g., "Is the woman in your picture wearing a hat?"), without showing each other their pictures. In another classic activity, students are given incomplete maps containing complementary information about landmarks, and they are asked to give each other directions to travel to a given destination—again without showing each other their copies. The former activity is expected to elicit interrogative patterns and the latter prepositions (*at, past, across, into*), certain verbs (e.g., *turn, pass, cross*) and perhaps even expressions such as *take a left turn at…* . The extent to which such classroom tasks should resemble communication outside the classroom is a matter of some debate. Imagine, for example, being asked for directions by tourists who have lost their way. If you happened to have a map with you, you would surely *show* them your map while explaining how to get to a certain destination. The point is that classroom tasks need not always imitate specific real-life situations but should at least reflect the broader communicative functions (such as exchanging information) that language serves in real life.

As mentioned above, task repetition offers an opportunity for students to apply the knowledge acquired during or after a first attempt at doing the same task. Another option is to engage students in a new task, but which bears close enough resemblance to the first to invite transfer of the newly acquired knowledge. While this may for variety's sake be preferred by some students (although see Ahmadian et al., 2017, for some evidence to the contrary), transfer cannot be taken for granted if the new task introduces too many new obstacles. To give just a simple example, students may be unable to adequately perform a follow-up task that could consolidate knowledge of a grammar pattern if the new task requires knowledge of topic-specific vocabulary they are not yet familiar with (e.g., Benson, 2016). It is therefore important for educators who wish to implement tasks as the main building blocks of their language course to sequence the tasks in a way that facilitates transfer of knowledge from one task to the next (Baralt et al., 2014; Bygate, 2018).

Recall that one of the characteristics of a task according to Ellis and Shintani (2013) is that learners should rely mostly on their own linguistic resources to complete the activity. A question this raises (e.g., Swan, 2005) is where those "own" linguistic resources should come from in the case of learners who have only just started learning a language. Engaging students in output activities from scratch is indeed counter-intuitive and difficult (Shintani, 2011). A related question is how even intermediate learners can be "pushed" to expand their linguistic resources if they manage to get a task done with the resources they already have. After all, while it is easy to design a communicative activity to create a need for certain items or patterns (such as comparative patterns in the example given earlier), for many other items and patterns this is far from straightforward (Loschky & Bley-Vroman, 1993). For instance, one could think of a task where students propose hypotheses as part of a collaborative effort to solve a mystery and expect this activity to elicit modal verbs such as *may have* + past participle, *might have* + past participle and *couldn't have* + past participle. However, learners may deploy simpler options they are already familiar with and which express essentially the same content, such as *perhaps* and *it is (not) possible that*. Ellis (2009) has responded to these lines of scepticism by clarifying that tasks can also be comprehension activities (which would be especially suitable for beginning learners) and also that output tasks can be based on samples of language input, or, as Ellis and Shintani (2013) put it: "Learners [...] may be able to 'borrow' from the input the task provides to help them perform it" (p. 135). This input may simply be the task prompts, or it could be textual input providing the students with the information they need to perform the task. For the above example about animal intelligence, for instance, different groups of students might read a text (or watch short documentaries) about the problem-solving skills demonstrated by a certain animal species, and they could use this information and the wording in which the information is presented to try and convince the other groups that species A must be more intelligent than species B. Learners are indeed known to spontaneously borrow language from task prompts, sometimes referred to metaphorically as "mining" the task prompts (e.g., Boston, 2008). This spontaneous recycling of language from input materials is especially likely for vocabulary. It is therefore helpful to include lexical items in the task prompts that are considered highly useful for the task at hand (Newton, 2013).

Conditions for mining input to fuel output are varied. Minimally, this may just be the use of words from a topic sentence (e.g., a statement for students to debate or write about). More often it will be words from the information given to students that is essential for doing the task (e.g., the words to refer to animal species in an agreement task about animals' intelligence). At other times, students are expected to first process a text and then produce output in relation to it. One example of this is the so-called continuation task, where students read or listen to an unfinished story and invent an ending to it (e.g., Wang & Wang, 2015). Another example is the use of an input text as a model of the type of discourse the students are expected to produce (e.g., Zhang, 2017). It is also common to ask students to retell a story or to sum up the contents of a text. Even the mere *expectation* of a text-based output task can make students more attentive to the language used in the text (Yoshimura, 2006). Whatever the implementation, the premise is that learners will treat the input materials as a helpful source of language elements and will feel free to recycle these elements in their own output. The latter cannot be taken for granted, because students are requested all too often by their teachers to use "their own words" to demonstrate text comprehension, a practice which risks leaving students with the impression that recycling words and phrases from an input text is akin to plagiarism rather than a useful strategy for language learning. However, some activities do instruct students explicitly to imitate input materials. An example is the so-called *dictogloss* (Wajnryb, 1990), where students try to reconstruct a text they have listened to several times. Unlike a standard dictation, where students immediately write down the chunks of language they have heard, dictogloss and *text-reconstruction activities* more generally (e.g., Pica et al., 2006) require students to recreate the text from memory. When such activities are done as pair work, they are likely to prompt LREs (e.g., Swain & Lapkin, 2001) first as the students discuss what they recall from the original text and later as they compare their reconstructed version to the original text. The input texts used for text-reconstruction activities should not be too long, because that would be too taxing on memory. They should not be too short either, lest students reproduce them verbatim from short-term phonological memory without any need to process meaning (e.g., Izumi & Izumi, 2004). Ideally, the students need to first un-pack the idea units of the text and then re-package them in a way that resembles the original. The activity thus requires students to reconnect *what* was said to *how* it was said.

Given the language-focused dimension of text-reconstruction activities, one may wonder if they truly belong to the realm of incidental acquisition, where learning is assumed to be a by-product of content-focused language use. This illustrates again that the distinction between incidental and intentional language learning can easily get blurred. Even though reconstruction activities could arguably be considered exercises rather than tasks (to use the distinction made in TBLT circles), I will discuss them in the present chapter because they were incorporated in some of the studies from the realm of TBLT that I will also review here.

Words and Phrases

Many studies have furnished evidence that vocabulary acquisition benefits from output activities. However, in most of them the students were explicitly told to use specific lexical items, thus turning the activity into vocabulary-focused work. I will review that line of research in chapter 6. There are in fact few studies to date which have examined the benefits of input-based output activities for vocabulary learning, and where the students were *not* told explicitly to use specific words or phrases. That is why I am including available research concerning the effects on word learning and on phrase learning in a single section here. A study where the benefits of an input-based output activity for vocabulary learning can still be considered a by-product of a content-focused activity is Nguyen and Boers (2019). A group of students of English were asked to watch a TED Talk video and to sum up its content. After giving their oral summary, the students watched the same video again. A comparison group also watched the same TED Talk twice, but they were not asked to summarize it in between the 2 viewings. A surprise vocabulary posttest on the meaning of 18 previously unfamiliar words used in the TED Talk revealed better recall (8 vs. 4.5, on average) by the students who had done the summary activity. Interestingly, it was when students incorporated a word in their summary that it was almost certain to be remembered in the posttest as well (see Joe, 1998, for similar findings). In addition, when learners attempted to use a word from the video in their summaries but failed to retrieve it from memory at that point, the second viewing gave them an opportunity to attend to the word again, and this was also strongly associated with the likelihood of correct recall in the posttest. This observation lends support to the tenet of the Output Hypothesis that output activities help students notice gaps in their L2 resources and that this will prime their interest in the linguistic means to fill those gaps when they next see or hear them. Worth mentioning here is that the students in this study prepared and delivered their summaries of the TED Talk individually. It might be interesting to see if more vocabulary could be acquired if the task were done collaboratively, as suggested by several studies reporting positive effects of student–student interaction (e.g., Adams, 2007; Dobao, 2014).

In 2 other studies (Niu & Helms-Park, 2014; Rott et al., 2002) students were asked to reconstruct reading passages from memory. In both studies, this led to better vocabulary learning than merely reading the same passages to answer comprehension questions. A feature worth mentioning in the way the activity was implemented in Niu and Helms-Park (2014) is that the target words were given on the students' worksheets. This means there was in fact no need for them to retrieve these words from memory as part of their text-reconstruction effort. It is conceivable that seeing these words preselected and spelled out for them was experienced by the students as an indication that these were considered important by their instructor.

Empirical studies on phrase learning through input-based output activities with a focus on content are rare as well. In Hoang and Boers (2016), students of English were presented with a short story on PowerPoint slides in a multimodal format: an audio-recording of the story, L2 captions of the text, and pictures on the slides to help the students follow the story line. The students listened to the story twice with a view to retelling the same story themselves shortly afterwards. The original text contained 35 phrases consisting of familiar words (e.g., *despite the fact that, get in touch with* and *one way or another*). While the story line was reproduced well and many content words were borrowed from the original text, the students reproduced on average just 2 of the 35 phrases. They often borrowed words from the phrases, but not the whole phrase. For example, the original phrase *he took no notice of...* was rendered as *he did not notice*. Often, the less distinctive elements in the phrases were replaced by incorrect substitutes, such as *look forward about* for *look forward to* and *earn the living* for *earn a living*. If learners do not spontaneously mine input texts for phraseology, this suggests there is a need for interventions to make phraseology more noticeable in the texts (such as typographic enhancement, as discussed in chapter 3). Note, however, that in Hoang and Boers (2016) the sequence of learning activities ended with the retelling of the story. In keeping with the idea that output activities can make students pay attention to language features in *subsequent* input texts, it would have been advisable to give students the opportunity to compare their own version of the story to the original text and then perhaps retell the story once more.

If learners tend to pay little spontaneous attention to phraseology in input texts, then perhaps instructing the students that they should try to reproduce a text so it resembles the original not only in content but also in wording will be more effective. Lindstromberg et al. (2016) explored this possibility by means of the dictogloss activity. While the results appear promising, they are difficult to put into perspective because the study design did not include a non-dictogloss comparison condition. There is one small-scale study (Reinders, 2009) which showed a marginal advantage of dictogloss over a standard dictation for students' acquisition of phrases with subject-verb inversion after certain adverbs, such as *Seldom had he + past participle* and *No sooner had he + past participle*. Subject-verb inversion after certain adverbs is a phenomenon that can be considered as belonging to the realm of grammar as well, to which I turn next.

Patterns

There are only a few empirical studies that investigate how content-focused output tasks can be framed such that learners will mine input texts for grammar patterns. One example is a classroom experiment by Van de Guchte et al. (2017), who created a task where Dutch learners of German were asked to describe a school canteen. This picture-based description necessitated use of spatial prepositions. One of the challenges of learning German is to know which grammatical case is associated with each preposition and accordingly how to change the form of the article in the noun phrase that follows it. For example, the (default) nominative form of the noun phrase 'the middle' in German is *die Mitte*, but after the preposition *in* the noun phrase adopts the dative case and as a result the article changes into *der* (*in der Mitte*). Before performing the description task, the students in the experiment watched 2 video-recorded models of a very similar task. One group of students was asked to evaluate these videos for their appeal (i.e., content and presentation). Another group was asked to pay attention to how the speakers in the videos described the location of objects. In other words, this second group's attention was oriented to the wording of place descriptions. The students then performed the canteen description task themselves (as an immediate posttest) and did so again 3 weeks later (as a delayed posttest). The students whose attention had been directed to the wordings used in the videos were found to use the dative case more accurately than the other group in the immediate posttest, but this advantage shrank in the delayed posttest. Overall, accuracy levels remained very low, even though the students were given ample pre-task planning time and could thus be expected to prepare grammatically accurate sentences—provided they understood the grammar pattern. It is important to note in this regard that these were low-proficiency learners of German, and it is possible that they had never been taught the grammar pattern targeted here. This is reminiscent of the research on the effects of textual enhancement (chapter 3) of grammar patterns, where I argued that, without prior explanations regarding a given pattern, learners may find it hard to discern and interpret it themselves from textual input alone. That said, textual enhancement may nonetheless influence students' experience of a subsequent output activity. Rassaei (2020) asked Iranian students of English to retell short stories which they had read either with the definite and indefinite articles (*the* and *a*) visually enhanced in the texts or without any enhancement. As the students reproduced the stories, they received feedback in the form of recasts on their incorrect use (or non-use) of the articles. The enhancement was found to improve the chances that students would recognize the purpose of the recasts, which, in turn, had a positive effect on the students' accurate use of articles in later story-telling activities. Rassaei (2020) also included a condition where students read the enhanced version of the stories but where no corrective feedback was given as they retold the stories. This did not lead to significantly more improvement in the students' article use than a parallel condition where non-enhanced text versions were used. This again illustrates what was said in chapter 3 about the limited impact on grammar learning of typographic enhancement on its own. At the same time, this study supports the suggestion made in chapter 3 that visual enhancement can be helpful if it is applied *in combination with* other steps.

Instead of providing corrective feedback on a retell task, learning can also be promoted by asking students to revisit the original ("model") text, so they can themselves detect differences between the model and their own version. In a series of small-scale studies in the context of L2 writing (Izumi et al., 1999; Izumi & Bigelow, 2000; Uggen, 2012), students wrote an essay on a topic that was likely to elicit a certain grammar pattern (e.g., writing about a hypothetical situation in the past is expected to elicit past counterfactual conditional sentences, such as *if I hadn't accepted the job offer, I wouldn't have met you*). They subsequently studied a model essay on a similar topic containing multiple examples of the target pattern before repeating the writing task. Overall, improvements in the use of the target grammar patterns from the first to the second essay were found to be marginal, possibly because the students did not focus specifically on the grammar pattern of interest when they read the model essay. Perhaps some form of attention-directing could again have made a difference in the activity sequence. Izumi (2002) explored such means of directing learners' attention to a grammar pattern in an input-output-input cycle. The target pattern was relative clauses in English (*[...] who...*, etc.). Students were given a text flooded with instances of relative clauses and divided into short subsections. After each subsection, some students were asked to reconstruct it from memory, then take another look at the original and reconstruct it again from memory, before moving on to the next subsection of the text. Other students were instead asked to answer content-related questions after each subsection. For half of the students in either condition, the relative pronouns were made visually salient by typographic means when they read the sections the second time. A series of tests to measure the students' mastery of relative clauses was administered before and after these activities. Interestingly, the visual enhancement of the target pattern in the input text was *not* found to have a significant effect on learning, but the text–reconstruction activity did make a significant difference: the average improvement in scores between the pretests and the posttests was 14%, compared to only 5.5% for the students who had not been asked to reconstruct the text passages. Similar results were found in a conceptual replication by Song and Suh (2008), with a focus on the English past counterfactual conditional (*if I hadn't..., I would have...*), and by Russell (2014), with a focus on the Spanish future tense.

Reconstructing short input texts from memory and comparing the reconstructed version to the original thus appears beneficial for the acquisition of grammar patterns. It is an activity that is quite time-consuming, however. In Izumi (2002), 5 sessions (spread over 2 weeks) were invested, and each session took between 30 and 60 minutes. This time investment puts the 14% learning gain into perspective. It also puts the very marginal gain (5.5%) of the comparison group into perspective. The latter gain is particularly unimpressive considering that a control group also improved their test scores by 3%, even though they did not even read the texts. The poor outcome for the comparison group demonstrates again that students are unlikely to acquire new grammar patterns when their attention is directed only to the content of a text and not to the language code. In any case, the question needs to be asked whether it is realistic for language teachers to create several texts flooded with instances of a grammar pattern and engage their students for so long and so repeatedly with the same type of activity for the purpose of fostering knowledge of one pattern. It seems likely that some explicit instruction about a given grammar pattern would accelerate the learning process and could help students reap the benefits of an input–output–input cycle with reduced time investment. A study supporting this—coincidentally also about English relative clauses—is Mochizuki and Ortega (2008), although in that case the explicit instruction was given *after* the students had listened to a story. The effect of explicit grammar explanations *before* engaging with the input text for a text-reconstruction activity was examined as part of a more recent study, by Li et al. (2016). In their experiment, Chinese students of English reconstructed (through the dictogloss procedure) 2 short texts that were flooded with instances of the passive voice (30 instances altogether, all in the simple past tense; e.g., *The car was hit by a truck*). The texts were presented several times orally and on PowerPoint slides, and potentially difficult words were pre-taught. Students worked in pairs to reconstruct the texts and they were also asked to invent an ending to the 2 stories. Then some students presented their stories to the class. The whole lesson took 2 hours. Learning of the passive voice was gauged by means of a grammaticality judgement test, where the students were asked to correct errors, and a so-called elicited imitation test. The latter is a time-pressured task where learners are required to repeat spoken sentences, some of which contain language errors. If the students spontaneously fix the error as they repeat the sentence, then this is taken as evidence of automatized knowledge of the grammar pattern. The tests were administered before the lesson (as a pretest), at the end of the lesson (as an immediate posttest) and again 2 weeks later (as a delayed posttest). On the grammaticality judgement test, the students improved their score from pretest to delayed posttest by only 3.5 out of 30 points on average (and ending up with an average test score of just 5/30). On the elicited imitation test the improvement in scores was even more marginal—by just 1.5 points out of 30. Clearly, these students had no or only minimal prior knowledge of the target grammar pattern and were perhaps unable to work it out independently from textual input alone. This then raises the question (again) whether prior instruction about the target pattern could make a difference, and this was in fact part of Li et al.'s (2016) study. There was another group of students who received a 15-minute introduction about the passive voice before they embarked on the dictogloss activity. These students' improvement on the grammaticality judgement test was twice as large as that observed for the students who had not received these explicit grammar explanations. This is reminiscent of a study about typographic enhancement (Indrarathne & Kormos, 2017) discussed in chapter 3, where pre-teaching the target grammar pattern was also found to generate far better learning outcomes than only doing a content-focused activity. The advantage of pre-teaching the target pattern was much less noticeable in the elicited imitation test used by Li et al. (2016), however, which indicates that it takes much more practice than what was done in the 2-hour lesson for grammar knowledge to become automatic. All the same, what Li et al.'s (2016) findings clearly suggest is that explicit explanations about a new grammar pattern can accelerate the development of declarative knowledge (i.e., the kind of knowledge one can deploy in a decontextualized test without time pressure). What is less clear is whether the better learning observed for the instructed group is to be attributed to the *combination* of the explicit explanations and the text-reconstruction activity or simply to the explicit explanations as such. The research design did not include a comparison group who only received the explicit explanations and who did not do the text-reconstruction activity.

In any case, the learning condition in Li et al. (2016) which brought about the best learning outcomes does clearly not fit the approach discussed in this part of the book—where the acquisition of words, phrases or patterns is meant to be a by-product of content-focused communication rather than language-focused teaching. I will therefore say more about Li et al. (2016) in the next part of the book, about language-focused learning.

Further Reflection

What Are the Output Activities in Your Textbook Like?

Examine a contemporary L2 textbook for the characteristics of output activities. Do these activities prompt language use for real communication, akin to the functions that language serves outside the language classroom? Do the output activities require students to express their own thoughts or do they present students with content to be reproduced? Do the activities require stretched output, beyond single sentences? Are the students encouraged to recycle language from input texts? Do the students engage in more than one communicative output activity meant to elicit the same vocabulary or grammar pattern? Do the activities involve preparation time and allow students to carefully monitor their language (as in prepared speeches and most writing tasks), or do they require "real-time" language use where students need procedural or automatized knowledge of the language to be able to balance fluency and accuracy?

Essential or Just Helpful?

Compile a list of grammar features of the target language you are likely to teach (you could also screen the table of contents of a grammar book or L2 textbook). For how many of these can you think of content-oriented output activities where the grammar feature is essential (i.e., without using the grammar feature, the task cannot be completed)? For how many would you consider it necessary to explicitly urge students to use the given grammar feature, lest they avoid using it altogether because other—simpler—language options suffice to get the task done?

When Do Recasts Have an Effect?

Recasts are correct reformulations of a learner's utterances. They are considered an implicit, non-face-threatening type of corrective feedback. Due to their nature, however, learners will not necessarily interpret recasts as feedback on language. Instead, learners may interpret reformulations as natural discourse moves, such as confirmation on the part of the interlocutors that they understand what is being said. So, what factors might influence the likelihood that recasts have an impact on learners' L2 development? Factors to be considered here include (a) the language target (e.g., does the recast concern a content word, a phrase or a grammar pattern?), (b) the learner's prior knowledge (e.g., does the learner already have sufficient knowledge of the grammar pattern to be able to interpret the feedback?), (c) the situational context (in the L2 classroom or elsewhere), (d) the way the recast is formulated (e.g., with prosodic stress on the reformulated part of the utterance), and (e) the profile of the individual learner. An additional factor is the teachers' openness about the feedback strategies that they will use with their students. Teachers may explain to their students early on in a course that they will be using recasts as their preferred feedback strategy, and so explain to the students that if they reformulate a student's utterance, this will often be intended as presenting them with an alternative way of packaging the same message. A study by Sato and Loewen (2018) has demonstrated that raising the students' awareness of the feedback function of recasts can indeed make a significant difference.

References

Adams, R. (2007). Do second language learners benefit from interacting with each other? In A. Mackey (Ed.), *Conversational interaction in second language acquisition: A series of empirical studies* (pp. 29–52). Oxford University Press.

Ahmadian, M. J., Mansouri, S. A., & Ghominejad, S. (2017). Language learners' and teachers' perceptions of task repetition. *ELT Journal*, 71, 467–477. https://doi.org/10.1093/elt/ccx011

Ammar, A. (2008). Prompts and recasts: Differential effects on second language morphosyntax. *Language Teaching Research*, 12, 183–210. https://doi.org/10.1177/1362168807086287

Baralt, M., Gilabert, R., & Robinson, P. (Eds.). (2014). *Task sequencing and instructed language learning*. Bloomsbury Academic.

Benson, S. D. (2016). Task-based language teaching: An empirical study of task transfer. *Language Teaching Research*, 20, 341–365. https://doi.org/10.1177/1362168815569829

Boers, F. (2014). A reappraisal of the 4/3/2 activity. *RELC Journal*, 45, 221–235. doi:10.1177/0033688214546964

Boston, J. S. (2008). Learner mining of pre-task and task input. *ELT Journal*, 62, 66–76. https://doi.org/10.1093/elt/ccm079

Brumfit, C. J., & Johnson, K. (1979). *The communicative approach to language teaching*. Oxford University Press.

Bui, G., Ahmadian, M. J., & Hunter, A.-M. (2019). Spacing effects on repeated L2 task performance. *System*, 81, 1–13. https://doi.org/10.1016/j.system.2018.12.006

Bygate, M. (Ed.). (2018). *Learning language through task repetition*. John Benjamins. https://doi.org/10.1075/tblt.11

DeKeyser, R. M., & Sokalski, K. J. (1996). The differential role of comprehension and production practice. *Language Learning*, 46, 613–642. https://doi.org/10.1111/j.1467-1770.1996.tb01354.x

de la Fuente, M. J. (2002). Negotiation and oral acquisition of L2 vocabulary. *Studies in Second Language Acquisition*, 24, 81–112. https://doi.org/10.1017/S0272263102001043

Dobao, A. F. (2014). Vocabulary learning in collaborative tasks: A comparison of pair and small group work. *Language Teaching Research*, 18, 497–520. https://doi.org/10.1177/1362168813519730

Ellis, R. (2009). Task-based language teaching: Sorting out the misunderstandings. *International Journal of Applied Linguistics*, 19, 221–246. https://doi.org/10.1111/j.1473-4192.2009.00231.x

Ellis, R. (2018). *Reflections on task-based language teaching*. Multilingual Matters. https://doi.org/10.21832/9781788920148

Ellis, R., & Shintani, N. (2013). *Exploring language pedagogy through second language acquisition research*. Routledge.

Ellis, R., Skehan, P., Li, S., Shintani, N., & Lambert, C. (2019). *Task-based language teaching: Theory and practice*. Cambridge University Press.

Indrarathne, B., & Kormos, J. (2017). Attentional processing of input in explicit and implicit learning conditions: An eye-tracking study. *Studies in Second Language Acquisition*, 39, 401–430. https://doi.org/10.1017/S027226311600019X

Foster, P., & Ohta, A. S. (2005). Negotiation for meaning and peer assistance in second language classrooms. *Applied Linguistics*, 26, 402–430. https://doi.org/10.1093/applin/ami014

Fujii, A., & Mackey, A. (2009). Interactional feedback in learner-learner interactions in a task-based EFL classroom. *International Review of Applied Linguistics*, 47, 267–301. https://doi.org/10.1515/iral.2009.012

Fukuta, J. (2016). Effects of task repetition on learners' attention orientation in L2 oral production. *Language Teaching Research*, 20, 321–340. https://doi.org/10.1177/1362168815570142

Hidalgo, M. A., & García Mayo, M. d. P. (2019). The influence of task repetition type on young EFL learners' attention to form. *Language Teaching Research*. https://doi.org/10.1177/1362168819865559

Hoang, H., & Boers, F. (2016). Re-telling a story in a second language: How well do adult learners mine an input text for multiword expressions? *Studies in Second Language Learning and Teaching*, 6, 513–535. doi:doi:10.14746/ssllt.2016.6.3.7

Izumi, S. (2002). Output, input enhancement, and the noticing hypothesis? An experimental study on ESL relativization. *Studies in Second Language Acquisition*, 24, 541–577. https://doi.org/10.1017/S0272263102004023

Izumi, S., & Bigelow, M. (2000). Does output promote noticing and second language acquisition? *TESOL Quarterly*, 34, 239–278. https://doi.org/10.2307/3587952

Izumi, S., Bigelow, M., Fujiwara, M., & Fearnow, S. (1999). Testing the Output Hypothesis: Effects of output on noticing and second language acquisition. *Studies in Second Language Acquisition*, 21, 421–452. https://doi.org/10.1017/S0272263199003034

Izumi, Y., & Izumi, S. (2004). Investigating the effects of oral output on the learning of relative clauses in English: Issues in the psycholinguistic requirements for effective output tasks. *Canadian Modern Language Review*, 60, 587–609. doi:doi:10.3138/cmlr.60.5.587

Joe, A. (1998). What effects do text-based tasks promoting generation have on incidental vocabulary acquisition? *Applied Linguistics*, 19, 357–377. https://doi.org/10.1093/applin/19.3.357

Kartchava, E. (2019). *Noticing oral corrective feedback in the second-language classroom: Background and evidence*. Lexington Books.

Kim, Y., & Tracy-Ventura, N. (2013). The role of task repetition in L2 performance development: What needs to be repeated during task-based interaction? *System*, 41, 829–840. https://doi.org/10.1016/j.system.2013.08.005

Li, S., Ellis, R., & Zhu, Y. (2016). Task-based versus task-supported language instruction: An experimental study. *Annual Review of Applied Linguistics*, 36, 205–229. https://doi.org/10.1017/S0267190515000069

Lindstromberg, S., Eyckmans, J., & Connabeer, R. (2016). A modified dictogloss for helping learners remember L2 academic English formulaic sequences for use in later writing. *English for Specific Purposes*, 41, 12–21. https://doi.org/10.1016/j.esp.2015.08.002

Littlewood, W. (1981). *Communicative language teaching*. Cambridge University Press.

Long, M. H. (1996). The role of the linguistic environment in second language acquisition. In W. C. Ritchie & T. K. Bhatia (Eds.), *Handbook of second language acquisition* (pp. 413–468). Academic Press.

Long, M. H. (2015). *Second language acquisition and task-based language teaching*. Wiley-Blackwell.

Loschky, L., & Bley-Vroman, R. (1993). Grammar and task-based methodology. In G. Crookes & S. M. Gass (Eds.), *Tasks and language learning: Integrating theory and practice* (pp. 123–167). Multilingual Matters.

Mackey, A. (1999). Input, interaction, and second language development: An empirical study of question formation in ESL. *Studies in Second Language Acquisition*, 21, 557–587. https://doi.org/10.1017/S0272263199004027

Mackey, A. (2006). Feedback, noticing and instructed second language learning. *Applied Linguistics*, 27, 405–430. https://doi.org/10.1093/applin/ami051

Mackey, A., Gass, S., & McDonough, K. (2000). How do learners perceive interactional feedback? *Studies in Second Language Acquisition*, 22, 471–497. https://doi.org/10.1017/S0272263100004010

McDonough, K. (2005). Identifying the impact of negative feedback and learners' responses on ESL question development. *Studies in Second Language Acquisition*, 27, 79–103. https://doi.org/10.1017/S0272263105050047

Mochizuki, N., & Ortega, L. (2008). Balancing communication and grammar in beginning-level foreign language classrooms: A study of guided planning and relativization. *Language Teaching Research*, 12, 11–37. https://doi.org/10.1177/1362168807084492

Muranoi, H. (2000). Focus on Form through interaction enhancement: Integrating formal instruction into a communicative task in EFL classrooms. *Language Learning*, 50, 617–673. https://doi.org/10.1111/0023-8333.00142

Musumeci, D. (1996). Teacher-learner negotiation in content-based instruction: Communication at cross-purposes? *Applied Linguistics*, 17, 286–325. https://doi.org/10.1093/applin/17.3.286

Nassaji, H., & Kartchava, E. (2017). *Corrective feedback in second language teaching and learning*. Routledge.

Newton, J. (2013). Incidental vocabulary learning in classroom communication tasks. *Language Teaching Research*, 17, 164–187. https://doi.org/10.1177/1362168812460814

Newton, J., & Nguyen, B. T. T. (2019). Task repetition and the public performance of speaking tasks in EFL classes at a Vietnamese high school. *Language Teaching for Young Learners*, 1, 34–56. https://doi.org/10.1075/ltyl.00004.new

Nguyen, C.-D., & Boers, F. (2019). The effect of content retelling on vocabulary uptake from a TED talk. *TESOL Quarterly*, 53, 5–29. https://doi.org/10.1002/tesq.441

Niu, R., & Helms-Park, R. (2014). Interaction, modality, and word engagement as factors in lexical learning in a Chinese context. *Language Teaching Research*, 18, 345–372. https://doi.org/10.1177/1362168813510383

Ohta, A. S. (2001). *Second language acquisition processes in the classroom: Learning Japanese*. Lawrence Erlbaum Associates.

Philp, J., & Iwashita, N. (2013). Talking, tuning in and noticing: Exploring the benefits of output in task-based peer interaction. *Language Awareness*, 22, 353–370. https://doi.org/10.1080/09658416.2012.758128

Pica, T. (1994). Research on negotiation: What does it reveal about second-language learning conditions, processes, and outcomes? *Language Learning*, 44, 493–527. https://doi.org/10.1111/j.1467-1770.1994.tb01115.x

Pica, T., Kang, H.-S., & Sauro, S. (2006). Information gap tasks: Their multiple roles and contributions to interaction research methodology. *Studies in Second Language Acquisition*, 28, 301–338. https://doi.org/10.1017/S027226310606013X

Rassaei, E. (2020). The separate and combined effects of recasts and textual enhancement as two focus on form techniques on L2 development. *System*, 89. https://doi.org/10.1016/j.system.2019.102193

Reinders, H. (2009). Learner uptake and acquisition in three grammar-oriented production activities. *Language Teaching Research*, 13, 201–222. https://doi.org/10.1177/1362168809103449

Rott, S., Williams, J., & Cameron, R. (2002). The effect of multiple-choice L1 glosses and input-output cycles on lexical acquisition and retention. *Language Teaching Research*, 6, 183–222. https://doi.org/10.1191/1362168802lr108oa

Russell, V. (2014). A closer look at the Output Hypothesis: The effect of pushed output on noticing and inductive learning of the Spanish future tense. *Foreign Language Annals*, 47, 25–47. https://doi.org/10.1111/flan.12077

Sato, M., & Loewen, S. (2018). Metacognitive instruction enhances the effectiveness of corrective feedback: Variable effects of feedback types and linguistic targets. *Language Learning*, 68, 507–545. https://doi.org/10.1111/lang.12283

Shintani, N. (2011). A comparative study of the effects of input-based and production-based instruction on vocabulary acquisition by young EFL learners. *Language Teaching Research*, 15, 137–158. https://doi.org/10.1177/1362168810388692

Shintani, N., & Ellis, R. (2010). The incidental acquisition of English plural -s by Japanese children in comprehension-based and production-based lessons: A process-product study. *Studies in Second Language Acquisition*, 32, 607–637. https://doi.org/10.1017/S0272263110000288

Song, M., & Suh, B. (2008). The effects of output task types on noticing and learning of the English past counterfactual conditional. *System*, 36, 295–312. https://doi.org/10.1016/j.system.2007.09.006

Springer, S., & Collins, L. (2008). Interacting inside and outside of the language classroom. *Language Teaching Research*, 12, 39–60. https://doi.org/10.1177/1362168807084493

Swain, M. (1995). Three functions of output in second language learning. In G. Cook & G. Seidhofer (Eds.), *Principles and practices in applied linguistics: Studies in honour of H. G. Widdowson* (pp. 125–144). Oxford University Press.

Swain, M., & Lapkin, S. (1998). Interaction and second language learning: Two adolescent French immersion students working together. *The Modern Language Journal*, 82, 320–337. https://doi.org/10.1111/j.1540-4781.1998.tb01209.x

Swain, M., & Lapkin, S. (2001). Focus on form through collaborative dialogue: Exploring task effects. In M. Bygate, P. Skehan, & M. Swain (Eds.), *Researching pedagogic tasks: Second language learning, teaching and testing* (pp. 99–118). Pearson Education.

Swan, M. (2005). Legislation by hypothesis: The case of task-based instruction. *Applied Linguistics*, 26, 376–401. https://doi.org/10.1093/applin/ami013

Thai, C., & Boers, F. (2016). Repeating a monologue under increasing time pressure: Effects on fluency, accuracy and complexity. *TESOL Quarterly*, 50, 369–393. https://doi.org/10.1002/tesq.232

Toth, P. D. (2008). Teacher- and learner-led discourse in task-based grammar instruction: Providing procedural assistance for L2 morphosyntactic development. *Language Learning*, 58, 237–283. https://doi.org/10.1111/j.1467-9922.2008.00441.x

Uggen, M. S. (2012). Reinvestigating the noticing function of output. *Language Learning*, 62, 506–540. https://doi.org/10.1111/j.1467-9922.2012.00693.x

Van de Guchte, M., Rijlaarsdam, G., Braaksma, M., & Bimmel, P. (2017). Focus on language versus content in the pre-task: Effects of guided peer-video model observations on task performance. *Language Teaching Research*, 23, 310–329. https://doi.org/10.1177/1362168817735543

Van den Branden, K. (1997). Effects of negotiation on language learners' output. *Language Learning*, 47, 589–636. https://doi.org/10.1111/0023-8333.00023

Wajnryb, R. (1990). *Resource books for teachers: Grammar dictation*. Oxford University Press.

Wang, C., & Wang, M. (2015). Effect of alignment on L2 written production. *Applied Linguistics*, 36, 503–526. https://doi.org/10.1093/applin/amt051

Widdowson, H. G. (1978). *Teaching language as communication*. Oxford University Press.

Willis, D., & Willis, J. (2007). *Doing task-based teaching*. Oxford University Press.

Yang, Y., & Lyster, R. (2010). Effects of form-focused practice and feedback on Chinese EFL learners' acquisition of regular and irregular past-tense forms. *Studies in Second Language Acquisition*, 32, 235–263. https://doi.org/10.1017/S0272263109990519

Yoshimura, F. (2006). Does manipulating foreknowledge of output tasks lead to differences in reading behaviour, text comprehension and noticing of language form? *Language Teaching Research*, 10, 419–434. https://doi.org/10.1191/1362168806lr204oa

Zhang, X. (2017). Reading–writing integrated tasks, comprehensive corrective feedback, and EFL writing development. *Language Teaching Research*, 21, 217–240. https://doi.org/10.1177/1362168815623291

PART III

LANGUAGE-FOCUSED LEARNING

5.

EVALUATING THE MERITS OF INFERENCING AND DISCOVERY LEARNING

Introduction

In this chapter I turn to procedures which turn language items or patterns into study objects. The items or patterns selected for students to examine and reflect about may be presented to the students in a decontextualized manner, but it is common to present them in context because this illustrates how they are used. A recurring question is whether it is best to inform students straightaway of the meaning and characteristics of items or patterns, or whether it is better to encourage the students to apply their inferencing skills first, in case they can figure things out themselves. Making inferences presumably requires more cognitive effort than merely taking in explanations. In keeping with the notion of *Desirable Difficulties* (e.g., Bjork & Bjork, 2014), one would expect more robust learning outcomes when students are asked to figure things out themselves than if they are spoon-fed the required information. This expectation is not always borne out by research findings, however. As always, several variables are at play. One of these is the accuracy of the inferences. Another is how effectively feedback overrides wrong inferences, especially in cases where the language items or patterns are highly confusable. A potential downside of inferencing is that wrong inferences linger in memory and interfere with the learner's recall of the correct knowledge further down the road.

Words

When working with textual input, it is common practice for teachers to draw their students' attention to unfamiliar words, and students themselves may also spontaneously ask their teacher to clarify unfamiliar words. On occasion, the meaning of words may be inferable from contextual clues (and, in addition, perhaps from known word parts or similarities with L1 words). If so, instead of simply informing their students about the word's meaning, teachers may want to encourage them to try and infer the meaning themselves, under the assumption that this active quest for meaning will leave stronger memories. A handful of studies have in recent years investigated whether word meanings are better retained by learners after they have tried to infer these from context. Overall, the findings have been mixed. Mondria (2003) presented Dutch students of French with sets of unfamiliar words embedded in sentences with enough clues to help the students infer the meanings. Either the students were asked to write down their inferences and then verify them by inspecting a word list with translations, or the translation of the words was presented alongside the sentences and so no inferences needed to be made. After this stage, the students were asked to memorize the words and their translations. The time spent by the students under the 2 learning conditions was recorded as well. A recall test administered 2 weeks later revealed no difference in effectiveness between the "meaning-inferred" and the "meaning-given" procedures. What was different, however, was the time invested under the 2 procedures: inferring and verifying the inferences naturally required more time than simply taking in the translations alongside the sentences. The meaning-given procedure should therefore be considered more efficient, since it brought about the same learning gains as the inferencing procedure but with less time invested. A similar study by Carpenter et al. (2012) also found that simply giving L1 translations was as effective as asking students to infer meanings and then verify their inferences, while the latter procedure took more time and can for that reason be considered less efficient.

Because the sentences in Mondria (2003) were designed such that wrong inferences were prevented most of the time, the study does not provide a lot of data to evaluate the side-effects of wrong inferences. Still, words which students failed to recall in the posttest were often the ones for which their inferences had needed to be rectified at the learning stage. More evidence that incorrect inferences can interfere with later recall despite corrective feedback was furnished by Elgort (2017). Chinese learners of English were presented with sets of 12 unfamiliar words, each word embedded in 3 sentences containing contextual clues. The learners were asked to infer the words' meanings, after which they were presented with dictionary-style definitions to verify their inferences. After dealing with a total of 48 words this way, the participants were presented with the same words but without contextual clues and asked to recall the meanings. Given the challenge of remembering as many as 48 new words in just one study session, it is not surprising that posttest scores were poor (about 15%). The relevant point here, however, is that meanings which the participants failed to infer in the study phase were especially poorly recalled in the posttest, which indicates that the feedback (presenting the learners with the correct meanings after their inferences) was not particularly effective. Unlike Mondria (2003), Elgort (2017) did not include a comparison condition where participants were given the word meanings from the start. A more recent experiment (Elgort et al., 2020), however, did compare inferencing and meaning-given procedures and found better learning gains for the former regardless of whether the inferences were incorrect and thus needed to be rectified through feedback. In this study, Chinese learners of English were presented with series of short text passages (about 120 words in length), each containing a new word 3 times and in contexts pointing to the meaning of the words. In one condition, the participants were asked to infer the meaning of the word after each passage, and they were then shown a dictionary-style definition of the word to verify their inferences. In another condition, the participants were first presented with the dictionary-style definition of the word before they read the passage. After reading the passage they were asked to recall the word's meaning. After having dealt with 45 words this way, the participants were presented with the target words again and asked about their meanings. The posttest performance was this time better after the inferencing activity. The meanings of words that were inferred correctly again stood a better chance of being recalled than those which were not inferred correctly, but even in the latter case recall was slightly better than in the meaning-given condition. This suggests that encouraging students to infer word meaning from supportive contexts is beneficial after all, even if the inferencing fails and needs to be rectified through feedback. It must be mentioned that, overall, posttest performance in Elgort et al. (2020) was again rather poor: success rates were 20% and 15% for the inferencing and the meaning-given condition, respectively. Again, this is not surprising, because the participants had been exposed to as many as 45 new words in one go, which must have been very taxing on memory. In addition, these were all technical words related to specialized domains such as building and construction, and the participants may have felt knowledge of such specialized vocabulary was not particularly relevant for them beyond the context of the experiment. In studies such as these, there is often a tension between experimental rigour (ensuring learner-participants do not yet know the target words and including enough target words for the sake of statistical power) and the learner-participants' needs and interests.

A striking observation in Elgort et al. (2020) was that participants in the meaning-given condition often (close to 20%) failed to accurately recall the meaning of a target word immediately after reading the text passage, even though they had been presented with its definition just before. Apparently, presenting a definition of a word prior to reading a passage did not guarantee adequate understanding. A closer look at the list of definitions made available in the online supplement (Appendix A) to the article helps to explain this. Take, for example, the following definition (Elgort et al., 2020): "a hand tool that is used to hold or twist a nut or bolt", which requires understanding *nut* and *bolt*. Similarly, "A decorative wooden border at the top of a window used to conceal curtain fittings" may not be immediately transparent if one is not familiar with the meanings of *fittings* and *border* in this description. Although care may have been taken in the experiment to use words in the materials which, according to corpus frequency data, should have been within the vocabulary range of the participants, the problem is that although learners may be familiar with the most common meaning of a word, they may not yet be familiar with its less common meanings. It could be interesting to replicate Elgort et al. (2020) but with easier elucidations of word meaning, such as L1 translations or pictures. Another modification could be to present the meaning of the target word alongside instead of before the text passage, as was done by Mondria (2003). The latter approach was also taken by Huang and Lin (2014), who gave Chinese students of English a text to read in which the same 8 target words were incorporated 3 times, but each time on a different page (displayed sequentially on a computer screen). In one reading condition, the learners did not need to infer word meanings, because the words were glossed (L1 translation) on every occurrence. In a second reading condition, however, the first instance of each word was not accompanied by a gloss and the students were required to infer its meaning before reading on. The inferences were subsequently confirmed or rectified on reading the glosses on the following pages. The third reading condition had a gloss for the first instance of the target but did not for the second instance. Students were required to supply the word's meaning before encountering the word a third time, this time again with a gloss. Posttests asking the students to recall the words' meanings were administered shortly after the reading activity and again 2 weeks later. The best results on both tests were obtained when students had seen the words explained first, then retrieved this information from memory on the second encounter with the words, and then saw the explanation again on the third encounter. This illustrates the positive effect of retrieval, about which more will be said in chapter 6. Posttest performance was poorer when students had first been required to infer word meaning before seeing the glosses, and this was due to the instances where students had started off with incorrect inferences. The latter suggests that, to reap the most benefit of inferencing, this should be done with a high success rate. Finally, the students who engaged in neither inferencing nor retrieval from memory obtained the poorest posttest scores. Just seeing the same information repeated without doing anything with it thus appears relatively ineffective (more evidence of which I will present in chapter 6).

For now, what can safely be concluded from the above collection of findings is that encouraging students to try and infer word meanings from context is beneficial *provided the inferencing is successful.* In the case of incorrect inferences, the available evidence is rather mixed, and when incorrect inferences seem likely, then clarifying word meanings from the start may well be the safer—and certainly less time-consuming—option. It is worth reiterating here that the text passages in the above experiments were specially created to offer contextual support for the inferences. The question this raises is how often students can be expected to infer word meanings *accurately* when they engage with other texts. After all, it is well documented that inferencing is error prone, and that this holds true even when texts are carefully selected to match the learners' proficiency level (e.g., Nassaji, 2003)—such as what could be expected of the input materials used in L2 classrooms. According to a review of available studies on this topic (van Zeeland, 2014), the average success rate when learners are asked to infer word meanings from comprehensible input is very seldom better than 60%.

Phrases

When it comes to phrases, it is useful to make a distinction between learning their meaning and learning their lexical composition (or form). This is because for some phrases (notably idioms and phrasal verbs), the first challenge is to establish their meaning (since their meaning does not follow straightforwardly from understanding the individual lexical components), while for others the meaning is already transparent. Let's start with the challenge for learners to establish the meaning of idioms. Analogous to the above discussion about word learning, one may wonder how successfully learners infer the meaning of idioms from context. Boers et al. (2007) presented English majors with 16 idioms (e.g., *hedge your bets, touch base* and *throw in your hand*) in supportive contexts—these were example sentences taken from an idiom dictionary and so presumably sentences which the dictionary makers considered illustrative of their use and meaning—and asked the students to guess the meaning of the expressions. The students managed to figure out on average only 24% of the idiomatic meanings they had no prior knowledge of. This is reminiscent of an earlier study by Cooper (1999), who also found that learners often fail to accurately infer the meaning of idioms from context, even if the context is quite informative. Without highly supportive contexts, inferencing is bound to be even less successful. Littlemore et al. (2011) found that international students at a British university not only failed to grasp the meaning of many of their lecturers' figurative expressions, but also that they were seldom aware of their misunderstanding. Martinez and Murphy (2011) found that intermediate-level learners sometimes take idiomatic expressions (e.g., *over the hill*—'growing too old for certain activities') literally ('on the other side of the hill'). When the literal reading is congruent with the idiomatic meaning, this can be helpful. However, if learners spontaneously try a literal interpretation of new idioms as a basis for inferring their idiomatic meaning, this will not always work well. There are several obstacles. One is that idioms may simply contain words that are unknown to the learner, either because they are low-frequency words (e.g., *tether* in *at the end of your tether* and *rein* in *keep a tight rein on someone*) or because they are obsolete outside the idiom in which they have been preserved (e.g., *doldrums* in *be in/out of the doldrums*). Another obstacle is the elliptic nature of many idioms. For instance, how can a learner be expected to guess what is cut in the expression *to cut and run*, what is chopped in *chop and change*, and what is thick in *through thick and thin*? Similarly, learners may be mystified by the proposition that a punch can be pulled in *pull no punches* and that a crop can be creamy in *cream of the crop*. In such cases, inferencing efforts are unlikely to lead anywhere. (Incidentally, note that the above examples of word strings display phonological patterns such as alliteration that probably helped them to become set phrases in the language—a notion I will pick up again in chapter 7, where I discuss ways of making phrases more memorable for learners.) The lexical composition of an idiom can also be deceptive and prompt inaccurate meaning inferences. For example, a learner may attach the wrong meaning to homonyms (i.e., different words that happen to share the same form). When encountering *to follow suit*, for instance, learners are likely to think of *suit* as something you can wear, and not its use in card games (Boers et al., 2004a). Learners may then wrongly infer that the idiom means something like *obeying authority*, given the observation that men in a position of status tend to wear suits. Polysemy (i.e., having different, but still related, meanings) and vagueness of meaning are also bound to lead learners astray. On encountering *to show someone the ropes*, the learner may think of the ropes used by a hangman or perhaps the ropes of a boxing ring instead of the ropes on a sailing vessel. The expression could then be interpreted as conveying a threat instead of an offer to teach someone a certain skill. Similarly, the *gun* in *to jump the gun* can easily be mistaken for a weapon rather than the pistol used to signal the start of a racing contest. This idiom may then be misinterpreted as referring to an act of bravery, as it may evoke the scene of someone trying to disarm a criminal holding a gun. In a similar vein, the *shot* in *a shot in the arm* may be mistaken for a shot from a weapon instead of an injection of medicine. Hearing or seeing the idiom *the gloves are off* may conjure up an image of someone who is taking a break from work that requires gloves. Even if learners were to correctly guess that the gloves in this expression originally refer to boxing gloves, they would still probably interpret the act of taking boxing gloves off as signifying that the fight is over, while the expression means the opposite—evoking the image of boxers using their bare fists to inflict more serious injury on each other.

Interference from L1 is an additional obstacle to L2 idiom interpretation (Boers, 2003). The meaning of a given idiom in L2 need not coincide with that of a similar expression in L1. Cross-cultural differences can also play a part. An example of this is the way different communities construe the domains of reason and emotion. The legacies of the Cartesian division between the mind and the body and the Jamesian view of emotions are still noticeable in the repertoires of European languages: the mind (associated with the head) is the seat of reason, while the emotions reside in the body, with the "higher" emotions more specifically residing in the heart. This is reflected in the high number of *heart* expressions used to talk about emotions (*a bleeding heart, a broken heart, to lose heart, to wear your heart on your sleeve, to eat your heart out, to win someone's heart* and so on). In many other cultures, a division between reason and emotion does not correspond to a mind/head versus body division. In Chinese culture, the concept of mind in fact coincides with the concept of heart (*xin*). It is not surprising, then, that Chinese learners of English can find it hard to make sense of English idioms containing the words *heart, mind* and *head* (Hu & Fong, 2010). Conversely, Westerners learning Chinese can be expected to be puzzled by Chinese idioms containing *xin*. Cultural variation may hinder L2 idiom comprehension even in the case of closely related languages (e.g., Boers & Stengers, 2008). Examples include idioms derived from sports that do not share the same popularity across cultures. For example, the Spanish stock of idioms contains many more expressions derived from bullfighting than, say, the English repertoire. Conversely, the English idiom repertoire contains more expressions derived from ball games such as cricket in British English (e.g., *off your own bat* and *hit someone for six*) and baseball in American English (e.g., *go in to bat for someone* and *touch all the bases*), which appear particularly hard to interpret for learners from communities where these sports are virtually unknown (Boers et al., 2004b).

It should be clear from the above that many obstacles can prevent successful interpretation of L2 figurative phrases if learners are left to their own devices. In some cases, inferences are barely possible; in other cases, the familiar-looking lexical constituents of the idiom do provide a basis for inferencing. When the inferencing goes wrong, however, the question is whether the inaccurate inference is easily eradicated through corrective feedback or if it will linger in memory and possibly interfere with recall of the correct meaning later. In one of the experiments reported in Boers et al. (2007), students tended to perform better on a posttest after a learning procedure where hints about the literal underpinnings of the idioms helped them to infer the idiomatic meanings. This is compatible with the view that it is judicious to avoid wrong inferencing lest they cause interference later. Note that this is different from the guessing that is sometimes required of participants in laboratory-type experiments where they are asked to blindly guess the meaning of lexical items they have never seen or heard before, without any clues (e.g., Potts & Shanks, 2014). In that case, the participants have no basis for inferencing at all and are unlikely to consider their guesses as remotely plausible. Such guesses may then easily be supplanted by the correct answer. In the case of idioms consisting of familiar-looking words, however, learners do have a platform to launch an inferencing effort that (by virtue of the effort being made) may leave more durable memory traces. If the inference turns out to be wrong, it may be more difficult to erase it from memory.

Another class of phrases where the lexical makeup does not always help to interpret the overall meaning is that of phrasal verbs (e.g., *turn down an offer, live up to expectations, carry on, pass away, give in to temptation, head off to work*). Moreover, a single verb-particle combination can express diverse meanings (e.g., *make up a story, make up after an argument, make up one's face*) (Gardner & Davies, 2007; Garnier & Schmitt, 2015; Liu & Myers, 2020). Still, many phrasal verbs consist of familiar, high-frequency words which put learners in a position where they can sometimes hazard a guess about the meaning of the phrases. This may appear feasible especially when the phrasal verb plausibly reflects a general "conceptual metaphor" (Lakoff & Johnson, 1980). For example, *up* often denotes something positive while *down* often denotes something negative. Perhaps it is because the form–meaning relation of at least some phrasal verbs appears guessable that many textbooks and websites introduce phrasal verbs to learners in a quiz format, where the learners are asked to match phrasal verbs with a paraphrase of their meaning or where the learners are asked to fill in the missing particle in gap-fill exercises (Strong & Boers, 2019a, b). In such cases, learners are invited to infer the meaning or predict the lexical makeup of phrasal verbs based on their understanding of the constituent words. Feedback in the form of an answer key (when available) then confirms or rectifies the learner's responses. The question this raises again is whether encouraging learners to make these inferences (or guesses) before presenting them with the correct answers is such a good idea. This question was addressed by Strong and Boers (2019a). Japanese students of English learned phrasal verbs in a computer-assisted learning experiment, where one group was simply given the phrasal verbs and their corresponding meanings, while another group was first asked to supply the missing particle for each phrasal verb. For example, in the former condition, the students were first shown the following information:

> *Hang out* = spend time with friends.
> Speaker A: Hey, Yuki, if you're not busy after work, do you want to hang out?
> Speaker B: I'm sorry, Tomoko, but I'm not feeling well today. How about tomorrow?

After receiving this type of input on 7 phrasal verbs, these students were invited to retrieve the particles from memory, in a gap-fill exercise, such as:

> Speaker A: Hey, Yuki, if you're not busy after work, do you want to hang _____?
> Speaker B: I'm sorry, Tomoko, but I'm not feeling well today. How about tomorrow?

For students in the other group, the sequence was reversed: they first tried the gap-fill exercise and were only then presented with the explanations. The 2 learning conditions may be characterized as study + retrieval (the former condition) and trial and error + feedback (the latter condition). The phrasal verbs were presented in sets of 7, because Strong and Boers (2019a) found this to be the average number of items per exercise in textbooks for students of English. When the students were asked to supply the missing particles again 2 weeks later, the score was 14% better when they had followed the study + retrieval procedure compared to the trial and error + feedback procedure. Interestingly, no fewer than 25% of the wrong responses given by students who had tackled the phrasal verbs in the trial-and-error fashion were duplicates of the wrong responses they had supplied in the exercise. This indicates that the corrective feedback on the exercises often failed to supplant the incorrect guesses in long-term memory. One may wonder if the feedback provided in the above experiment was ineffective because it came after the students had completed an exercise on 7 phrasal verbs, and thus with a delay. Perhaps immediate corrective feedback after each exercise item is more effective as it might prevent wrong responses from lingering in memory. This was part of a follow-up study (Strong & Boers, 2019b), which used essentially the same procedures as described above, with the difference that the phrasal verbs were tackled one at a time. So, the study + retrieval group saw information about a phrasal verb, and this was followed immediately on the next screen by the gap-fill exercise pertaining just to that phrasal verb. In the trial and error + feedback condition, the students supplied the missing particle of a phrasal verb in a gap-fill exercise and then saw the correct information for that same item straightaway on the next screen. This mimics web-based exercises which also sometimes provide immediate feedback per exercise item. Unfortunately, this immediate feedback did not work wonders either: the posttest scores were again poorer after the trial-and-error procedure, and again many of the wrong exercise responses re-emerged in the test. Altogether, then, it seems more judicious to first give students the opportunity to take in correct information about a phrasal verb and then provide retrieval practice to consolidate the newly acquired knowledge.

In the case of phrasal verbs, the confusability concerns both idiomatic meaning (what do *hang out* and *hang on* mean?) and lexical composition (why *hang out* rather than *hang in* or *hang about*?). Another type of highly confusable phrases, but where the confusability concerns mostly lexical composition rather than meaning, are collocations (e.g., why *slim chance* rather than *narrow chance* and why *deeply religious* rather than *highly religious*?). A class of collocations whose confusability for learners has been well documented (Laufer & Waldman, 2011; Nesselhauf, 2003; Peters, 2016) are verb–noun collocations (e.g., *conduct research, commit a crime, run a business, make a comment, take a break, have a dream, do a good job*). With the growing recognition more generally of the important role of multiword expressions in language, textbook authors have also started to give due attention to such phrases. Often this is again through procedures where students are first invited to guess which words belong together, after which they check their answers (Boers & Strong, 2016). Most of the exercises are essentially matching activities, where students connect words from different columns, choose words from a list to complete gapped sentences, circle the correct option from a list of candidate collocates, choose between 2 synonyms preceding a given noun (e.g., choose the correct option in *say/tell the truth*) and so on. In other words, such exercises require students to assemble phrases before being informed which combinations of the words are appropriate. Unless the students already know the collocations, they are thus expected to learn though trial and error, akin to some of the types of exercises on phrasal verbs discussed above. Boers et al. (2014) put several of such exercise formats concerning verb-noun collocations to the test with intermediate students of English. The students did the exercises, verified their answers with reference to the answer key and took a test on the same collocations 2 weeks later. This posttest was a gap-fill test where they were required to supply the missing verbs (e.g., *I'll _____ a picture of you standing in front of the fountain*). The test scores were generally only marginally better (by 5 to 10%) than the scores on the same test administered a month earlier. Interestingly, while students did recall a few new collocations from the exercise procedures, they also made mistakes on some posttest items even though their pretest response had been correct. For example, in the pretest a learner correctly supplied *take* to complete the phrase *take a new approach to [...]* but wrote *give* (resulting in the non-conventional combination *give a new approach*) in the posttest. *Give* was one of the options to choose from presented on the worksheet 2 weeks previously. The student might perhaps never have made this specific mistake had she not contemplated the wrong word combination in the exercise. There were countless instances where the learners duplicated the mistakes they had made in the exercise, again indicating that the feedback often failed to replace the wrong guesses in long-term memory.

Simply comparing one's exercise responses to an answer key and then copying the correct answers on the worksheet does perhaps not require enough engagement on the student's part. Giving the students a more active role in finding the correct answers, for example by having them consult dictionaries, might work better. This was tried out by Laufer (2011), who first invited students of English to try and supply the verbs of 15 verb–noun collocations in gapped sentences (e.g., *make* in [...] ____ *headlines*) and then gave them copies of dictionary entries for confirmation or correction of their answers. The students were then asked to do the completion exercise again. Surprisingly, over half of the exercise items remained incorrect despite the availability of the dictionary pages. A posttest one week later yielded a mean score of only 4 out of 15, which was hardly better than the students' initial performance in the exercise. A partial replication was conducted by Chen (2016), who directed the students to online dictionaries instead of handing out paper copies. The results were similarly disappointing: on average only 2 out of 12 collocations were correctly recalled shortly after the dictionary-assisted exercise. A plausible explanation for these disappointing learning gains is that the students failed to find the information they needed in the dictionaries. Successful extraction of collocations from a general dictionary will inevitably depend on the amount of attention the dictionary gives to collocations and on how it presents this information (Dziemianko, 2014). Even if students consult a specially designed collocation dictionary, there is no guarantee that they will find the sub-entries they need (Komuro, 2009). Perhaps information about collocation is easier to extract from online corpora—a possibility which I will return to below. Another explanation for the poor outcomes in Laufer (2011) and Chen (2016) is that looking up information and copying it down is one thing, but committing the information to memory is quite another.

From the above reviews, it appears that trial-and-error exercises where students are invited to re-assemble broken-up collocations are not efficient for improving the students' collocational accuracy. If so, then it is probably safer to present the collocations to the students in their intact, complete forms from the very start. Textbooks indeed also occasionally include exercises where students are shown a collection of intact collocations to select from, for example to insert the appropriate intact collocations in gapped sentences. Boers et al. (2017) compared the learning gains obtained from this exercise format where collocations are presented as intact units, with the gains from the format discussed above where students are required to select verbs to be matched with their noun collocates. Working with intact collocations was found to generate better learning. Again, after doing the verb-noun matching exercise, several students repeated their incorrect answers in the posttest despite the corrective feedback given at the exercise stage. For instance, the list of verbs to choose from included the near synonyms *speak* and *talk*, and a student would wrongly remember *talk volumes* instead of *speak volumes*. But the confusion was not only due to near synonyms. For example, a student produced *cast fault with* instead of *find fault with* (*cast* was meant to complete _____ *doubt on* in the exercise) and *pay his bluff* instead of *call his bluff* (*pay* was meant to complete _____ *tribute to*). Again, it might never have occurred to this student to combine these verbs and nouns had it not been for the exercise. An additional advantage of asking students to select *intact* phrases to complete a given context is that this exercise necessitates a focus on meaning (because the phrase should fit the semantics of the given context). Many expressions which may seem transparent to an L1 user are not necessarily so for L2 learners (Boers & Webb, 2015). For example, the collocation *close the meeting* may not be transparent to a learner for whom this conjures up an image of closed doors (and thus possibly an interpretation as 'meeting behind closed doors'). Even a phrase like *pay tribute* may be misunderstood if a learner thinks of *pay* in the financial transaction sense. Using the transparency criterion to distinguish collocations from idioms gets problematic once we take the perspective of L2 learners and ask the question "transparent to whom?" In any case, the results of the above classroom experiments suggest that wrong responses made in a collocation exercise risk leaving undesirable traces in memory. If so, then it is probably best to minimize the risk of error at the exercise stage. One way of doing this is to present learners with example sentences featuring the target expressions alongside the exercise, as is done in some resources for independent study such as McCarthy and O'Dell (2005). Stengers and Boers (2015) compared this example-guided implementation of gap-fill exercises for learning verb-noun collocations in Spanish with a trial-and-error implementation. They indeed found the former to be slightly more beneficial, again because many wrong exercise responses generated through trial and error re-emerged in the posttest. At the same time, the learning gains brought about by the examples-guided procedure were still far from impressive (18%). An explanation may be that this activity just required the students to browse through the list of example sentences and to copy the appropriate collocations from them. Had the students been required to first read the examples and then retrieve the collocations from memory to complete the exercise, the learning gains would possibly have been better (see chapter 6 on the benefits of retrieval practice).

Another way of engaging learners with intact phrases is to have them explore authentic texts for examples (Lewis, 1997). This also serves the purpose of awareness-raising about the phraseological dimension of discourse more generally and could foster greater learner autonomy. It also has the advantage that the phrases are met in actual discourse, which may help learners to appreciate their pragmatic functions. Boers et al. (2006) tried this approach. Two groups of students majoring in English used the same in-class reading and listening texts over the course of a school year. One group was regularly asked to identify phrases in these texts after which the result of their exploration was compared to the teacher's. The other group was not explicitly alerted to the phraseological dimension of the texts. At the end of the course, the students' oral proficiency was gauged in an interview. The phrase-focused group was found to use more phrases than the comparison group. However, this greater number did not actually reflect greater uptake of phrases from the texts they had explored in class. Instead, the phrases used in the interview were mostly expressions borrowed from a text given as prompt for the interview (see chapter 4 on recycling or "mining" language from input texts). So, it seems the intervention equipped the students with a *strategic* advantage, but it is not clear from this classroom study how well it helped them to remember the phrases they encountered as they explored the course texts in class. When the study was replicated with a new cohort of students (Stengers et al., 2010), but *without* the use of an L2 text prompt in the end-of-course interview, the number of phrases used by both groups was very similar, and again few of the phrases were ones that had been encountered in the course texts. It needs to be acknowledged, though, that an interview is probably too crude an elicitation instrument to reveal the true extent to which items were learned from the course materials. The students may in theory have picked up a substantial number of phrases from these materials, but the end-of-course interview topics did not require their use—put differently, they were not "task essential" (see chapter 4). As argued by Thomson et al. (2019), replication studies should add tests specifically on the phrases from the course materials.

A practical problem with asking learners to identify phrases in texts is how learners can be expected to recognize phrases unless they are already (somewhat) familiar with them. After all, any word sequence could theoretically be a conventional multiword expression, and it may be naïve to expect L2 learners to have reliable intuitions about which sequences are more likely candidates than others. It is conceivable that raising students' awareness that a large proportion of natural discourse consists of phraseological units will make them consider more word sequences as *potential* instances of this broad phenomenon (e.g., Jones & Haywood, 2004), but there is no guarantee that all of them will truly qualify as such. Eyckmans et al. (2007) asked students of English who had regularly explored texts for phrasal units over the course of a school year to underline such items in a new text. These students indeed underlined significantly more segments of the text than a comparison group did. On the downside, this included many segments that were *not* considered English phrasal units by native speakers.

Instead of expecting learners to identify phrases themselves, this can of course also be done for them. Peters (2009, 2012), for instance, presented students with texts in which some words and phrases were typographically enhanced (underlined and in bold font) and glossed in the margin. Posttests showed substantial learning (50–70%) of these items, far more substantial than the gains attested in other studies of typographic enhancement and glossing (see chapter 3). Unlike those other studies, however, the text was introduced as material for intentional vocabulary learning, and the students knew a test would follow. The typographic enhancement thus helped the students to focus their attention on the lexical items that—having been preselected by the instructor—were to be expected in the test. The posttests in fact also targeted items which were *not* enhanced in the text, and these were recalled more poorly.

Nonetheless, further endeavours to foster learner autonomy must be worthwhile, since learners will not always be in a position where they can rely on a teacher to point out useful word strings. A possibility here is to familiarize students with resources such as online dictionaries and online corpora to help them verify their hunches about the phrase status of the word strings they come across. This approach was tried by Bui et al. (2020). Upper-intermediate students of English in Vietnam were familiarized with online versions of dictionaries such as *Macmillan English Dictionary* and *Cambridge English Dictionary*, which provide easily accessible information on a good range of fixed expressions, and with the collocation query functions of COCA (Corpus of Contemporary American English). They then explored authentic texts in 10 successive classes (one per week) for instances of phraseological units or strong collocations, verifying their intuitions by consulting these online resources. They were asked to make notes of the phrases they discovered, and later analysis of these notes showed that the students were quite successful at distinguishing phrases from "free" word combinations, although they also overlooked many phrases in the texts. The next question is how well the students *remembered* the new phrases from the texts. For this purpose, a gap-fill test was administered before and after the 10-week course. The students improved their score by 32%. Predictably, it was especially the phrases which the students had engaged with during the classroom activities and taken notes about that stood the best chance of being recalled. The learning gain needs to be put into perspective, however, because a comparison group that had used the same texts as input for content-oriented interactive activities and whose attention had not been directed to phraseology in the 10-week course also improved their knowledge of the phrases, by 20%. Again, detecting phrases in input texts is a useful initial step in a learning process, but learners will often need to do more with the phrases—such as incorporating them in their own output—in order to retain them in long-term memory.

If the comparison group borrowed lexical items from the input texts for their content-oriented interactive output activities, this may help to explain that they also recalled quite a few of them. Another thing to bear in mind is that, in experiments such as this, the learning gains that are measured concern just one knowledge domain (here: knowledge of phrases). It is conceivable that the comparison group developed other aspects of knowledge and enhanced their communication skills in their content-oriented interactive classes to a greater degree than the phrase-discovery group did, but such other improvements were not measured. This comment holds true for the majority of classroom experiments where the merits of language-focused interventions are examined.

Although the students in the classroom experiment just discussed tended to consult dictionaries first and foremost and the online corpus to a lesser extent, they did regularly examine concordance lines (i.e., examples of authentic language use extracted from the corpus) to find out about the phraseological patterning of words. This use of a corpus for discovery learning is often referred to as *Data-Driven Learning* (DDL) (Johns, 1991). Collocations have attracted a fair amount of attention from researchers interested in DDL, and according to meta-analytic reviews of the available research (Boulton & Cobb, 2017; Lee et al., 2019), learners tend to remember collocations better after they have discovered them in concordance lines (or through other corpus queries) than after receiving teacher-led instruction. Whether this discovery learning necessarily requires corpus-based examples rather than, say, examples created by a teacher or course writer is not clear. The merits of DDL may well be attributed to the discovery dimension rather than corpus use *per se*. The advantage of using a corpus is that many examples are readily available, and these will at least be authentic (in contrast to contrived-looking examples one occasionally finds in textbooks). That said, this authenticity can also make examples extracted from a corpus difficult to process for non-advanced learners, due to the presence of unfamiliar words and references to unfamiliar people and events. Teachers and researchers may then decide to select concordance lines they consider the most helpful and to edit concordance lines to make them easier to understand, in which case the distinction between authentic and made-up examples naturally gets blurred. A thing worth pointing out as well is that the favorable conclusion about DDL drawn by the aforementioned meta-analytic reviews is to some extent due to inclusion of studies where the comparisons were not exactly "fair". For instance, in some of the studies, collocations-focused DDL was compared to activities without any attention to collocations, and so it is no wonder that the DDL groups performed better on collocations-focused tests (see Boers et al., 2020, for additional critique). It is also important to make a distinction between effectiveness (i.e., how much learning occurs) and efficiency (i.e., the time invested to obtain good learning outcomes). A study by Lee and Lin (2019), for example, found very similar learning gains for students who were asked to use a corpus for discovery learning and students who used the corpus to find examples of word uses they were first informed about, but the former learning procedure took twice as long as the latter. Clearly, more empirical work to gauge the benefits of discovery learning would be welcome. Collocation does seem to be well suited to this approach because it is relatively straightforward to discover from a series of examples that 2 words often co-occur, and, in the case of transparent phrases, there is no additional challenge to figure out their meaning. This is rather different when it comes to a discovery approach to grammar patterns, to which I turn next.

Patterns

In the realm of grammar learning and teaching, a common label for discovery learning is *guided inductive learning*. In this approach, learners are presented with examples of a pattern and directed to relevant characteristics of the examples to help them discern the pattern (or the grammar "rule"). For example, students might be asked to consider instances of comparative forms (e.g., *Tom is tall, but Bill is even taller; Jane is smart, but Lucy is smarter; Tom is helpful, but Bill is even more helpful; Jane is talkative, but Lucy is more talkative*), and be given the guiding question "How are comparisons expressed in English with short (one-syllable) adjectives, and how is it done with longer (multi-syllable) ones?" This differs from a deductive approach, where the "rule" is presented first (e.g., "To express comparison in English, one usually adds –er to one-syllable adjectives; in the case of multi-syllable adjectives, one instead puts 'more' before the adjective"), and learners next apply this rule knowledge to instances. After students have been invited to "induce" a grammar rule, verification normally follows to make sure they arrived at the right conclusion. If they have not, more examples and more guidance may be required (and, if that fails, the instructor may eventually need to clarify the pattern). It stands to reason that applying an inductive approach is likely to take longer than applying a deductive approach, especially in the case of relatively complex grammar patterns. Still, as discussed at the beginning of this chapter, the inductive approach looks appealing because it is expected to stimulate more cognitive engagement, and cognitive engagement is expected to lead to better retention of knowledge. Contemporary L2 textbooks vary as to whether they give precedence to guided inductive learning of grammar (e.g., Crace & Acklam, 2011; Cunningham et al., 2013; Soars & Soars, 2016) or to a deductive presentation of grammar patterns (e.g., Kerr & Jones, 2012; Richards et al., 2017). This variation suggests that not all language teaching professionals are convinced that guided inductive grammar learning is always the most suitable approach, and so examining its effectiveness (and efficiency) is certainly of practical value. However, it turns out there is no abundance of empirical studies to support the prediction that guided induction will bring about greater gains in grammar knowledge than a deductive presentation. An early, small-scale study (Herron & Tomasello, 1992) showed an advantage for inductive over deductive grammar learning in a French course, but this could be due to the type of practice which followed the grammar explanations in the deductive procedure. According to the example given in the article, the exercises were oral drills which required hardly any effort from the students to retrieve the learned patterns from memory (see chapter 6 about the importance of retrieval). These drills were possibly too shallow to serve the purpose of consolidating the new knowledge. A comparison of deductive and inductive learning was also included in an early study by Robinson (1996), who, by contrast, found deductive learning to be much more effective. In that study, however, it is far from certain whether the participants in the inductive learning condition managed to discover the grammar rules from the examples given. As these participants were not subsequently presented with these rules to verify their hypotheses, it is not surprising that they performed poorly on the posttests.

Among the few more recent studies reporting evidence in favour of guided induction is a study by Cerezo et al. (2016), who examined ways of teaching Spanish *gustar* patterns. The Spanish counterpart of "I like this red wine" is "Me gusta este vino tinto" (literally, "to me pleases this red wine") or "Este vino tinto me gusta" (literally, "this red wine pleases me"). Because the sentence constituent that functions as subject (or nominative case) in English is assigned the role of indirect object (or dative case) in Spanish *gustar* patterns, such patterns are understandably confusing for English learners of Spanish. Cerezo et al. (2016) compared 2 instructional interventions to address this problem. In their guided induction lesson, the students played a video game specially designed to help them master the *gustar* patterns in a stepwise fashion, where the students received feedback on their choices and with guiding questions about what they should pay attention to. The students were then presented with potential rules for the *gustar* pattern they had been working on and asked to choose the correct rule. The deductive lesson, by contrast, took place in a regular classroom where the teacher explained the rules and illustrated them using the same sentences that were part of the video game. Completing the video game took about 20 minutes; the deductive presentation took about 15 minutes. The students who had received the guided induction lesson (through playing the video game) outperformed the group that had received the teacher-fronted deductive lesson on both immediate and 2-week delayed productive knowledge tests. While this finding is in accordance with the thesis that guided induction is preferable to deductive rule presentation (at least in the case of the grammar pattern examined), it is not clear whether the results should necessarily be attributed to the cognitive operations of induction versus deduction or perhaps rather to the difference in time investment and the engaging nature of a video game in comparison to a teacher-led lesson. It is also worth noting that the deductive lesson seems to have involved less productive practice than what was done in the video game, and the posttests where an advantage for guided induction was attested concerned productive knowledge.

More direct comparisons of guided induction and deductive treatments of grammar patterns have been reported by Haight et al. (2007) and by Vogel et al. (2011). In both studies, some of the grammar patterns covered in a French course were taught deductively and the others inductively. This was done in a counter-balanced fashion, so that for the first grammar pattern half of the students received the inductive treatment while the others learned the pattern deductively, but this was switched for the second pattern, switched again for the third and so on. The students were tested immediately at the end of each lesson and again at the end of the term. The immediate test results showed an advantage for guided induction, but this advantage became marginal in the end-of-term test in Haight et al. (2007) and it disappeared altogether in Vogel et al. (2011), thus casting doubt over the durability of the benefits of inductive grammar learning in the language classroom. In fact, regardless of treatment condition, the average test score in Vogel et al. (2011) improved from the pretest (administered at the start of the term) to the end-of-term test by fewer than 3 out of 20 multiple-choice test items (resulting in a final average score of 10.5/20). Interestingly, a debriefing questionnaire revealed that most of the students preferred a deductive approach to grammar lessons.

While the studies by Haight et al. (2007) and Vogel et al. (2011) are informative because they examined effects of different instructional methods implemented in a real, full-term language course, it is somewhat unfortunate that they did not report treatment effects separately for each of the grammar patterns. It is conceivable, after all, that some patterns are better suited than others to guided induction, and this may well be the reason why some studies (e.g., Erlam, 2003, to be reviewed further below) have not furnished evidence in favour of inductive grammar learning. At one extreme, a certain pattern (e.g., question formation) may be too complex to guarantee accurate rule induction despite stepwise guidance. Students may even wonder whether the time invested in trying to figure out a complex pattern is worth their while, especially if a teacher is present who could simply explain the pattern to them. At the other extreme, a certain pattern (e.g., add –s to pluralize nouns) may be so straightforward that the effort to discover it is too minimal to make a difference as far as the creation of strong memories is concerned. The picture is further complicated by the quality of the deductive instruction against which the benefits of guided induction are weighed. If a rule explanation given at the beginning of a lesson is too abstract, vague or hard to follow, then it is unlikely to accelerate learning because time will need to be invested in studying the examples and figuring out what the explanation is saying about them. In a similar vein, the quality of the activities that follow the rule presentation matters, if the purpose is for learners to apply the newly learned rule and entrench it in memory (see chapter 6).

The fact that not all research reports include much information about the instructional treatment against which the benefits of an experimental treatment are weighed can render a proper evaluation of the latter difficult. For example, Smart (2014) reported a small-scale study where students appeared to benefit more from 4 hours of guided inductive learning about the English passive voice than their peers who were taught according to a deductive approach. Unfortunately, how the latter was implemented is described in broad-brush strokes, and no sample materials are included (unlike for the inductive lesson). Smart's (2014) work is worth mentioning for an additional reason, however. Whereas the previous studies discussed in this section used examples of a chosen grammar pattern that were created for instructional purposes, Smart used examples extracted from an online corpus. As already mentioned above, corpus consultation has in recent years become a major trend in discovery learning. However, according to Boulton and Cobb's (2017) meta-analysis of studies where learners worked with corpus-based materials, comparatively few such investigations have focused on grammar patterns. Instead, the focus has mostly been on vocabulary, especially collocation (see previous section). It is, of course, easier to query a corpus for examples of single words or short phrases than for examples of syntactic patterns. Using certain words that are associated with a given grammar pattern as query terms will bring up instances of the pattern but likely also additional, irrelevant material. For example, using "if" as a query term will bring up instances of conditionals (*if ..., then ...*) but also of reported speech (e.g., *She asked if ...*). Using "which" as a query term to obtain instances of relative clauses (e.g., *This guitar, which I bought in Spain, ...*) will inevitably also generate instances of its use in questions (e.g., *Which one would you like?*). However, as demonstrated by Boulton (2010) and Smart (2014), corpus-based DDL does not necessarily require the direct consultation of online corpora by the students themselves. Instead, teachers (or materials developers) can select examples from a corpus that look the most helpful. As already mentioned, the great advantage of using corpus data as input for discovery learning activities is indeed that a corpus query can generate ample authentic examples of a given pattern in a few steps, thus bypassing the need to invent examples (some of which risk being contrived and not representative of how language is really used). On the downside, not all concordance lines brought up by a corpus query will necessarily be easy for learners to understand, due to the inclusion of proper nouns, specific cultural referents, technical terms and low-frequency vocabulary. Several of the corpus-extracted examples of active and passive voice in Smart (2014, p. 200) illustrate this issue (e.g., "*Kashlinsky's team measured cluster motions relative to the cosmic microwave background*"; "*The height values were measured as recommended by the CDC*") as do some of the sentences in the test used to gauge the students' progress (including low-frequency words such as *pivotal*). The participants in Smart (2014) are described as advanced learners of English, and so presumably they coped with these vocabulary demands. When working with less advanced learners, however, teachers may decide to ensure comprehensibility by excluding or editing opaque or confusing concordance lines. If so, the incorporation of corpus-derived examples instead of invented examples in one's language course will not be as time-saving as might initially be assumed. Inevitably, there are also limitations to what students can discover from concordance lines, even if these have been carefully selected and edited. One limitation is that a few concordance lines alone are unlikely to clarify the discourse function of a given grammar pattern (e.g., when and where to use the passive voice). Wider contexts would need to be explored for this sort of insight. Another limitation is that samples of language can only show speakers' or writers' language choices, but not the reasons or intentions behind those choices (e.g., why they chose to use the passive voice). Discovering recurring patterns in samples of language is one thing; determining the whys and where-fores of said patterns is quite another. Finally, samples of language can show how a given pattern is used, but not what its usage restrictions are. It will therefore often require a fair amount of guidance for students to work out when a given pattern is *not* appropriate. For example, it may take contrasting a series of concordance lines with the relative pronouns *which* and *who* to help students realize that the former is not used with a human antecedent (*My sister, who...*; not **My sister, which...*). In sum, it appears that guided inductive learning of grammar—with or without the use of examples extracted from a corpus rather than textbook or teacher-made examples—will often need to be complemented by information beyond what learners can reasonably be expected to figure out from samples of language alone. If so, guided induction and deductive teaching of grammar should not be considered as mutually exclusive options. Instead, examples may serve the purpose of discovery learning of certain new aspects of a given target pattern (where this is considered feasible), while they may at other times serve the purpose of illustrating aspects about which students have already been given information.

In chapter 3, I discussed textual enhancement as a way of directing learners' attention to selected *forms* in the input. I mentioned there that enhancement alone offers no guarantee that the learner will also fully appreciate the *meaning* or function of the highlighted forms. Here, I will discuss an intervention that puts the meaning of grammar features centre stage—*Processing Instruction* (PI), an intervention originally proposed by Bill VanPatten (VanPatten, 1996). The rationale for this intervention is as follows. Learners pay relatively little attention to inflectional morphology (e.g., verb endings, plural −s ending) and function words (e.g., articles, auxiliaries, relative pronouns), because they rely most on content words to interpret messages. For example, the presence of *Yesterday* in an utterance is sufficient for the learner to figure out that the utterance is about the past, and so the −ed ending of the verb in that utterance may be ignored by the learner since it makes no further contribution to the interpretation process. In addition, learners may rely on word order in a sentence to interpret the semantic roles of sentence constituents. For example, the word order in the German sen-tence *Den Sohn ruft der Vater* (literally 'the son calls the father') may lead learners to the default interpretation that it is the son who calls the father. However, the case markers of the definite articles (*den* and *der*) indicate that it is actually the other way around (i.e., it is the son who is called by the father). Similarly, learners unfamiliar with the English passive voice might wrongly assume that in *Tom was kicked in the stomach by Pauline* it was Tom who did the kicking and Pauline was on the receiving end, again because of an inclination to associate the first noun phrase of a sentence with the semantic role of agent (i.e., the 'doer'). It is therefore important to caution learners that word order can be misleading and that they should pay attention to morphological clues and function words that signal the semantic roles of sentence constituents. After alerting learners to the semantic relevance of such grammar features, PI will proceed with sentence-interpretation exercises (called "structured input"). A crucial characteristic of these exercises is that the interpretation question requires the learners to pay attention to the grammar feature of interest because no lexical elements are present that allow learners to bypass said feature. For example, learners might be asked if a given sentence refers to the present or to the past, and the sentence will *not* contain any adverbs such as *yesterday* that give away the answer. Instead, the learners will need to focus on the presence (or absence) of an –ed verb ending. Similarly, learners might be asked who is performing a given action according to a sentence which contains 2 equally plausible agents (as in the German example above), and so they will need to focus on grammar clues (morphological case markers) to determine this. After each sentence, feedback is given to inform the learner if their answer was correct.

What these interpretation exercises do, in essence, is to contrast the form-meaning correspondence of a grammar pattern that is already familiar to the students (e.g., present tense, active voice, the *der* article in German) with the form-meaning correspondence of a new pattern (e.g., past tense, passive voice, the *den* article in German). Some of the sentences to be interpreted will exhibit the new pattern while others will exhibit the familiar one. Students are then asked to choose between 2 answer options. For example, they may be presented with *The boy is kissed by a girl*, and asked which of 2 pictures this sentence corresponds to, one picture of a boy kissing a girl on the cheek and another picture of a girl kissing a boy on the cheek. Similarly, students may be presented with *Kate and Bill have been married for 14 years* and asked whether or not Kate and Bill are still married.

A PI lesson, as originally proposed, has 4 components:

1. explicit explanation about the grammar feature or pattern of interest;
2. a warning for learners that their default sentence-interpretation strategies, such as relying on content words and word order, are not reliable and that they should therefore pay closer attention to the grammar pattern just explained to them;
3. sentence-interpretation exercises of the kind mentioned above (so-called *referential activities* or *structured input*);
4. more examples of sentences featuring the pattern of interest, but now for learners to express agreement/disagreement with or tick whether or not they like the statements. This part of a PI lesson is called *affective activity*.

According to a study by Marsden and Chen (2011), the fourth component (i.e., affective activity) does not add much to the learning of the target feature. A group of students who only did interpretation exercises (i.e., the referential activity using structured input) learned the meaning of the English regular past tense as well as did a group whose interpretation exercises were followed by sentences to react to with like/dislike responses (i.e., the affective activity). Another group of students who were only presented with the latter type of exercise did not show evidence of learning the past tense any better than did a group that received no input about the past tense at all. Because the fourth component seems to be redundant, not all studies that investigate the effectiveness of PI include it anymore. Also, the second component is sometimes no longer included—if students receive a teacher's explanations about a grammar feature and its meaning, then they probably realize this must be relevant for their language processing even if the teacher does not tell them so explicitly. The 2 core components of PI, then, are the explicit rule explanation and the interpretation exercises. Whether explicit explanations about the grammar pattern of interest are always necessary before the interpretation exercises is a question that has been raised as well—and this relates to the question about the effectiveness of guided inductive learning—but I will return to that question further below. First we need to examine some of the evidence of the effectiveness of PI when it is implemented in the way it was originally proposed.

There have been numerous experiments testing the effectiveness of PI since the 1990s (e.g., Benati, 2019; DeKeyser & Botana, 2015, for reviews). A useful example to illustrate the nature of this line of research is a study by Benati (2005), who applied it to English regular past tense. The intervention was spread over 6 hours, and its outcome was compared to lessons where, instead of doing the interpretation exercises, students did exercises that required them, for example, to turn infinitives into the past tense (a mechanical transformation operation which in fact requires no engagement with the meaning of the grammar pattern) and to make lists of past events. Learning gains were gauged by means of 2 tests: a test where the students needed to determine whether sentences referred to the present or the past without any lexical clues to help with this, and a sentence-writing test. The PI group outperformed the other groups on the interpretation test but not on the sentence completion test, where performance was similar. It therefore looks as though sentence-interpretation exercises using structured input foster better understanding of a grammar feature while at the same time bringing about roughly the same gain in productive knowledge as production-oriented practice. A number of caveats need to be mentioned here, however. One is that the sentence-interpretation posttest closely imitated what students in the PI group had been practising. This practice-test congruency may therefore have put the PI group at an advantage in this posttest—after all, one gets better at what one practises. Moreover, part of the test involved aurally presented sentence prompts, which was also the case in the PI learning condition, but not, so it seems, in the comparison conditions. Since the –ed ending of verbs is not always easy to hear, having had practice in detecting it in aural prompts may have given an edge to the PI group as well. One might argue that, conversely, practice-test congruency should have given an edge to the comparison groups when it came to the sentence-writing posttest, because these had done productive work whereas the PI group had not. However, it is worth evaluating the exercises given to the comparison groups. As already mentioned, one exercise was a mechanical transformation exercise which did not require processing of meaning. The other task was to draft a list of past events, but a list is usually comprised of noun phrases, not conjugated verbs. It is therefore doubtful whether this exercise elicited many past tense verbs in the first place, because these were not task essential (see chapter 4). Similar observations can be made about other studies where PI was found to bring about better learning gains than a comparison condition. For instance, in Benati and Batziou (2019), where the target pattern was the causative *have* construction (e.g., *My mom had the windows of her house cleaned every month*), the activity given to the comparison group did not necessitate use of this target pattern either. When students in a comparison group *are* pushed to produce the target grammar pattern during practice (Chan, 2019; Qin, 2008; Toth, 2006), they do stand a better chance of improving their productive knowledge. For example, Suzuki and Sunada (2020) compared the effects of comprehension practice (operationalized as sentence-picture matching) and production practice (operationalized as picture description) on learners' mastery of relative clauses (e.g., *the girl who is watching the cat* vs. *the girl whom the cat is watching*) and found clear benefits of productive practice for the development of productive knowledge. Studies on PI are in fact often couched in a debate around whether comprehension-based instruction is superior to production-based instruction (DeKeyser & Botana, 2015; Shintani, 2015). From a practitioner's perspective, this debate may appear rather bizarre. After all, comprehension-oriented and production-oriented activities are not mutually exclusive but instead complementary, with receptive knowledge typically preceding productive knowledge. The most useful finding from the collection of studies about PI, then, is that PI is indeed quite effective at helping learners improve their understanding (i.e., receptive knowledge) of a given grammar pattern. That said, it does not work wonders either. In the aforementioned study by Benati (2005), for example, the average score on the interpretation test (which followed shortly after the instructional intervention) was about 7.5 out of 10 items. Evaluating this outcome should take into account that the whole intervention took 6 hours and that deciding whether a given sentence has past or present reference entails a pretty high chance of guessing correctly.

The observation that learning gains from PI are not always impressive when the amount of time invested is taken into account applies to several more studies. For example, Marsden (2006) applied PI to help young students of French come to grips with part of the French verb conjugation system. The whole intervention, including all 4 original components of PI, took almost 10 hours. Students who had little knowledge of this aspect of French grammar before the intervention improved their scores on interpretation tests by about 10% on average (and their success rate in the posttest was still below 50%). This is arguably poor return on investment. Similarly disappointing learning gains were found in a recent partial replication, again with young learners of French receiving interpretation practice regarding part of the French verb conjugation system (Kasprowicz et al., 2019). Granted, a 10% improvement is certainly better than no improvement at all. In fact, Marsden's (2006) study included a comparison group whose activities paralleled those of the PI group with the exception of the interpretation exercises. This comparison group showed hardly any improvement in their knowledge of the target patterns. When the experiment was repeated with more proficient students who were more aware of the French verb conjugation system at the start of the intervention, the learning gains (by about 16%) of the PI group were slightly better. Interestingly, however, the comparison group also improved this time, similarly to the PI group. This suggests that these students were better prepared to cope with the material than the less advanced learners in the earlier trial (recall similar reflections about learner-participants' "readiness" to acquire a selected grammar pattern in the preceding chapters).

Studies on the effectiveness of PI have tended to present explicit explanations about the grammar pattern of interest just once at the start of the intervention. In real classroom practice, however, teachers may find it useful to remind students of the grammar rule they are working on. Addressing this possibility, Kasprowicz and Marsden (2017) spread interpretation exercises over 5 lessons and occasionally reiterated the explicit grammar explanations between these exercises. The participants in their study were young learners of German, and the target grammar feature was the distinction between the definite articles *der* and *den*, where the former is used to precede a masculine noun when it is the subject of the sentence, and the latter precedes a masculine noun when it is the object. For example, in *der Lehrer ruft den Jungen* ('the teacher calls the boy'), *der Lehrer* (the teacher) is the subject of the sentence while *den Jungen* (the boy) is the object. German has relatively flexible word order, however, and one may also come across *den Jungen ruft der Lehrer* ("it is the boy who is called by the teacher'). In spoken German, prosody helps to interpret a sentence such as this (Henry et al., 2017), but when meeting such a sentence in writing, learners may ignore the form of the articles and may mistakenly assume that the first noun phrase is the subject of the sentence and the agent (or 'doer') of the action described. All of this was explained to the students in Kasprowicz and Marsden's (2017) experiment before and between sets of interpretation exercises where the students were to determine for each sentence (a grand total of 212 items) who did what to whom. Diverse tests were administered before and after the experiment, with a delayed test after 9 weeks. These tests included interpretation tasks and choosing between *der* and *den* in gapped sentences describing pictures. The tests were also given to a group of students who did not receive any instruction about the *der* versus *den* distinction. No learning of this distinction was observed in this group, which indicates yet again that purely incidental acquisition of L2 grammar is a very slow process even when it concerns items as frequent as definite articles. The PI group did show significant improvement, although the average success rate across the various tests fell to around 60% nine weeks after the experiment. Considering the time invested (five 50-minute lessons) as well as the fact that most of the test formats entailed a 50% chance of correct guessing, this is not as encouraging an outcome as one might have hoped.

Because feedback is received on each sentence-interpretation item, the question can be asked if students could not discover the form-meaning relation of the target grammar feature themselves through doing the exercise and learning from the feedback, thus bypassing the explicit explanations about it (e.g., Benati, 2020; Sanz & Morgan-Short, 2004; VanPatten & Oikkenon, 1996; also see Herron & Tomasello, 1992, which I mentioned earlier). Imagine, for example, an interpretation exercise on the *der/den* distinction in German. After being informed several times in a row that they mistook the object of the sentence for the subject, students with the necessary analytic ability could be expected to figure out the function of *den*. This amounts to guided inductive learning from a series of trial-and-feedback cycles, where the feedback serves as guidance towards the correct conclusion about the meaning of the grammar feature. Similarly, after receiving feedback on a series of sentences that these have past time instead of present time reference, a learner can be expected to realise that the –ed ending to verbs indicates past time reference in English (e.g., Marsden & Chen, 2011). If so, perhaps the cognitive effort invested in this inductive process is beneficial for retention. Several studies have indeed explored the possibility of bypassing the explicit explanation phase of PI. The results have been somewhat mixed, and this is not very surprising because successful induction of the form-meaning correspondence will inevitably depend on how straightforward it is.

For example, Erlam (2003) incorporated exercises resembling PI in a classroom-based experiment with L1 English students of French with the aim of helping them discover the system of French object pronouns (as in *Je les ai vu*—I've seen them), which they had not yet received any instruction about. This is a complex system, because the choice of pronoun depends on various factors: gender (*le* vs. *la*), person (e.g., *me* vs. *te*) and number (e.g., *le/la* vs. *les; te* vs. *vous*). In addition, learners may struggle with word order (e.g., **j'ai les vu* instead of *je les ai vu*). The students in Erlam's (2003) study who did the PI-type exercises received feedback on their responses but were *not* given explicit explanations about the rules that govern object pronoun use in French. This practice was spread over three 45-minute lessons in one week. Posttests in which the students were required to reformulate sentences by using object pronouns (e.g., *Je vois Anne et Nathalie* → *Je les vois*) were administered 1 week and 6 weeks later. The average improvement from the pretest to the immediate and the delayed posttest was under 10%, leaving more than 90% of the posttest responses flawed. Erlam's (2003) study also included a group of students who did receive explicit explanations about the French object-noun system at the start of the lesson series, and who were regularly reminded of these. Their improvement on the tests was significantly better, which indicates there is an important role for such explicit explanations where students find it hard to work out a grammar system by themselves. It needs to be mentioned here that this second group was also given a different kind of exercise (not resembling PI), notably transformation practice which resembled what was required in the tests. Another classroom experiment in which PI activities were used (but called input-based tasks by the authors) was conducted by Erlam and Ellis (2019). This resembled Erlam's (2003) experiment, but this time the grammar feature of interest was a bit simpler. Beginning learners of French were trained to distinguish plural articles (*les, des*) and the plural form *sont* of the verb *être* ('to be') from their singular counterparts (*un, une, le, la, est*) during aural interpretation exercises spread over three 50-minute classes. Again, no explicit rule explanations were given. Instead, it was assumed the students would work out what forms referred to plural versus singular referents through interpreting utterances and through being told their interpretations were correct or not. The pretests and posttests required matching spoken utterances to pictures of single or plural referents. The students improved their average score from the pretest to a 2-week delayed posttest by 4 out of 30 test items (reaching a final average score of 21/30). Considering the 50% chance of correct guessing in this test, such an improvement is again not quite spectacular. It was nonetheless significantly better that what was attested for a control group who had not done any activities with a special focus on the singular-plural distinction, and who showed hardly any improvement.

A crucial question to be asked in classroom experiments such as these is, again, how successful and efficient participants in a discovery learning or inductive learning condition are at figuring out the patterns. One way of finding out how easy it is for learners to work out the nature of the form–meaning correspondence through interpretation exercises such as those used in a PI lesson is to investigate how long (i.e., how many exercise items) it takes them to get their interpretations consistently right. Once they have worked out the pattern, the remainder of the exercise may serve the purpose of consolidating the newly acquired insights. The more opportunity for such consolidation through repeated practice, the less effortful accessing the acquired knowledge will become in the longer run (see chapter 6). If learners have just received an explicit explanation about the form and meaning of the grammar pattern of interest, it will save them time to figure this out themselves through doing the interpretation exercises, and so more of the exercise items will subsequently serve as knowledge consolidation. This helps to explain why presenting students with the explicit explanations before the interpretation exercises can lead to better posttest results than having students tackle those exercises without prior explanation, even if the form–meaning connections of interest are gradually worked out successfully by the students through the feedback they receive on each response. This is illustrated, for example, by Henry et al. (2017), another experiment where students of German studied the *der* versus *den* distinction. Although it was clear that a group of students who had not received an explicit explanation managed to figure out the meaning of *den* after a dozen or so exercise items, they nonetheless performed less well on posttests than did their fellow students who had received the explanation prior to tackling the same exercise. In fact, their average score for comprehending *den* in a test 4 weeks later was just 2.7 out of 6 test items. For the group that had received the explanation beforehand, the average score was 4.1. From the vantage point of the inductive versus deductive learning debate, Henry et al.'s (2017) findings can thus be taken as evidence in favour of a deductive learning procedure. Recall the study by Indrarathne and Kormos (2017), reviewed in chapter 3, where explicit explanations about a target pattern were found to significantly benefit learners' subsequent processing of typographically enhanced instances in a text, and also the study by Li et al. (2016), reviewed in chapter 4, where explicit explanations about a target grammar pattern prior to a text-reconstruction task led to better learning outcomes. It is also worth noting that the intervention tried in Henry et al. (2017) was relatively short (under 50 minutes) and in that sense much closer than some of the other experiments reviewed above (such as Kasprowicz & Marsden, 2017) regarding what time investment teachers would find feasible in a regular language course.

A question that needs to be asked as well is how many grammar patterns in a target language lend themselves to developing PI exercises. Given the nature of PI, it has greater scope of application in target languages that are relatively rich in inflectional morphology. Investigations of PI indeed often concern target languages such as German, French, and in several studies Spanish (the language taught by VanPatten—the founder of PI—himself: e.g., VanPatten & Cadierno, 1993; VanPatten et al., 2009). Regardless of language typology, creating sentences whose interpretation hinges on inflectional morphology or function words can be challenging as well. Many grammar features are intrinsically bound to the characteristics of content words, after all. Take, for example, relative pronouns (*who, that, which,* etc.) as candidates for PI. One may wish to design sentence-interpretation exercises to foster an understanding that *who* refers to human antecedents, but such sentence prompts will then inevitably contain a content word denoting a human antecedent (e.g., *My father, who* …)—unless one decided to substitute those words by ones the students do not yet know or by pseudowords. Not only can it be challenging to create suitable sentence prompts for the interpretation exercise, the prompts may not exemplify how the target language is typically used in natural discourse and how the grammar feature of interest performs specific pragmatic functions. For example, the word order in German where the object of the sentence is fronted (as in *Den Jungen ruft der Lehrer*) would typically be used to repair a misunderstanding (e.g., "It is the boy, not the girl, who the teacher is calling"), and it would be uttered with a different prosody from the default word order. This may well be part of the explanation given to students at the start of the PI lesson, but being presented with a considerable number of examples of the pattern in the subsequent exercises may leave the student with the impression it is more common than it actually is in real discourse. Similarly, when PI is applied to the English passive voice, and learners are asked to determine who did what to whom according to given sentences (e.g., Uludag & VanPatten, 2012), these sentences will often contain a by-phrase to indicate the agent role (e.g., *Ben was bullied at school by Eric*). However, this is but one discourse function of the passive voice—emphasizing the identity of the agent. Most often the passive voice is used *without* the by-phrase, when there is no need to specify the agent (e.g., *Obama was re-elected*), when we do not know the identity of the agent (e.g., *Their daughter's been kidnapped*) or when we do not wish to state the identity of the agent. Again, information about these pragmatic functions of the target pattern may be explained prior to the exercises, but the sentence-interpretation exercises will not illustrate them. Despite such limitations, PI indisputably has many merits. Most importantly, it makes learners deeply aware of the fact that grammar conveys meaning, and it can alter learners' habitual allocation of attention to language features (Cintrón-Valentín & Ellis, 2015). As explained, it typically does so by contrasting an already familiar grammar feature to a new target feature. In order to help learners recognize the target feature (e.g., –ed ending) and its meaning (past time), sentences that instantiate the feature are mixed with sentences that do not (e.g., with verbs in the present tense). This makes the exercise essentially a discrimination task, where the learner identifies the target feature by contrasting it with another, already learned feature, a feature with a different semantic function. It is important to emphasize that the contrast is typically made with an already learned pattern. Presenting different new target patterns at the same time would make it harder for learners to establish the correct form-meaning relations. It is worth noting in this regard that the study by Marsden (2006), which we reviewed above, is an outlier within the strand of PI research because it targeted multiple components of the French verb conjugation system that were as yet unfamiliar to the students, and this may help to explain why the learning outcomes were so modest.

PI does not appear to have exerted much influence on mainstream textbooks. This illustrates the slow rate at which research findings are translated into professional practice. It may also be due to the fact that designing PI lessons is far from easy, because for many grammar features it is hard to invent sentences for the referential interpretation exercises where only the grammar feature provides the clue (e.g., Sanz & Morgan-Short, 2004). Even researchers examining the effectiveness of PI may fail to implement it optimally—see, for example, VanPatten et al.'s (2009) critique of Qin (2008). All the same, the use of contrasting sentence pairs to raise learners' awareness of grammatical meaning is something that many language teachers (and learners) will recognize, even if they have never heard or seen the terms "Processing Instruction" or "Structured Input". For example, teachers might present their students with (a) *She drowned* and (b) *She was drowning*, and ask which is most likely to be followed by *and so I jumped into the pool.* Similarly, they might present students with (a) *She's studying very hard* and (b) *She studies very hard*, and ask which is most likely to be followed by *and that's a trait that will help her a lot when she enters university.* And they might contrast (a) *I'm used to getting up early* and (b) *I used to get up early*, and ask which is most likely to be followed by *and so I don't mind an early start tomorrow morning.*

What remains more controversial, however, is the claim by proponents of PI that the purely input-based interpretation practice is sufficient not only to foster good receptive knowledge of grammar but also to foster productive knowledge. This is controversial because of a general tenet in *Skill Acquisition Theory* (e.g., DeKeyser, 2015) which holds that what you can do with acquired knowledge will be determined by the way in which you acquired that knowledge and how you have practised deploying it. If so, knowledge that was acquired exclusively through receptive activities may not be straightforwardly deployable for smooth productive purposes. It may take extra steps to stimulate this transfer. I therefore turn in the next chapter to language-focused learning with a stronger orientation towards output practice. Before doing so, it needs to be mentioned that PI could easily be adapted so as to include some output practice as well. It is somewhat surprising that even the fourth component of a PI lesson as originally proposed— the affective activity where students react to the content of statements—is designed as a purely receptive exercise. In a classroom setting, this could easily be turned into an interactive activity where students not only decide whether or not they agree with a given statement, but they also present their reasons. In some cases, this could then elicit active use of the target pattern (possibly prompted by the teacher; Toth, 2006). Imagine if learners are asked to react to a statement such as *I enjoyed my science classes last year* (exemplifying past tense). Giving reasons for their (dis)agreement with this statement is likely to involve use of past tense as the student recalls events from last year's science classes—which would perhaps not be dissimilar from the use of communicative tasks with a planned focus on a preselected grammar pattern which I discussed in chapter 4. In sum, elements of PI could easily be incorporated in an ensemble of activities, in symbiosis with elements from other instructional approaches.

Further Reflection

Can You Get Better at Guessing Word Meanings?

Read a text in a second language that you are sufficiently proficient in and try to guess the meaning of words you do not know. Alternatively, read a text about a specialized topic you know little about and guess the meaning of terms you are not familiar with. How often do you find enough contextual clues? How often are your guesses confirmed by a dictionary? Are you conscious of the strategies you use to infer word meanings from context? There are claims that learners will guess word meanings from context more successfully if they are taught certain strategies. For example, Clarke and Nation (1980) proposed to teach the follow- ing steps: (1) decide on the part of speech of the unknown word, (2) look at the immediate context of the word, (3) look at the wider context of the word, that is, the adjoining sentences or clauses, (4) guess, (5) check the guess by asking the following questions: Is the guess the same part of speech as the unknown word?

Does the sentence make sense if you substitute the guess for the unknown word? Does it fit comfortably into the context? Does the meaning of the parts of the word support the guess? Then check the dictionary. This procedure has even inspired the design of a "guessing from context test" (Sasao & Webb, 2018), which learners can use to assess their inferencing abilities and to practise the strategy. When you tried to guess word meanings before, did you perhaps spontaneously use strategies such as the ones proposed by Clarke and Nation (1980)? There do not appear to be many empirical investigations of the effect of strategy training on learners' ability to infer word meanings (where this ability is tested before and after the training). At a future opportunity, you may want to ask your students to first guess the meaning of words from context without any guidance and then ask them to try again but using the steps suggested by Clarke and Nation (1980). Do you think the success rate will increase?

Does Breaking up Words Help to Infer Their Meanings?

One of the final steps in Clarke and Nation's (1980) procedure that I mentioned above is to break up the word into parts, because some parts (typically affixes, such as *anti-, inter-, mono-, trans-, un-, pre-, -er* and *-less*) provide clues which can be used in conjunction with contextual clues. Knowledge of such word parts is indeed very useful. There is now even a test which focuses exclusively on knowledge of affixes (Sasao & Webb, 2017). Unfortunately, looking for known word parts in a new lexical item and using this to infer the item's meaning is not always a reliable strategy. For one thing, a single affix can have varied meanings. For example, although *in-* often means something negative (e.g., *invalid, incorrect, insecure*), it does not convey that meaning in *invaluable, insert* and *integrate*. Parts of a word may also be mistaken for known affixes, as in *remark* and *resent* (which could be misinterpreted as 'mark again' and 'sent again'). The same holds true for other word parts which resemble words the learner is already familiar with. Imagine a learner using knowledge of the adjective *gross* in the sense of 'repulsive' to guess the meaning of being *engrossed* in an activity. Put yourself in the shoes of a learner of English and anticipate what may go wrong if this learner were to rely on presumed knowledge of word parts to guess the meaning of the following lexical items: *coaster, comprehensive, dandelion, distress, fearsome, flatulent, predominant, priceless, pursuit, shortcut, unnerving, miscarriage* and *inmates*.

Does Your Textbook Use a Trial-and-Error Approach?

Examine a contemporary textbook for exercises on phrases such as *partitive* expressions (e.g., *a bar of chocolate, a clove of garlic, a flock of birds, a pack of wolves*) and other word partnerships. Do these exercises ask students to assemble (match) the constituents of the expressions? If options to choose from are given, do these include easily confusable words (such as near synonyms; e.g., *say* and *tell*)? Does the textbook provide any opportunities for learning the phrases in the pages prior to the exercise? Put differently, does the textbook implement exercises in a trial-and-error fashion (where, in the case of incorrect answers, learning is expected to happen through corrective feedback)? Or does the book implement exercises as retrieval opportunities (following study material)? In the latter case, is it truly retrieval from memory (which is known to be beneficial), or can the students simply copy answers from the study material presented on the same page?

Inductive or Deductive? Form or Meaning?

What approach do you (or your textbook) take to grammar instruction? Are students first presented with examples for them to figure out the "rule" themselves? If so, how much guidance is given for students to work it out? Do such activities focus on the meaning (or function) of the grammar pattern, or is the focus mostly on formal features? Do any of the exercises that follow require students to interpret the grammar features, akin to what is done in *Processing Instruction*? Are grammar patterns contrasted with each other concerning their meaning (or function)? If so, does this concern a contrast between a new pattern and a pattern that is already familiar?

References

Benati, A. (2005). The effects of processing instruction, traditional instruction and meaning-output instruction on the acquisition of the English past simple tense. *Language Teaching Research*, 9, 67–93. https://doi.org/10.1191/1362168805lr154oa

Benati, A. (2019). Classroom-oriented research: Processing Instruction (findings and implications). *Language Teaching*, 52, 343–359. https://doi.org/10.1017/S0261444817000386

Benati, A. (2020). The effects of structured input and traditional instruction on the acquisition of the English causative passive forms: An eye-tracking study measuring accuracy in responses and processing patterns. *Language Teaching Research*. Online early view. https://doi.org/10.1177/1362168820928577

Benati, A., & Batziou, M. (2019). Discourse and long-term effects of isolated and combined structured input and structured output on the acquisition of the English causative form. *Language Awareness*, 28, 77–96. https://doi.org/10.1080/09658416.2019.1604721

Bjork, E. L., & Bjork, R. A. (2014). Making things hard on yourself, but in a good way: Creating desirable difficulties to enhance learning. In M. A. Gernsbacher & J. Pomerantz (Eds.), *Psychology and the real world: Essays illustrating fundamental contributions to society* (2nd ed., pp. 59–68). Worth.

Boers, F. (2003). Applied linguistics perspectives on cross-cultural variation in conceptual metaphor. *Metaphor and Symbol*, 18, 231–238. https://doi.org/10.1207/S15327868MS1804_1

Boers, F., Bryfonski, L., Faez, F., & McKay, T. (2020). A call for cautious interpretation of meta-analytic reviews. *Studies in Second Language Acquisition*. Online early view. https://doi.org/10.1017/S0272263120000327

Boers, F., Dang, T. C. T., & Strong, B. (2017). Comparing the effectiveness of phrase-focused exercises. A partial replication of Boers, Demecheleer, Coxhead, and Webb (2014). *Language Teaching Research*, 21, 362–380. https://doi.org/10.1177/1362168816651464

Boers, F., Demecheleer, M., Coxhead, A., & Webb, S. (2014). Gauging the effects of exercises on verb–noun collocations. *Language Teaching Research*, 18, 54–74. https://doi.org/10.1177/1362168813505389

Boers, F., Demecheleer, M., & Eyckmans, J. (2004a). Etymological elaboration as a strategy for learning figurative idioms. In P. Bogaards & B. Laufer. (Eds.), *Vocabulary in a second language: Selection, acquisition and testing* (pp. 53–78). John Benjamins.

Boers, F., Demecheleer, M., & Eyckmans, J. (2004b). Cultural variation as a variable in comprehending and remembering figurative idioms. *European Journal of English Studies*, 8, 375–388. https://doi.org/10.1080/1382557042000277449

Boers, F., Eyckmans, J., Kappel, J., Stengers, H., & Demecheleer, M. (2006). Formulaic sequences and perceived oral proficiency: putting a Lexical Approach to the test. *Language Teaching Research*, 10, 245–261. https://doi.org/10.1191/1362168806lr195oa

Boers, F., Eyckmans, J., & Stengers, H. (2007). Presenting figurative idioms with a touch of etymology: More than mere mnemonics? *Language Teaching Research*, 11, 43–62. https://doi.org/10.1177/1362168806072460

Boers, F., & Stengers, H. (2008). A quantitative comparison of the English and Spanish repertoires of figurative idioms. In F. Boers & S. Lindstromberg (Eds.), *Cognitive Linguistic approaches to teaching vocabulary and phraseology* (pp. 355–373). De Gruyter Mouton.

Boers, F., & Strong, B. (2016). An evaluation of textbook exercises on collocations. In B. Tomlinson (Ed.), *Second language acquisition research and materials development for language learning* (pp. 139–152). Routledge.

Boers, F., & Webb, S. (2015). Gauging the semantic transparency of idioms: Do natives and learners see eye to eye? In R. Heredia & A. Cieslicka (Eds.), *Bilingual figurative language processing* (pp. 368–392). Cambridge University Press. https://doi.org/10.1017/CBO9781139342100.018

Boulton, A. (2010). Data-driven learning: Taking the computer out of the equation. *Language Learning*, 60, 534–572. https://doi.org/10.1111/j.1467-9922.2010.00566.x

Boulton, A., & Cobb, T. (2017). Corpus use in language learning: A meta-analysis. *Language Learning*, 67, 348–393. https://doi.org/10.1111/lang.12224

Bui, T., Boers, F., & Coxhead, A. (2020). Extracting multiword expressions from texts with the aid of on-line resources: A classroom experiment. *ITL International Journal of Applied Linguistics*, 171, 221–252. https://doi.org/10.1075/itl.18033.bui

Carpenter, S. K., Sachs, R. E., Martin, B., Schmidt, K., & Looft, R. (2012). Learning new vocabulary in German: The effects of inferring word meanings, type of feedback, and time of test. *Psychonomic Bulletin & Review*, 19, 81–86. https://doi.org/10.3758/s13423-011-0185-7

Cerezo, L., Cara, A., & Leow, R. P. (2016). The effectiveness of guided induction versus deductive instruction on the development of complex Spanish "gustar" structures: An analysis of learning outcomes and processes. *Studies in Second Language Acquisition*, 38, 265–291. https://doi.org/10.1017/S0272263116000139

Chan, M. (2019). The role of classroom input: Processing Instruction, traditional instruction, and implicit instruction in the acquisition of the English simple past by Cantonese ESL learners in Hong Kong. *System*, 80, 246–256. https://doi.org/10.1016/j.system.2018.12.003

Chen, Y. (2016). Dictionary use for collocation production and retention: A CALL-based study. *International Journal of Lexicography*, 30, 225–251. https://doi.org/10.1093/ijl/ecw005

Cintrón-Valentín, M., & Ellis, N. C., (2015). Exploring the interface: Explicit focus-on-form instruction and learned attentional biases in L2 Latin. *Studies in Second Language Acquisition*, 37, 197–235. https://doi.org/10.1017/S0272263115000029

Clarke, D. F., & Nation, I. S. P. (1980). Guessing the meaning of words from context: Strategy and techniques. *System*, 8, 211–220.

Cooper, T. C. (1999). Processing of idioms by L2 learners of English. *TESOL Quarterly*, 33, 233–262. https://doi.org/10.2307/3587719

Crace, A., & Acklam, R. (2011). *New Total English, upper intermediate: Students' book*. Pearson Education.

Cunningham, S., Moor, P., & Bygrave, J. (2013). *Cutting Edge, intermediate: Students' book* (3rd ed.). Pearson Education.

DeKeyser, R. M. (2015). Skill acquisition theory. In B. VanPatten & J. Williams (Eds.), *Theories in second language acquisition: An introduction* (2nd ed., pp. 94–112). Routledge. https://doi.org/10.4324/9780203628942

DeKeyser, R., & Botana, G. P. (2015). The effectiveness of Processing Instruction in L2 grammar acquisition: A narrative review. *Applied Linguistics*, 36, 290–305. https://doi.org/10.1093/applin/amu071

Dziemianko, A. (2014). On the presentation and placement of collocations in monolingual English learners' dictionaries: Insights into encoding and retention. *International Journal of Lexicography*, 27, 259–279. https://doi.org/10.1093/ijl/ecu012

Elgort, I. (2017). Incorrect inferences and contextual word learning in English as a second language. *Journal of the European Second Language Association*, 1, 1–11. https://doi.org/10.22599/jesla.3

Elgort, I., Beliaeva, N., & Boers, F. (2020). Contextual word learning in the first and second language: Definition placement and interference error effects on declarative and non-declarative knowledge. *Studies in Second Language Acquisition*, 42, 7–32. https://doi.org/10.1017/S0272263119000561

Erlam, R. (2003). The effects of deductive and inductive instruction on the acquisition of direct object pronouns in French as a second language. *The Modern Language Journal*, 87, 242–260. https://doi.org/10.1111/1540-4781.00188

Erlam, R., & Ellis, R. (2019). Input-based tasks for beginner-level learners: An approximate replication and extension of Erlam & Ellis (2018). *Language Teaching*, 52, 490–511. https://doi.org/10.1017/S0261444818000216

Eyckmans, J., Boers, F., & Stengers, H. (2007). Identifying chunks: Who can see the wood for the trees? *Language Forum*, 33, 85–100.

Gardner, D., & Davies, M. (2007). Pointing out frequent phrasal verbs: A corpus-based analysis. *TESOL Quarterly*, 41, 339–360. https://doi.org/10.1002/j.15457249.2007.tb00062.x

Garnier, M., & Schmitt, N. (2015). The PHaVE List: A pedagogical list of phrasal verbs and their most frequent meaning senses. *Language Teaching Research*, 19, 645–666. https://doi.org/10.1177/1362168814559798

Haight, C., Herron, C., & Cole, S. P. (2007). The effects of deductive and guided inductive instructional approaches on the learning of grammar in the elementary foreign language college classroom. *Foreign Language Annals*, 40, 288–310. https://doi.org/10.1111/j.1944-9720.2007.tb03202.x

Henry, N., Jackson, C. N., & Dimidio, J. (2017). The role of prosody and explicit instruction in Processing Instruction. *The Modern Language Journal*, 101, 294–314. https://doi.org/10.1111/modl.12397

Herron, C., & Tomasello, M. (1992). Acquiring grammatical structures by guided induction. *The French Review*, 65, 708–718.

Hu, Y.-H., & Fong, Y.-Y. (2010). Obstacles to conceptual-metaphor guided L2 idiom interpretation. In S. De Knop, F. Boers, & A. De Rycker (Eds.), *Fostering language teaching efficiency through cognitive linguistics* (pp. 293–317). De Gruyter Mouton.

Huang, L.-L. & Lin, C.-C. (2014). Three approaches to glossing and their effects on vocabulary learning. *System, 44*, 127–136. https://doi.org/10.1016/j.system.2014.03.006

Indrarathne, B., & Kormos, J. (2017). Attentional processing of input in explicit and implicit learning conditions: An eye-tracking study. *Studies in Second Language Acquisition, 39*, 401–430. https://doi.org/10.1017/S027226311600019X

Johns, T. (1991). Should you be persuaded: Two examples of data-driven learning. *English Language Research Journal, 4*, 1–16.

Jones, M., & Haywood, S. (2004). Facilitating the acquisition of formulaic sequences: An exploratory study. In N. Schmitt (Ed.), *Formulaic sequences* (pp. 269–300). John Benjamins. https://doi.org/10.1075/lllt.9.14jon

Kasprowicz, R., & Marsden, E. (2017). Towards ecological validity in research into input-based practice: Form spotting can be as beneficial as form-meaning practice. *Applied Linguistics, 39*, 886–911. https://doi.org/10.1093/applin/amw051

Kasprowicz, R. E., Marsden, E., & Sephton, N. (2019). Investigating distribution of practice effects for the learning of foreign language verb morphology in the young learner classroom. *The Modern Language Journal, 103*, 580–606. https://doi.org/10.1111/modl.12586

Kerr, P., & Jones, C. (2012). *Straightforward, intermediate: Student's book* (2nd ed.). Macmillan Education.

Komuro, Y. (2009). Japanese learners' collocation dictionary retrieval performance. In A. Barfield & H. Gyllstad (Eds.), *Researching collocations in another language: Multiple perspectives* (pp. 86–98). Palgrave Macmillan. https://doi.org/10.1057/9780230245327_7

Lakoff, G., & Johnson, M. (1980). *Metaphors we live by.* Chicago University Press.

Laufer, B. (2011). The contribution of dictionary use to the production and retention of collocations in a second language. *International Journal of Lexicography, 24*, 29–49. https://doi.org/10.1093/ijl/ecq039

Laufer, B., & Waldman, T. (2011). Verb-noun collocations in second language writing: A corpus analysis of learners' English. *Language Learning, 61*, 647–672. https://doi.org/10.1111/j.1467-9922.2010.00621.x

Lee, H., Warschauer, M., & Lee, J. H. (2019). The effects of corpus use on second language vocabulary learning: A multilevel meta-analysis. *Applied Linguistics, 40*, 721–753. https://doi.org/10.1093/applin/amy012

Lee, P., & Lin, H. (2019). The effect of the inductive and deductive data-driven learning (DDL) on vocabulary acquisition and retention. *System, 81*, 14–25. https://doi.org/10.1016/j.system.2018.12.011

Lewis, M. (1997). *Implementing the Lexical Approach: Putting theory into practice.* Language Teaching Publications.

Li, S., Ellis, R., & Zhu, Y. (2016). Task-based versus task-supported language instruction: An experimental study. *Annual Review of Applied Linguistics, 36*, 205–229. https://doi.org/10.1017/S0267190515000069

Littlemore, J., Chen, P. T., Koester, A., & Barnden, J. (2011). Difficulties in metaphor comprehension faced by international students whose first language is not English. *Applied Linguistics, 32*, 408–429. https://doi.org/10.1093/applin/amr009

Liu, D., & Myers, D. (2020). The most-common phrasal verbs with their key meanings for spoken and academic written English: A corpus analysis. *Language Teaching Research, 24*, 403–424. https://doi.org/10.1177/1362168818798384

Marsden, E. (2006). Exploring input processing in the classroom: An experimental comparison of Processing Instruction and enriched input. *Language Learning*, 56, 507–566. https://doi.org/10.1111/j.1467-9922.2006.00375.x

Marsden, M., & Chen, H.-Y. (2011). The roles of structured input activities in processing instruction and the kinds of knowledge they promote. *Language Learning*, 61, 1058–1098. https://doi.org/10.1111/j.1467-9922.2011.00661.x

Martinez, R., & Murphy, V. A. (2011). Effect of frequency and idiomaticity on second language reading comprehension. *TESOL Quarterly*, 45, 267–290. https://doi.org/10.5054/tq.2011.247708

McCarthy, M., & O'Dell, F. (2005). *English collocations in use*. Cambridge University Press.

Mondria, J.-A. (2003). The effects of inferring, verifying, and memorizing on the retention of L2 word meanings: An experimental comparison of the "meaning-inferred method" and the "meaning-given method." *Studies in Second Language Acquisition*, 25, 473–499. https://doi.org/10.1017/S0272263103000202

Nassaji, H. (2003). L2 vocabulary learning from context: Strategies, knowledge sources, and their relationship with success in L2 lexical inferencing. *TESOL Quarterly*, 37, 645–670. https://doi.org/10.2307/3588216

Nesselhauf, N. (2003). The use of collocations by advanced learners of English and some implications for teaching. *Applied Linguistics*, 24, 223–242. https://doi.org/10.1093/applin/24.2.223

Peters, E. (2009). Learning collocations through attention-drawing techniques: A qualitative and quantitative analysis. In A. Barfield & H. Gyllstad (Eds.), *Researching collocations in another language: Multiple perspectives* (pp. 194–207). Palgrave Macmillan. https://doi.org/10.1057/9780230245327_15

Peters, E. (2012). Learning German formulaic sequences: The effect of two attention-drawing techniques. *Language Learning Journal*, 40, 65–79. https://doi.org/10.1080/09571736.2012.658224

Peters, E. (2016). The learning burden of collocations: The role of interlexical and intralexical factors. *Language Teaching Research*, 20, 113–138. https://doi.org/10.1177/1362168814568131

Potts, R., & Shanks, D. R. (2014). The benefit of generating errors during learning. *Journal of Experimental Psychology: General*, 143, 644–667. https://doi.org/10.1037/a0033194

Qin, J. (2008). The effect of processing instruction and dictogloss tasks on acquisition of the English passive voice. *Language Teaching Research*, 12, 61–82. https://doi.org/10.1177/1362168807084494

Richards, J. C., Hull, J., & Proctor, S. (2017). *Interchange 3: Student's book* (5th ed.). Cambridge University Press.

Robinson, P. (1996). Learning simple and complex second language rules under implicit, incidental, rule-search, and instructed conditions. *Studies in Second Language Acquisition*, 18, 27–67. https://doi.org/10.1017/S0272263100014674

Sanz, C., & Morgan-Short, K. (2004). Positive evidence versus explicit rule presentation and explicit negative feedback: A computer-assisted study. *Language Learning*, 54, 35–78. https://doi.org/10.1111/j.1467-9922.2004.00248.x

Sasao, Y., & Webb, S. (2017). The word part levels test. *Language Teaching Research*, 21, 12–30. https://doi.org/10.1177/1362168815586083

Sasao, Y., & Webb, S. (2018). The guessing from context test. *ITL – International Journal of Applied Linguistics*, 169, 115–141. https://doi.org/10.1075/itl.00009.sas

Shintani, N. (2015). The effectiveness of Processing Instruction and Production-based instruction on L2 grammar acquisition: A meta-analysis. *Applied Linguistics*, 36, 306–325. https://doi.org/10.1093/applin/amu067

Smart, J. (2014). The role of guided induction in paper-based data-driven learning. *ReCALL*, 26, 184–201. https://doi.org/10.1017/S0958344014000081

Soars, L., & Soars, J. (2016). *American Headway* 3 (3rd ed.). Oxford University Press.

Stengers, H., & Boers, F. (2015). Exercises on collocations: A comparison of trial-and-error and exemplar-guided procedures. *Journal of Spanish Language Teaching*, 2, 152–164. https://doi.org/10.1080/23247797.2015.1104030

Stengers, H., Boers, F., Housen, A., & Eyckmans, J. (2010). Does 'chunking' foster chunk uptake? In S. De Knop, F. Boers, & A. De Rycker (Eds.), *Fostering language teaching efficiency through cognitive linguistics* (pp. 99–117). De Gruyter Mouton. https://doi.org/10.1515/9783110245837.99

Strong, B., & Boers, F. (2019a). The error in trial and error: Exercises on phrasal verbs. *TESOL Quarterly*, 53, 289–319. https://doi.org/10.1002/tesq.478

Strong, B., & Boers, F. (2019b). Weighing up exercises on phrasal verbs: Retrieval versus trial-and-error practices. *The Modern Language Journal*, 103, 562–579. https://doi.org/10.1111/modl.12579

Suzuki, Y., & Sunada, M. (2020). Dynamic interplay between practice type and practice schedule in a second language: The potential and limits of skill transfer and practice schedule. *Studies in Second Language Acquisition*, 42, 169–197. https://doi.org/10.1017/S0272263119000470

Thomson, H., Boers, F., & Coxhead, A. (2019). Replication research in pedagogical approaches to spoken fluency and formulaic sequences: A call for replication of Wood (2009) and Boers, Eyckmans, Kappel, Stengers & Demecheleer (2006). *Language Teaching*, 52, 406–414. https://doi.org/10.1017/S0261444817000374

Toth, P. D. (2006). Processing Instruction and a role for output in second language acquisition. *Language Learning*, 56, 319–385. https://doi.org/10.1111/j.0023-8333.2006.00349.x

Uludag, O., & VanPatten, B. (2012). The comparative effects of Processing Instruction and Dictogloss on the acquisition of the English passive by speakers of Turkish. *International Review of Applied Linguistics*, 50, 189–212. https://doi.org/10.1515/iral-2012-0008

VanPatten, B. (1996). *Input processing and grammar instruction: Theory and research.* Ablex Publishing Corporation.

VanPatten, B., & Cadierno, T. (1993). Explicit instruction and input processing. *Studies in Second Language Acquisition*, 15, 225–241. http://dx.doi.org/10.1017/S0272263100011979

VanPatten, B., Inclezan, D., Salazar, H., & Farley, A. P. (2009). Processing Instruction and Dictogloss: A study on object pronouns and word order in Spanish. *Foreign Language Annals*, 42, 557–575. https://doi.org/10.1111/j.1944-9720.2009.01033.x

VanPatten, B., & Oikkenon, S. (1996). Explanation versus Structured Input in Processing Instruction. *Studies in Second Language Acquisition*, 18, 495–510. https://doi.org/10.1017/S0272263100015394

van Zeeland, H. (2014). Lexical inferencing in first and second language listening. *The Modern Language Journal*, 98, 1006–1021. https://doi.org/10.1111/modl.12152

Vogel, S., Herron, C., Cole, S. P., & York, Y. (2011). Effectiveness of a guided inductive versus a deductive approach on the learning of grammar in the intermediate-level college French classroom. *Foreign Language Annals*, 44, 353–380. https://doi.org/10.1111/j.1944-9720.2011.01133.x

6.

WHAT PRACTICE MAKES (ALMOST) PERFECT (AND FOR WHAT PURPOSE)?

Introduction

Newly acquired knowledge can decay and vanish from memory unless it is reactivated. This is reflected, for example, in the fact that scores on delayed posttests are almost always markedly poorer than scores on (near-)immediate posttests when no reviewing is done in the time span between them. In this chapter, I turn to ways of re-activating knowledge of items or patterns. With repeated activation (i.e., with repeated practice), newly acquired declarative knowledge is consolidated in memory and may gradually be transferred to procedural knowledge, so that its use may ultimately become effortless or automatic (Anderson, 2005). Questions addressed here include not only what practice procedures are comparatively effective, but also what type of practice is best suited for a particular purpose. To give just one example for now, it is very doubtful if multiple-choice exercises resemble communicative use of language sufficiently to directly foster students' smooth use of newly learned items or patterns in conversation. So, the question is not just what practice works best, but also what practice works best to develop a specific skill (Lightbown, 2008; Lyster & Sato, 2013). The corollary question is how well practice in one skill can be expected to benefit the development of additional skills. If one gets better at one type of activity, does that improvement transfer to other activities? An analogy could be drawn here with developing skills at playing certain sports. If one has learned to play tennis well, this skill will probably help if one next tries a game of squash because tennis and squash share similarities (they both involve use of a racket to hit a ball)—although one will certainly need to adjust to several differences between the 2 sports as well. Being a skilful tennis player may even help a little bit if one were to try baseball (which still involves hitting a ball, albeit with a bat). However, tennis skills cannot be expected to help much in a game of soccer, nor in a game of ice-hockey if one does not know how to skate. Toward the end of the chapter, I will discuss some of the implications of the research on practice for a re-appraisal of lessons that follow the *Present-Practice-Produce* sequence. In this type of lesson, the "controlled practice" stage supposedly prepares students for the "free production" stage, where the students are expected to use the learned items or patterns communicatively. However, the practice stage can only serve this purpose well if the specific skills it fosters sufficiently resemble the skills that the students will be needing in the communicative activity (DeKeyser, 1998). If not, the practice stage could in extreme cases be likened to doing snooker practice as preparation for a swimming race.

Another recurring theme of this chapter is the implementation of retrieval practice. There is abundant evidence from research that retrieving information from memory consolidates knowledge far better than, for example, re-reading the same information (Karpicke et al., 2014; Roediger & Butler, 2011). The question, then, is how retrieval schedules should be organized. For example, is it best to ask learners to repeatedly recall newly acquired items or patterns shortly after the initial study episode, or is it best to spread the retrieval attempts over time, with relatively long intervals between each attempt? On the one hand, recall shortly after a study episode is more likely to be successful. On the other hand, recall after a time interval will be more effortful, and this is believed to be beneficial too, according to the notion of desirable difficulties (e.g., Bjork, 1994, 2018). A balanced approach involving effort but with a high probability of successful retrieval would appear ideal (e.g., Bahrick & Phelps, 1987), but operationalizing this is far from straightforward. For instance, the chances of accurate retrieval will also depend on how much there is to be remembered and on how difficult (and confusable) the items or patterns to be remembered are.

Words and Phrases

In chapter 3, it was mentioned that the rate of incidental uptake of new words from reading texts tends to be rather slow, even when the new words are explained in glosses or when learners are given resources to look up their meanings. It was also mentioned that learners' engagement with new words in a text can be increased by making the words relevant to complete a given task. In Peters et al. (2009), one of the studies reviewed in chapter 3, this was done through text-comprehension questions which necessitated engagement with the target words. Another way to increase engagement with new words is to ask students to *do* something more with the words than merely taking in their meaning for the purpose of text comprehension, such as using the words in their own communicative output. That adding an output activity is beneficial for vocabulary retention was illustrated, for instance, by Eckerth and Tavakoli (2012). Students of English read a series of texts each of which was accompanied by glosses explaining the meaning of 10 unfamiliar words. In some lessons this was followed by a composition task, where the students were required to incorporate the glossed words in their own writing. As expected, students retained the meaning of these words better than the words which they had not been required to engage with beyond the reading tasks. Explicit directions that the students should incorporate newly learned words in their own output is important for this to happen. Although learners do sometimes recycle language from input texts spontaneously (see chapter 4), they are also likely to shy away from using what they are not yet familiar with. In a study by Yang et al. (2017), students of English were given a composition task related to the topic of a glossed text they had just read, but they were *not* explicitly told to use the glossed words in their own writing, and so they probably did not. Two weeks later, these students did not recall the meaning of the target words any better than students who had not even read the text. So, although the writing task may have been beneficial for the students in other regards, it did not serve the purpose of consolidating new vocabulary knowledge in this case.

Meaningfully integrating new words in one's own writing requires more cognitive effort than merely processing information presented in the glosses that assist reading comprehension. Put differently, it invites a higher degree of "task-induced involvement" (Laufer & Hulstijn, 2001). Adding this output activity also increases the total time spent on the target words. From a theoretical standpoint it could therefore be argued that the better retention of the target words after an output activity need not be ascribed to the *nature* of the output activity, as it might also be attributed to the greater investment of time. To resolve this ambiguity, some researchers have compared learning conditions with and without output activities that are more similar in time investment. One approach has been to bypass the reading activity in the output condition. Instead of first giving the students a glossed text and comprehension questions, they can simply be given a list of target words with information about their meaning and part of speech. Hulstijn and Laufer (2001) and Laufer (2003) found that if students incorporate new words presented this way in their own composition writing, they will indeed retain their meaning significantly better than if they engage with the words in a glossed text for the purpose of reading comprehension. They conceded that the writing activity still took considerably longer than the reading activity, however. Kim (2008) tried to amend this by adding an activity to the reading comprehension condition with a view to engaging the students for a longer time with the reading text. These students were asked to complete a "graphic organiser" to sum up the text content. The writing activity with incorporation of the target words again helped students to remember the meaning of the words far better than this more expanded reading-based activity.

Other researchers have substituted the composition writing activity by less time-consuming writing exercises, such as inventing separate sentences that incorporate the target words. This is less time-consuming because these sentences need not be integrated into a coherent stretch of discourse. Keating (2008) partially replicated Hulstijn and Laufer (2001) but replaced the composition writing by a sentence-writing task. The latter again yielded significantly better scores on recall tests than reading a glossed text and answering comprehension questions. It thus appears that incorporating new words in one's own output, or the "generative" use of new words (Joe, 1998), is indeed an effective learning procedure, even if it just involves inventing a sentence. Whether the latter is as beneficial for vocabulary retention as incorporating the new words in a longer, coherent piece of writing is not certain. Kim (2008) found no difference in learning outcomes between a sentence-writing and a composition-writing condition, but a more recent study by Zou (2017) did find better learning outcomes for the latter. Integrating a set of new words in a coherent stretch of discourse requires greater cognitive effort, more associative thinking, and may consequently leave stronger memories.

Still, if inventing separate sentences helps to remember new words better than reading glossed texts, then perhaps other vocabulary exercises can serve the same purpose—and possibly with less time required. One possibility is to give students a list of words and their meanings to select from to complete blanks in a text or gapped sentences, because matching a new word to a context where it fits also requires engagement with the word's meaning. Many of the aforementioned studies in fact compared the benefit of such a fill-in-the-blanks exercise to reading a glossed text for comprehension and to generating written output with the target words (Eckerth & Tavakoli, 2012; Hulstijn & Laufer, 2001; Laufer, 2003; Keating, 2008; Kim, 2008; Yang et al., 2017). Blank filling was consistently found to be more beneficial for vocabulary retention than only reading the glossed text, but less beneficial than the generative use of target words in sentence or composition writing—likely because the latter indeed requires greater cognitive engagement (Zou, 2017).

The activity types mentioned so far can therefore be ranked for relative effectiveness (for vocabulary retention) in the following ascending order: reading a glossed text for comprehension < blank filling < sentence writing < composition writing. That said, this does not mean that the sentence- and composition-writing activities in the above studies always brought about spectacular results—scores on immediate meaning-recall tests were seldom higher than 60%. It also needs to be mentioned that, when delayed posttests (typically 1 or 2 weeks after the learning activities) were administered, these showed high attrition rates. In some cases, the delayed test scores were only half as high as the immediate posttest scores (e.g., Hulstijn & Laufer, 2001; Keating, 2008; Kim, 2008). This illustrates the need for reviewing opportunities after an initial learning episode.

The fact also remains that the activities ranked as comparatively *effective* are also the ones that take the most time, and so one might wonder if they are also comparatively *efficient* (in terms of return on time investment). If a single blank-filling operation takes so little time, then performing this operation more than once will be no more time-consuming than a creative writing exercise. Folse (2006) and Lu (2013) compared learners' retention of new words after they had invented one sentence for each word and after they had completed 3 gapped sentences with each word. The latter led to significantly better learning outcomes, which shows that it is not only the nature of the cognitive operation required by an exercise but also the number of times learners engage with a target word that matters (see Peters, 2012, for an additional example).

If the delayed posttests revealed high attrition rates in the studies reviewed here, this is not surprising because memories left by a single episode or just a few episodes of engagement with a set of new words can easily dissipate unless the new knowledge is reactivated soon enough. In a real language course, teachers are likely to revisit vocabulary that was introduced in a previous class. Textbooks contain pages where students are encouraged to review previously introduced items as well, or they will have a companion "workbook" for this purpose. It is also worth bearing in mind that in a real course, teachers and textbooks are likely to use more than a single activity with a focus on certain target words (and they will include several other exercise formats than the ones mentioned above). Determining the effectiveness of a specific type of practice necessitates the kind of experimental control exhibited in the studies mentioned earlier, but it is also useful to examine the benefits of an ensemble of activities that more closely resembles what is done in actual language courses. For example, contemporary textbooks typically introduce new words in context (e.g., a reading text), and some teachers may prefer to present their students with additional input texts in which the same words re-occur repeatedly, while others may believe it is necessary to give their students discrete vocabulary-focused exercises to supplement input-oriented activities. Min (2008) and Laufer and Rozovski-Roitblat (2011, 2015) compared these 2 broad approaches and found better outcomes for vocabulary retention under the latter approach (i.e., the use of various vocabulary-focused exercises after the reading texts). In Laufer and Rozovski-Roitblat (2015), students in an extensive reading course were exposed to target words 3 times as often as students who did less reading but instead did vocabulary-focused exercises, and yet the latter remembered significantly more of the target words at the end of the course. This again demonstrates the merits of deliberate language-focused learning activities as compared to text-comprehension activities alone.

In the above studies which examined the benefits of using target words in writing activities, these words and their meaning (and additional information such as their part of speech) were provided, and the students could consult these explanations as they performed their output tasks. Put differently, there was no incentive for the students to retrieve the information from memory. Similarly, in the blank-filling activities they could copy the words in the appropriate blanks, without any need to recall the orthographic form of the words from memory. Although there is some evidence that copying a newly learned word can be beneficial for the retention of its form (e.g., Candry et al., 2017; Thomas & Dieter, 1987; Webb & Piasecki, 2018), knowledge is known to be consolidated in memory more robustly through retrieval efforts (e.g., Candry et al., 2020; McNamara & Healy, 1995; Smith et al.,

2013). It is therefore possible that the learning gains attested in some of the studies reviewed above could have been more robust had the learning procedures included a retrieval component, such as an exercise where learners no longer have the handout with target words at their disposal but instead need to recall the words from memory to complete blanks or to generate sentences.

The benefits of retrieval for L2 word learning have been illustrated, for example, by Barcroft (2007) and Karpicke and Roediger (2008). In Barcroft (2007), participants either studied and re-studied L2 words and their meanings presented together, or they studied them and then tried to recall them. The latter condition led to significantly better retention. Similar results have been found when the retrieval procedure is implemented as part of a reading activity. In Barcroft (2015a), students read either a text version including 3 instances of new L2 words accompanied by their L1 translation or a text version where the second and third instance of the L2 words was replaced by a blank for the students to fill in with the missing word (cued by the L1 translation). The latter reading condition was found more effective. Its superiority over the condition which did not require retrieval was particularly pronounced on a L1-to-L2 translation posttest, showing that the effort to recall the *form* of the L2 words in the blank-filling task often fostered productive knowledge where merely encountering the items during reading failed to do so. That said, retrieval during reading has also been found to be beneficial at the receptive level. Van den Broek et al. (2018) first asked their participants to study the meaning of a set of new words and then gave them sentences to read which included these words. The sentences were either contextually informative so that the meaning of the new target words could easily be inferred (and so no retrieval from memory was necessary) or lacking in contextual clues (thus requiring retrieval of word meaning from memory). The latter condition brought about significantly better posttest results, *provided* the retrieval of word meaning during the sentence-reading activity was successful. In case retrieval fails, feedback reminding the learner of the correct response will be required. If retrieval fails completely because the learner has totally forgotten the item, then taking in the feedback is comparable to an initial study episode of the item—the learner is back at square one, so to speak. Successful and unsuccessful retrieval are not dichotomous, however. Retrieval may also be partly successful (e.g., when a learner recalls some but not all the facets of a word's meaning or reproduces only part of the word accurately). The feedback will then serve the dual purpose of consolidating knowledge of the aspects which were correctly recalled and extending knowledge where it was incomplete.

Retrieval practice has been operationalized mostly as paired-associate learning, which in our discipline typically involves the memorization of L2-L1 word pairs through a series of retrieval trials. This is what many learners do, for instance, when they first study a list of L2 words laid out on the page as one column and with their L1 translations in an adjacent column, and then cover one column to check if they can recall either the L2 words or their L1 translations. This is also what learners do when they use flashcards with the target word written on one side of the card and its translation (or other clarification) on the other side. This type of retrieval practice is now commonly applied also in computer-assisted vocabulary learning (Nakata, 2011). The questions addressed in this specific strand of research concern how retrieval practice should be implemented to obtain the best results. For example, teachers may wonder if it is best to have their students review a set of words shortly after they studied the words or if they should leave a longer interval between study and review sessions (e.g., Rogers & Cheung, 2020a, b; Sobel et al., 2011). On the one hand, a short interval is likely to make retrieval easier and thus more successful during the practice session. On the other hand, a longer interval will make retrieval more effortful, and effortful retrieval is believed to entrench knowledge more deeply in long-term memory (Pyc & Rawson, 2007). In addition, the learner is likely to attend more to feedback given after an unsuccessful retrieval attempt than to feedback which simply affirms a response the learner already felt confident about (Bahrick & Hall, 2005).

A related question is how many new items should be included in a study-and-practice session, because the more items that need to be recalled, the more challenging this will be. Again, retrieval of a small set of studied items (e.g., a stack of just 5 flashcards) is likely to be successful, but it may not require the amount of cognitive effort that is believed to strengthen memories. All these things considered, optimal retrieval practice is probably a matter of striking a balance between practice that is too easy and practice that is too hard. In other words, it should have a desirable level of difficulty (Bjork, 1994, 2018; Bjork & Bjork, 2014). Asking learners to study a single word (e.g., English *squirrel* = Dutch *eekhoorn*), and recall it immediately afterwards (*squirrel* = ___; feedback: *squirrel* = eekhoorn) will not induce much cognitive engagement. At the other extreme, asking learners to study, say, 50 new words in one go and then recall them a week later is obviously too challenging, and so the learning process will need to start anew for most of the words.

In the literature, the insertion of time intervals between study and retrieval sessions is often referred to as "spacing". For example, one might study a set of words and review it on the same day, or one may postpone the reviewing until the following day. The latter is the recommended option, according to the findings of several experiments (e.g., Cepeda et al., 2009; Küpper-Tetzel et al., 2014). Spacing thus concerns the distinction between "cramming" in a short span of time versus distributing study and review work over a longer stretch of time. Because cramming involves retrieval shortly after studying the items, it may seem efficient to learners—the successful retrieval leaves learners with the impression that the new knowledge is acquired. However, longer-term benefits of retrieval have almost consistently been shown to be greater after distributed or spaced practice (e.g., Bloom & Schuell, 1981; Kornell, 2009).

A notion associated with spacing is "interleaving". Interleaving means that a single item is not studied or retrieved consecutively because other items in the set of to-be-learned items are mixed in between. For example, when learners study

10 new words and then try to recall the words in the same order, they will have attended to 9 other words before attempting to recall the first word in the list. The greater the number of items to be learned, the more challenging retrieval will be. Deliberate vocabulary learning usually involves both spacing and interleaving. For example, textbooks typically introduce several new words per unit or lesson and will provide activities concerning this set of words rather than focus on just one single word. The reviewing may be done relatively soon after the words were introduced (as part of the activities included in the same lesson), but it may also be done later, for example, as homework. If a first round of retrieval practice is organized soon after the new words were introduced and more practice follows with a delay, then such a scenario essentially corresponds to what is called "expanding spacing" in the literature. Expanding spacing means that a first practice session follows a study phase after a relatively short lag, but subsequent practice sessions follow with increasing intervals (e.g., Kang et al., 2014). When expanding spacing is implemented well, the first retrieval practice will have a good success rate while nonetheless inducing cognitive effort (it should therefore not be done *too* soon after the study phase). Gradually expanding the interval afterwards helps to keep the retrieval practice sufficiently challenging. Ultimately, however, it is hoped that, as a result of ample practice of the right kind, accurate retrieval will become effortless— and this also during communicative use of the language.

Nakata et al. (2020) applied the recommendations derived from the above strand of research to a real language course. The students learned 10 new words per weekly class and were also quizzed each class on previously studied words. For one group of students, these quizzes were exclusively about the 10 words learned in the immediately preceding class, while for another group the quizzes included some of the most recently learned words but also some words from earlier classes. Put differently, the latter group's vocabulary practice schedule was more distributed and more interleaved than the former group's schedule. At the end of the course, the students were tested on the whole collection of target words. The group that did the mixed quizzes performed significantly better on this end-of-course test. It is worth mentioning that the students were told in advance about the weekly vocabulary quizzes and that they counted toward the course grades. This was thus an incentive for the students to review the vocabulary in between classes as well. Importantly, the students were explicitly told whether the quizzes would only be about the words learned in the most recent class (in one group) or would include words from earlier classes as well (in the other group). The students who were expecting the mixed quizzes were thus given an incentive to regularly review the vocabulary from earlier classes instead of just focusing on the words from the most recent class. If they remembered more target words overall at the end of the course, this may well be due to their greater investment in review work. Two other classroom-based experiments (Rogers & Cheung, 2020a, b), both conducted with young learners of English, did *not* furnish evidence that a long lag between initial learning and reactivation of knowledge is better for retention than a short lag. In these experiments, teachers taught 10 new words to their students either a day of a full week before reviewing the words in another class. The results of a surprise posttest administered 4 weeks later indicated an advantage for the one-day lag in the first experiment, but no difference in effectiveness between the one-day lag and the one-week lag in the second. In sum, the few experiments which have investigated study-and-practice schedules in real language courses have thus far yielded rather mixed results, which is not surprising given the diverse ways in which such schedules can be implemented in practice.

Study-and-practice schedules can also be manipulated *within* a single learning session (or lesson). Nakata (2015) is one of several useful evaluations by the same author of within-session retrieval schedules. This was a computer-assisted experiment where Japanese students of English first studied new words paired with their L1 translations, and then tried to retrieve the words 3 times following schedules which varied in the amount of interleaving/spacing. For example, in one condition, students would try to recall a given word after tackling 5 other words in between, while in another condition there would be as many as 30 other words in between. For half of the words the number of intervening items was kept constant, while for the other half the number increased after each retrieval episode. Nakata (2015) found a relative advantage for a practice schedule with a moderate amount of interleaving (10 words on average). The advantage was the greatest when this was implemented as expanding spacing, where the first retrieval attempt came relatively early (after 5 other items mixed in between) and subsequently with an increased delay (10 and then 15 other items in between). These findings support the above rationale that, after a successful first retrieval effort, knowledge of the items can be entrenched through practice especially if that additional practice remains effortful for a while. Nakata (2015) also included a condition where students recalled each word 3 times *without* other items mixed in between. This condition yielded the poorest posttest scores, which supports the notion that immediate retrieval practice regarding just one lexical item is too effortless and unengaging to leave robust memories.

It needs to be said that a situation where learners try to memorize as many as 30 words in one go is not common outside experiments such as the above. According to Strong and Boers (2019a), for example, exercises in textbooks typically have about 7 items. Yet, almost all of the experiments on retrieval practice to date have subjected participants to study-and-retrieval schedules involving at least 20 new words, with several involving as many as 40 or more (e.g., Bahrick & Hall, 2005; Cepeda et al., 2009; Kang et al., 2014; Kornell, 2009). With so many new items to be remembered, it may take quite a few retrieval trials followed by feedback before participants manage to successfully recall all of them. In some of the experiments, participants were prompted to recall the items 3 times in the training schedule, which was probably not enough to establish accurate memories for all the target words. In Nakata (2015), for example, the "best" learning schedule yielded a score of about 70% on the immediate posttest (whose format was identical to the retrieval trials which the students had previously performed). In another experiment, Nakata (2017) found that, after 7 retrieval trials, students managed to recall almost all of 16 target words (>95%) in the immediate posttest. The addition of retrieval trials inevitably increases the total amount of time invested. It may be worth replicating some of the experiments cited above which compared the effectiveness and efficiency of different practice schedules, but with sets of items of a more realistic size.

Another option may be to cut up a large set of new items into more manageable blocks for learners to study and practise one at a time. Kornell (2009) explored this possibility in 3 experiments. Participants studied and practised 20 new words either as an integral package or in blocks of 5 at a time. No advantage was found for the latter schedule. The practice schedule included up to 8 retrieval trials, and it is likely that, after the first couple of trials, retrieval of just 5 items per block became too easy to induce any more cognitive engagement. Nakata and Webb (2016) also compared the effects of doing retrieval practice on a whole set of 20 target items or on separate blocks of 4 words at a time. After the initial study phase, students did 4 retrieval trials (each followed by feedback). These trials varied in whether they prompted receptive or productive recall, and thanks to this variation they probably remained rather challenging even when the students were recalling just a handful of items at a time. Still, no statistically significant advantage was observed for the schedule where students studied and retrieved the words organized in small blocks of 4. The retrieval practice with all 20 words together was arguably better preparation for the posttest, because the posttest was in effect a continuation of the same procedure—all 20 words mixed. Put differently, for the students who studied and practised the words exclusively in small blocks, the test procedure was less congruent with the practice they had done. It might be interesting to investigate the effectiveness of a procedure where learners initially study and retrieve words in blocks, and then move on to retrieval practice where the items from different blocks are mixed. This would be a way of increasing the success rate of the first retrieval trials, preserving a challenge in later retrievals and helping the learners to progress from segmented to integrated knowledge. I will return to this proposal further below, in the section on grammar practice.

The nature of the retrieval operation matters in other ways as well. For example, productive retrieval (i.e., recall of word form) is harder and thus more error-prone than receptive retrieval (i.e., recall of word meaning). Because it is more challenging, entrenching productive knowledge is likely to take more practice (i.e., more retrieval trials). If the objective is to foster productive knowledge, then productive retrieval is preferable, as it fosters knowledge of word form where receptive retrieval alone might not suffice (e.g., Griffin & Harley, 1996; Mondria & Wiersma, 2004; Nakata, 2016; Webb, 2005). More generally, the specific nature of a learning activity (e.g., meaning oriented vs.

form oriented) will influence the nature of the resulting knowledge and what skills this knowledge serves best (Barcroft, 2015b; Lightbown, 2008; Morris et al., 1977; Webb, 2009). Finding the optimal implementation of study + practice schedules is further complicated by the nature of the lexical items the learners are presented with. As discussed in chapter 2, some words are harder to learn than others. For example, remembering a set of abstract words is likely to take more effort than remembering a set of words with concrete meanings. Including cognates in a set of to-be-learned words is likely to alleviate the learning burden, while inclusion of so-called false friends may increase the burden. When productive recall is the objective, then word length and formal complexity will be a variable, too. Inclusion of look-alikes (e.g., *precede* and *proceed, shirt* and *skirt, stalactite* and *stalagmite*) is also likely to increase the risk of inter-item confusion.

A question that has attracted considerable interest in this context is whether learning semantically related words together increases the risk of inter-item confusion. Instructional materials often present vocabulary items together that belong to the same superordinate category, such as a set of nouns for items of clothing, jobs, vehicles, fruit, body parts and so on. Learning new words belonging to the same semantic category may be relatively challenging, because the learner may find it hard to discriminate between the related meanings. Put differently, they not only need to put effort into remembering new form-meaning pairings, but also into keeping these similar pairings apart from one another. Some studies have indeed shown that it tends to take more retrieval trials for learners to correctly memorize sets of semantically related words than to memorize sets of unrelated words (Tinkham, 1993; Waring, 1997). Some studies have also found that later recall of the related words is poorer (e.g., Erten & Tekin, 2008; Finkbeiner & Nicol, 2003; Wilcox & Medina, 2013). The latter is perhaps surprising in the light of what was said above about desirable difficulties (i.e., the benefits of making a learning task challenging). After all, if it takes longer and more effort to memorize a set of semantically related words, then one might expect relatively good longer-term outcomes. There are in fact also studies in which studying semantically related words led to better posttest scores (Hashemi & Gowdasiaei, 2005; Hoshino, 2010; Schneider et al., 2002). According to a meta-analytic review (Nakata & Suzuki, 2019a), memorizing sets of words is harder if the words are semantically clustered, but the evidence to suggest that they will then also be remembered less well afterwards is much weaker. Part of the explanation for the mixed findings may lie with the nature of the semantic clustering (e.g., Ishii, 2015). Words may be semantically related at a rather generic level, where cross-item interference is less likely because the referents are quite distinct. For example, although the referents of *orange, strawberry, grape* and *banana* belong the category of fruits, they are clearly more distinct from one another than the referents of *orange, grapefruit, mandarin, lemon* and *lime*, which belong to the more specific category of citrus fruits and which bear a stronger resemblance to one another. Adding, for example, *melon* to the list would increase the challenge of avoiding inter-item interference due to its phonological resemblance to *lemon*. An even more extreme example of semantic clustering might be a set of words referring to different kinds of berries: *strawberries, raspberries, blueberries, cranberries, gooseberries, blackberries, boysenberries*. In a similar vein, learning a set of words belonging to the rather generic category of vehicles need not carry much risk of inter-item confusion if the referents are quite distinct (e.g., *car, airplane, train, ship, bike*), but this will be different at a less generic level, where the referents resemble one another much more (e.g., different types of car, such as *sedan, SUV, hatchback, minivan, station wagon, pickup, coupe* and *convertible*).

In case learning semantically related words together increases the risk of inter-item interference, then one option is to avoid presenting learners with such combinations of words in one and the same lesson, textbook unit, handout or web page. This is difficult in practice, however, because many language courses and instructional materials are organized around certain real-world topics or themes (e.g., jobs, travelling, food), and with those themes come related words (e.g., various jobs, various means of transport, foods). Another option might be to design study and retrieval practice concerning the related words that reduces the clustering by mixing the words with many other, non-related words. This possibility was investigated by Nakata and Suzuki (2019a). Japanese students of English studied 48 English words and their Japanese translations and then engaged in 3 retrieval trials (each trial followed by feedback—a re-study opportunity). The 48 words included 4 sets of 6 words each belonging to the same category. For example, there were 6 words referring to mammals and 6 words referring to plants. The other 24 words were not semantically related. Half of the students studied and then tried to recall the meaning of the words per block of 6 items. For example, they studied the 6 words for mammals and then did 3 retrieval trials for those 6 items before moving on to the next set of 6 words. The other students studied and tried to retrieve the words in 2 sets of 24 items, with items from the various categories mixed. Unsurprisingly, the third retrieval attempt was more likely to be successful in the former schedule (83%) than in the latter (50%), and yet, the immediate posttest performance (where the students were presented with all 48 words and asked to provide the L1 translation) was similar for both conditions (54% and 56%, respectively). In a one-week delayed posttest, it was the group which studied the mixed sets (i.e., with greater interleaving and thus with longer spacing between re-encounters with the same words) that performed best (17% vs. 27%). Interestingly, there was more evidence of within-set confusion (e.g., confusing the word for one mammal or plant with that for another mammal or plant) when students had studied and practised these words in blocks instead of mixed with various other themes. It needs to be noted that 3 retrieval trials were insufficient to guarantee correct recall on the third trial even in the blocked condition. It is therefore difficult to tell how successful recall in the posttests might have been had the students had the opportunity to more firmly entrench knowledge of the related words through further retrieval practice. Still, Nakata and Suzuki's (2019a) findings clearly indicate that the semantic relatedness of target words is a factor that should be considered as one tries to design study and practice schedules which strike a good balance between success rates and cognitive effort. Their results also support the findings from several other experiments (see above) that on delayed posttests it is typically the spaced or distributed learning schedules that trump the cramming schedules. At the same time, it needs to be said that the delayed posttest scores in this strand of inquiry are typically quite low (e.g., <20%). Different outcomes under various study schedules, while significant in statistical terms, are not always highly pertinent in pedagogical terms when the observed longer-term outcomes turn out poor overall, regardless of the schedule followed. Perhaps the plain paired-associate learning (or rote learning) that is used in these experiments is insufficiently engaging. How lexical items are clarified to learners is likely to matter as well. That, however, is a topic to be discussed in chapter 7.

In comparison to the above collection of studies, empirical investigations of practice schedules concerning *phrases* are still rare. While strictly speaking not about practice *schedules*, there are nonetheless some studies which indicate that similar factors to ones identified above play a part in phrase learning as well. For example, Steinel et al. (2007) demonstrated that productive knowledge of idioms is fostered better by presenting the meaning of idioms to prompt recall of their L2 form than by presenting the idioms to prompt recall of their meaning. This is reminiscent of studies of paired associate learning which found that the direction of association at the learning phase matters (e.g., Griffin & Harley, 1996; Mondria & Wiersma, 2004; Nakata, 2016; Webb, 2005, 2009). Also reminiscent of the research reviewed above about the potential downside of presenting semantically similar words together, Webb and Kagimoto (2011) found that memorizing sets of adjective-noun phrases where the adjectives bear semantic resemblance (e.g., *narrow escape* and *slim chance, tall order* and *high spirits*) is harder and more error-prone than learning sets of phrases where the risk of inter-item interference is smaller. L2 textbooks (e.g., Crace & Acklam, 2011) nonetheless include exercises that require students to choose between near synonyms—an approach which may need to be re-assessed. Finally, Szudarski (2012) and Laufer and Girsai (2008) compared how well learners remembered verb-noun collocations included in a reading text with or without additional decontextualized exercises concerning these collocations. The addition of collocation-focused practice led to the better outcome, which is akin to what was found in numerous studies of word learning reviewed above.

Again, the type of the exercise may matter as well. Exercises which require students to produce the target phrases are more likely to foster productive knowledge than exercises which require only processing of the meaning of given phrases (e.g., Peters & Pauwels, 2015). Even so, the kind of "production" in output-oriented exercises will matter, too. Copying given phrases into gapped sentences (Webb & Kagimoto, 2009) or saying the given phrases aloud repeatedly (Alali & Schmitt, 2013) is probably less effective for knowledge consolidation than generating new sentences or texts with the phrases (Teng, 2020; Zhang, 2017) and less effective also than retrieving the phrases from memory (Alali & Schmitt, 2013).

Since repeated practice gives smoother access to knowledge in memory, investigating practice schedules for phrase learning would be particularly welcome given the connection between learners' mastery of phrases and their ability to produce language fluently (e.g., Tavakoli & Uchihara, 2020; Wood, 2010). Suggestions for classroom activities entailing repeated use of the same phrases are available in manuals for teachers (e.g., Lindstromberg & Boers, 2008), but most of these activities have yet to be put to the test in empirical research. It should be pointed out here that having learners re-use a set of newly learned phrases need not amount to decontextualized drill exercises. Neither should it amount to reading scripted dialogues aloud, since this mimicry does not necessarily help students appreciate the meaning of the language forms they are imitating. Instead, meaningful re-use of the same phrases can be encouraged, for example, when students repeat the same communicative activity several times but each time with different interlocutors (Gatbonton & Segalowitz, 2005; Lynch & Maclean, 2000). In fact, it is the increased ease with which students reproduce the same word strings as they repeat a communicative task that helps to explain the improvements in speech fluency that have been attested in studies of task repetition (e.g., de Jong & Perfetti, 2011; Thai & Boers, 2016).

Patterns

I already discussed grammar practice of a receptive nature (i.e., focusing on comprehension) in chapter 5, as part of the review of the teaching method known as *Processing Instruction*. Here, I will discuss mostly grammar practice oriented towards accuracy in language production. In the realm of grammar, teachers will likely associate this practice with the second component of a traditional *Present-Practice-Produce* lesson (PPP), as described, for example in Ur (1996). In such a lesson design, the "controlled" practice stage (i.e., the second P in the sequence) is meant to provide a bridge between the introduction of the grammar pattern where learners develop declarative knowledge of the pattern (the first P) and their use of the pattern in communicative activities (the third P). The practice stage is controlled in the sense that students are given limited options, and it allows the students to focus on the new language pattern because they do not need to provide (much) content themselves. In the third P (i.e., "free" production), the students do need to express their own thoughts. Thanks to the preceding practice stage, the multi-tasking that is inherent in genuine communication (thinking about content *and* its linguistic packaging) will be more manageable, so the reasoning goes. For example, a PPP lesson about the simple past tense could start with examples and explanations about this tense (its form, function and usage), continue with a series of exercises where the students need to use past tense forms to complete sentences with past time reference (e.g., *My Dad _____ the saxophone in a band when he was younger*) and retell a past narrative with the aid of picture cues, and end with communicative activities where the students draft a short text about the history of their home town as a contribution to a new tourist information brochure and/or share memories of their best (or worst) holidays. It is hoped that, after ample practice in using past tense forms at the practice stage, the students will find it easier to perform the communicative tasks. In this light, a PPP sequence is compatible with *Skill Acquisition Theory* (Criado, 2016; DeKeyser, 2010; Johnson, 1996), according to which most skills are initially supported by declarative knowledge but can over time get deployed more smoothly thanks to repeated practice—practice which gradually makes the learner less dependent on the initial, declarative knowledge. An analogy can be drawn here with learning to drive a car. One will initially learn what to do with the gear stick to get into reverse, to distinguish between the brake pedal and the accelerator pedal, and so on, and learn these operations in a safe environment such as the practice area of a driving school. It is after one has become familiar with these operations that due attention can in addition be given to traffic signs, what other drivers around you are doing and where one needs to change lanes in order not to miss the right exit. Like communicative language use, driving is a multi-componential skill, and if some of the constituent micro-skills are executed without requiring conscious thought anymore, then the multi-tasking will become more manageable, because it frees up mental resources to be allocated to the other components of the skill set.

If the practice stage (i.e., the second P in PPP) is intended to gradually prepare learners for the communicative use of a newly learned grammar pattern (the third P), then the kind of exercises included in the practice stage should be designed such that they foster knowledge that is likely to serve that ultimate purpose in some way. Unfortunately, it is questionable if all the exercise formats in contemporary textbooks are truly very useful in this regard. For example, textbooks abound with exercises where the students are required to examine instances of incorrect language. Common formats of this kind include find-and-correct-the-errors exercises (e.g., *6 out of the following 8 sentences have a mistake; find the mistakes and correct them: 1. Would you mind to switch off the light, please? 2. ...*) and compare-and-choose-the-correct-option exercises (e.g., *Cross out the wrong word: 1. She is very interesting / interested in science; 2. ...*). These exercises invite students to evaluate incorrect language forms, non-standard word combinations and wrong form-meaning pairings. After being asked to contemplate them, they are expected to erase these incorrect forms, combinations or pairings from memory. It is important to add here that the incorrect options which the students are presented with are not necessarily ones that they would have been inclined to produce spontaneously themselves. Put differently, these exercises do not necessarily serve the purpose of "remedial" teaching—authors of internationally marketed textbooks would find it hard to anticipate the likely language errors made by learners with diverse L1 backgrounds. I already questioned the usefulness of such exercise formats in chapter 5, in connection with collocations (e.g., Boers et al., 2017; Boers et al., 2014) and phrasal verbs (Strong & Boers, 2019a, b). These studies indicated that exercises which require learners to distinguish right word combinations from wrong ones carry a risk of wrong options lingering in the learner's memory and causing interference further down the road. It seems plausible that exercises that ask students to examine instances of incorrect language (which they have not even produced themselves) carry such a risk also when it comes to grammar. And yet, some popular contemporary textbooks abound with such exercises. In the students' book for upper-intermediate learners of the *New Total English* series (Crace & Acklam, 2011), for example, 24% of the grammar practice consists of find-and-correct-the-error exercises. In addition, 27% requires students to distinguish right from wrong language in dual-choice or multiple-choice exercises. In sum, over half of the controlled grammar practice in this book engages the students with instances of language they should in fact avoid. In the students' book for intermediate students of the *Cutting Edge* series (Cunningham et al., 2013), 15% of the grammar practice consists of find-and-correct-the-errors exercises, and 21% consists of choose-the-correct-option exercises. Students using this book will thus be examining incorrect instances of grammar in over a third of the exercises. Some textbook series include minimal controlled practice in the students' book but instead refer the students to a companion "workbook". Such workbooks also tend to make extensive use of exercises that require learners to find and correct errors or to choose the correct form from 2 (or sometimes 3) adjacent options. For example, approximately half of the grammar exercises in the workbook for intermediate students of the *Straightforward* series (Waterman, 2012) are of this kind. If students use this companion workbook in conjunction with the student's book (Kerr & Jones, 2012), chances are that for certain grammar patterns they will meet more wrong instances than appropriate ones. For example, the unit on expressing future reference in the students' book (unit 6) has students identify the correct form (e.g., *going to* vs. *will*) in 7 sentences as the controlled practice component. This is complemented in the workbook by another 6 items of the same kind, followed by 6 correct-the-mistakes items. The only exercise where the students themselves produce a future-reference expression is a completion exercise consisting of 6 items. Even if future research reveals that I have been overestimating the risk of interference from these exercises, one must still wonder why students should spend time and effort contemplating language features that they are subsequently expected to *avoid* using. Surely, what learners need first and foremost is a repertoire of language items and patterns which *are* appropriate means of communication. If so, exercises which entrench knowledge of what is right without requiring the students to also contemplate what is wrong probably provide a more direct way of building that repertoire. It is worth reiterating that the multiple-choice exercises and formats such as find-and-correct-the-error exercises that one finds in textbooks and other practice materials present learners with errors which these learners themselves might never have made. This is very different from teachers giving feedback on their own students' language (see chapter 4) and from using their own students' errors to inform remedial teaching (Richards & Reppen, 2014). I am by no means questioning the value of corrective feedback. My point is that giving feedback on students' own output is very different from asking students to examine inappropriate language choices which they themselves did not make and were perhaps never going to make. Asking students to discriminate between what is right and what is wrong, such as find-and-correct-errors in sentences and choosing the appropriate form from a set of options, is perhaps better suited for *testing* purposes. In many countries, these are indeed still the kinds of formats that occur in high-stakes tests (such as university entrance exams), and many teachers feel morally obliged to prepare their students for these important milestones. It needs to be asked, however, whether such test formats are optimal *teaching* instruments to foster the kind of skills that students need to become proficient language users—not just successful test takers.

With the growing popularity of *Task-Based* and *Task-Supported Language Teaching*—paradigms which eschew controlled practice—few researchers now find it worth evaluating the effectiveness of various grammar-oriented exercises. This is regrettable, because PPP-type language courses are still very common around the world—although the educators who designed them tend to use more fashionable labels to describe them—and so an empirical investigation of their comparative effectiveness is long overdue. A common complaint about PPP is that students often fail to successfully incorporate the grammar pattern in the free production stage of such lessons (the third P), despite the controlled practice (the second P). In other words, there is insufficient transfer of knowledge from the practice to the production stage. As I have just argued, however, this may be due to the nature of the exercises that are often used in the practice stage. If the second P in PPP were implemented more adequately, that is, with repeated use by the students of what is right, without distracting them with what is wrong, transfer of knowledge to the third P (i.e., the communicative activity) might be smoother. This practice could give precedence to activities such as sentence completion, picture description, and story retelling. It is worth noting in this context that language teaching methods such as *Situational Language Teaching* and the *Audio-Lingual Method*, which were widely used in the West until the early 1970s, also promoted repeated use of correct patterns without presenting students with erroneous examples. While I am by no means pleading for a return to the sort of unengaging, mechanical drill exercises associated with such methods, it might nonetheless be worth exploring how some such exercise types could be adapted and integrated in a package of *meaningful* practice activities in a manner that is more compatible with current views of learning—including recognition of the importance of retrieval practice (instead of mere imitation practice).

What *has* attracted a fair amount of research effort is the question of practice *schedules*, but mostly with little consideration to the *kind* of practice being implemented. Analogous to the lines of inquiry concerning vocabulary learning schedules, several researchers interested in L2 grammar learning have investigated whether it is best to teach and practise grammar patterns in a distributed fashion ("spaced" over time) or whether a more intensive schedule (a lot of practice in a shorter time span) could be more beneficial. Additionally, some researchers have addressed the question whether it is best to introduce and practise one grammar pattern at a time, or whether it is more useful to introduce 2 or more patterns simultaneously and then interleave this practice, so that the learners engage in compare-and-contrast operations early on. Answers to these questions have important implications for course and curriculum design. For example, schools may schedule regular language classes, such as 2 classes per week, throughout a school year, or they may decide to schedule the whole course in one single term of the school year. Some schools may offer an even more intensive language course, typically as some sort of "summer camp" where the target language is used almost non-stop for a month or so. While not specifically focused on grammar learning, some large-scale studies have been conducted to compare the outcomes of these curricular choices. Collins et al. (1999) and Collins and White (2011) found slightly better outcomes for intensive English programs compared to regular ones at schools in Quebec. Serrano and Muñoz (2007) and Serrano (2011) found a similar advantage for intensive English programs over regular ones in Spain. One difficulty with interpreting these findings is that other factors than just the distribution of classes over time are likely to have influenced the learning outcomes. The courses were taught by different teachers, the nature of the lessons inevitably varied to some extent (e.g., some may have been more language focused than others), the amount of out-of-class exposure to the target language may have varied, and the total number of class hours was not necessarily the same in the programs being compared. A second difficulty with interpreting the findings concerns the time of assessing the learning outcomes. The students were tested at the end of their respective programs, but there was no further delayed test to ascertain if the advantage of the intensive programs was preserved over time. It is conceivable that students tested at the end of an intensive program are better able to recall words and phrases they learned in the first half of that program simply because the time lag between learning and the test is shorter than is the case with words learned in the first half of a distributed program. In Serrano (2011) it is indeed striking that the intensive programs led to the better performance especially on tests that required good vocabulary knowledge. When it comes to grammar, however, this effect seems less likely because most grammar patterns are frequent enough to recur throughout a course, and instruction that successfully raises students' awareness of a given pattern (e.g., the past tense) early on may raise the students' awareness of the pattern when they re-encounter it during the remainder of the school year. More tightly controlled experiments with the addition of delayed posttests may be helpful to compare the effects of distributed and intensive practice on L2 learners' mastery of specific grammar patterns.

Some such experiments (Bird, 2010; Miles, 2014) have shown a slight advantage for intensive practice schedules in posttests administered shortly after completion of the schedules but, conversely, an advantage for the more distributed schedules in delayed posttests. Bird (2010) gave adult, intermediate-level learners of English practice in distinguishing between the simple past tense (e.g., *I saw a great movie last night*), the present perfect tense (e.g., *I've seen that movie many times*) and the past perfect tense (e.g., *I hadn't seen that movie before she recommended it*). The practice sessions took 10 hours in total and consisted of grammaticality-judgement exercises followed by feedback. Per session, the students were presented with 20 sentences most of which were incorrect (e.g., *Thomas Edison has invented the light bulb), asked if they could detect errors in these sentences and, if so, to correct them. At the end of the exercise, feedback with explanations (or reminders) about the use of the respective tenses followed. The pretest, a posttest one week after completion of the series of practice sessions, and a delayed posttest after 60 days were of the same, grammaticality-judgement format. Depending on the learning schedule which the learners were assigned to, the practice sessions were either 3 days apart or 14 days apart. Scores were slightly higher on the one-week delayed posttest after the former practice schedule, but the further delayed posttest revealed a significantly greater rate of forgetting compared to the schedule where the practice sessions had been 14 days apart, suggesting a long-term advantage for spreading practice sessions over time. It is worth mentioning that, altogether, the improvements from the pretest to the posttest were far from impressive. The scores on the one-week delayed test were, on average, only 28% better than the pretest scores (and leaving over 25% of the responses incorrect). Considering the generous time investment (a total of 10 hours of practice), the fact that the learners practised exactly what they were going to be tested on, and the fact that, according to their pretest performance, these learners already had appreciable prior knowledge of the target grammar, it is surprising that the test scores did not improve more than this. The explanation may be found in the nature of the exercises that were used in the practice sessions. As I noted above, find-and-correct-the-mistakes exercises require learners to contemplate erroneous sentences and to decide whether they are incorrect and in what respect. The learners are also presented with correct sentences, but the nature of the test invites them to wonder if these are truly correct. Unless the learners have already developed reliable and stable knowledge of the target patterns, such exercises potentially cause competition in memory between what is right (and thus what is meant to be consolidated in memory) and what is wrong (and thus meant to be suppressed). One might argue that such interference was prevented thanks to the feedback which the students received at the end of the practice sessions. As discussed previously, however, this cannot be taken for granted, especially in the case of language features that are inherently confusable. Moreover, the students were at the start of the experiment given a pretest consisting of 35 grammaticality-judgement items, and these items were of course *not* followed by feedback. A second study claiming superiority of distributed practice for L2 grammar learning is Miles (2014). Students of English received instruction and exercises on word order, more specifically the place of adverbs such as *almost, never* and *usually* in sentences. For one group, this was distributed over 3 sessions with at least one week in between. For another group, the whole battery of instruction and practice was organized as a single session. In both cases, the total time spent was 65 minutes. Most of the exercises required the students to detect and correct errors again, and this was also what they were required to do in pretests and posttests. Again, a delayed posttest administered 5 weeks after the practice sessions indicated less forgetting after the distributed practice sessions. This was a rather small-scale experiment, however, with only 16 participants per condition. Besides, there was also a test of productive knowledge (a sentence-translation test scored for the correct placement of the adverb), and this did not show an advantage for distributed practice—the test scores were barely over 60% regardless of the practice schedule.

Other studies regarding grammar practice have not revealed an advantage of distributed practice. In Suzuki and DeKeyser (2017), beginner-level students of Japanese learned and practised a set of rules regarding verb morphology in 2 sessions (each about 45 minutes) one day apart or one week apart. Productive knowledge tests (including a picture-description test) showed no significant difference in effectiveness between the 2 practice schedules shortly afterwards or 3 weeks later. The learning gains were in fact quite remarkable in both conditions, with average improvements of over 70% from the pretest to the immediate and delayed posttests. It is noteworthy that neither the tests nor the practice sessions made use of exercises such as error correction, but instead focused the learners' attention exclusively on correct applications of the grammar rules. The same approach was taken in Suzuki (2017), where grammar practice was also implemented mostly through picture-description exercises. In this study, learners studied and practised verb morphology rules in 5 sessions (each about 40 minutes), which were either 3 or 7 days apart. Tests followed 7 days after completion of the schedules and again after 3 weeks. The learning gains were again substantial under both conditions (60% to 70%), but this time it was the students who had done the practice sessions with the shorter intervals who obtained the highest scores on both the immediate and the delayed tests.

Given the mixed findings, it is impossible to tell at this point what the optimal practice schedule for grammar learning might be. Considering the findings by Miles (2014), distributed practice is probably preferable to uninterrupted practice of the same grammar topic in a single session (if only to avoid boredom and fatigue). But how long the interval between sessions should be will inevitably depend on many factors, including how well learners recall what they learned in the previous session(s). As discussed regarding retrieval practice for vocabulary, the optimal schedule probably requires a fine balance between effort and success. For example, Kasprowicz et al. (2019) found a significant association between students' success rates during practice sessions and their learning gains. Unsurprisingly, the success rates during practice were higher when the time lag between the practice sessions was 3 days as compared to a full week. Success rates during practice will of course not only be influenced by how much time has passed since the previous learning session, but also by how much practice has previously been done. The complexity of the pattern to be mastered and the nature of the practice and the test format will undoubtedly matter as well.

In all the studies reviewed here, the practice sessions involved different grammar patterns (e.g., simple past and present perfect) and the learners were required to distinguish between them. This makes pedagogical sense because in real communication one also needs to decide when to use one pattern (e.g., simple present tense) rather than another (e.g., present progressive tense). The question this raises is how soon in the process of learning related grammar patterns the practice in contrasting such pairs should start. For example, is it more judicious to introduce and practise each pattern one at a time before alternating between them in exercises, or is it better to start alternating early on? Put differently, is it best to teach and practise each pattern first in separate blocks, or is it more beneficial to interleave the practice on different patterns shortly after the patterns were introduced? This is a pertinent question, because the approach taken by course designers and textbook authors varies in this regard. Yet, only a few studies to date have addressed this question. Nakata and Suzuki (2019b) conducted a computer-assisted experiment where Japanese students of English did practice concerning 5 grammar patterns (simple past tense, present perfect tense and 3 conditional sentence patterns). The exercises used a multiple-choice format. After each exercise item, feedback with explanations was provided. For one group, all the exercise items per grammar pattern (10 items) were tackled in a single block before moving on to the next grammar pattern. For a second group, the exercises on the various patterns were interleaved from the very beginning. For a third group, half of the exercise items per pattern were first tackled in blocks, and after this the remaining items were interleaved. Learning gains were assessed by means of a grammaticality-judgement test. The gains were greater for the 2 conditions that included interweaving. The scores on the one-week delayed posttest were on average only 10% higher than the pretest scores, however. In fact, the high pretest scores (around 70%) suggest these learners already had fair knowledge of the target grammar patterns before the actual experiment. These were intermediate learners of English with at least 6 years of experience studying English at school, and so there was probably no need to re-introduce and practise each pattern separately in blocks. Textbooks for intermediate-level learners of English also tend to address more than one tense (e.g., past simple and past continuous) in a single unit or chapter (e.g., Cunningham et al., 2013; Richards et al., 2017), because most tenses were already introduced in one way or another in the textbooks for beginners and low-intermediate-level students. As the students could rely on prior knowledge, they were probably ready to cope with the interleaved practice from the start. The learners' success rate during practice was in fact already over 60% for the first 5 items in the interleaved practice schedule (and it climbed to about 80% by the end of the schedule as a result of repeated practice).

A similar research design was used by Suzuki and Sunada (2020). Japanese learners of English did computer-assisted exercises to help them distinguish between 4 relative clause patterns (e.g., *The girl who is watching the cat* vs. *The cat which is watching the girl* vs. *The girl whom the cat is watching* vs. *The cat which the girl is watching*). The study involved both comprehension practice (sentence-picture matching resembling the interpretation practice used in *Processing Instruction*; see chapter 5) and production practice. For the sake of simplicity, I will focus on the latter for now. The students were shown pictures (e.g., of a girl who is watching a cat) which they were asked to describe by completing a sentence prompt (e.g., *That is the girl* _____; expected response: *who is watching the cat*). There were 16 exercise items per pattern. The correct sentence was shown as feedback. One group of participants practised each of 4 relative clause patterns one at a time in a single block of 16 exercise items. A second group practised the 4 patterns in an interleaved schedule from the start, while a third group first tackled blocks of 8 items per pattern before interleaving began for the remaining items. This third group was found to make the greatest improvement (by 44%) from the pretest to a one-week delayed posttest, which used the same picture-description format. This suggests that it is beneficial to first entrench knowledge of a new pattern on its own and only subsequently alternate the pattern with others to help learners discriminate among them and refine their understanding of when to use which. The learning gains were quite substantial also for the other 2 groups (both >40%). Again, it is likely that many of the participants (students at university with several years of experience learning English) had enough prior knowledge of relative clauses to be able to cope with interleaving early in the practice schedule (also see Suzuki et al., 2020, for a replication study showing an advantage of interleaving over blocking when students already have fair knowledge of the grammar pattern). It would be interesting to test whether interleaving is as effective in the case of new grammar patterns, and this was in fact done in a series of experiments by Pan et al. (2019). The participants in each of these experiments were introduced to Spanish verb conjugation patterns for 2 tenses, and they then practised these under different schedules. In the first experiment, this was organized for one group in a blocked fashion (one tense at a time), without any interleaving, whereas the practice was organized in an interleaved fashion from the start for a second group. This time, it was the blocked condition that brought about the better scores on a test (a multiple-choice test), which was administered 2 days later. In the second experiment, the interleaving was introduced later, after some of the exercises had first been tackled separately for each tense, and the advantage for the totally blocked schedule disappeared. Experiments 3 and 4 differed from the first 2 experiments in that the learning schedule was divided over 2 sessions, with a 7-day lag between them. The 2 Spanish tenses were introduced and practised one tense per session, or they were introduced one at a time in the first session with interleaved practice following at the end of that session and throughout the second session. The latter schedule generated the better learning gains according to a one-week delayed posttest. It is important to note that in all these experiments, the different target patterns were also mixed in the posttest, and so doing interleaved practice would appear to be better preparation for these tests for that reason, too. As said, real communication at a discourse level requires use of diverse grammar patterns, and so it is indeed important for learners to appreciate the differences between available patterns in both form and usage. From this perspective, interleaved practice is certainly recommendable, but it appears advisable to include at least a little bit of blocked practice at the beginning of the learning process to ensure enough familiarity with the new pattern to increase the success rate of subsequent compare-and-contrast operations.

In most of the experiments reviewed here, repeated practice was implemented at the sentence level, and with minimal context. This is quite different from how language is used in real communication. More research would be welcome to evaluate learning outcomes from various types of practice, and what specific skills certain types of practice foster the most. After all, what you practise is what you get better at. For example, in the study by Suzuki and Sunada (2020), which I reviewed earlier, students who had done productive practice outperformed students who had done only comprehension practice on a productive test, but not on a comprehension test (see Mahmoudi-Gahrouei et al., 2020, for similar findings). To reiterate my earlier comment, what also remains to be established with greater certainty is how well the kinds of practice implemented in experiments such as the above contribute to learners' ability to make good use of the specific micro-skills they have practised when they need to engage in real communication. Several of the studies reviewed above used multiple-choice formats or grammaticality-judgement formats, but the mental operations performed in such kind of practice need not resemble the mental operations needed in real communication (where speakers express their own thoughts and need to orchestrate multiple micro-skills at the same time). Practice should be a means to an end, not an end itself. Surely, the final goal for language learners is not to get better skilled at, say, detecting errors in made-up sentences, but to become proficient communicators in their target language. Some of the studies did use practice formats and test formats that better resemble communicative language use, such as describing pictures, but even in those cases we cannot be sure that good performance in such discrete-item exercises and tests is a strong predictor of learners' ability to transfer what they have learned to real communication. Incidentally, even in the realm of *Task-Based Language Teaching*, where controlled practice is eschewed, learning outcomes are often assessed by means of discrete knowledge tests instead of actual task performance (Plonsky & Kim, 2016).

There may be an additional reason for re-evaluating the choice of test formats in experiments that use a pretest–posttest design. Unless the learners already know the correct responses to the test items, a pretest is akin to a trial-and-error activity—but without feedback. On the one hand, a pretest can pique a learner's curiosity, and so it may positively influence subsequent learning during the instructional intervention. On the other hand, the trial-and-error nature of a pretest raises the question whether incorrect responses given by learners in a pretest might interfere with later learning. This is probably unlikely when the learner has no inkling at all of what the right response could be, but it is more likely if a wrong response does seem plausible to the learner. In the case of a multiple-choice format, for example, learners are invited to consider the available options and pick the one they find the most plausible. The extent to which wrong choices or even the mere contemplation of the lures in such a test may leave traces in a learner's memory invites much more research. Using eye-tracking data (as a proxy of what options in a multiple-choice test a learner gives special attention to) to predict later recall from memory might be a fruitful avenue to find out more about this. A format that seems particularly problematic to me when it is used as a *pretest* is the grammaticality-judgement test. This is a test which requires learners to inspect a series of incorrect sentences to decide if they are correct or not. When used as a pretest, it is unlikely that the learners have already developed reliable intuitions to guide their evaluations, and so they will be inspecting numerous sentences without knowing what is right and what is wrong. For example, toward the end of chapter 4, I reviewed a classroom study by Li et al. (2016) about the effectiveness of a task-supported lesson concerning the English passive voice. In this experiment, the students were presented in the grammaticality-judgement pretest with as many as 60 incorrect examples of the passive voice. Altogether, the students were in fact exposed over the course of the whole experiment to more wrong examples than correct examples. In this light, it is not so surprising that the scores in the posttests were unimpressive (<35%), despite 2 hours' worth of instruction and practice. A replication study could be useful to examine what the learning outcome could be like if the students are *not* exposed to such an abundance of wrong examples of the grammar pattern. The same considerations about the potential negative side effects of grammaticality-judgement pretests and find-and-correct-the-mistakes exercises apply to some of the other studies reviewed above, such as Bird (2010).

Further Reflection

What Sort of Exercises Are Common in Your Textbook?

Examine a contemporary textbook (or other language learning materials, such as online resources) for the kind of exercise formats they include. If the textbook has a "workbook" companion, this could be worth examining, too. Do the exercises require learners to discriminate between right and wrong options, or do they steer clear of such exercise formats? If students are asked to distinguish the correct option from incorrect ones, are the incorrect options the sort of mistakes that your students are likely to make themselves?

What Type of Learning and Practice Schedules Does Your Textbook Implement?

Does the textbook introduce one language pattern at a time and provide blocked practice, or does it introduce language patterns in a compare-and-contrast fashion? Or does the compare-and-contrast stage only follow when each pattern has been introduced and practised separately for a while? Can you find patterns where co-presentation from the start is inevitable? For example, it would be difficult to introduce the English past continuous tense (e.g., *I was mowing the lawn*) without involving the past simple tense (*there was a power cut*) because the former typically occurs in combination with the latter. It would be even harder to introduce the past perfect tense without involving the past simple tense. The relevant question in such cases, then, is whether the contrast created is between something new and something that is already familiar. Turning to vocabulary, do the materials engage the learner repeatedly with the same words or phrases? How many lexical items are tackled in a single exercise? Are the items semantically related or confusable for some other (e.g., formal) reasons? Do the activities involve the generative use of new words and expressions, that is, integration of the items in the students' own output?

Same Product, New Label?

Unlike the strong version of *Task-Based Language Teaching*, *Task-Supported Language Teaching* uses communicative tasks in conjunction with explicit language-focused instruction. Li et al. (2016), for example, describe a lesson where students first received explicit explanations about a grammar pattern (passive voice) and then engaged in a story-telling activity in which they could use this pattern. These 2 stages of the lesson are not dissimilar from the first and the third stages of a *Present-Practice-Produce* (PPP) lesson. Moreover, the explanations about the grammar pattern were followed by find-and-correct-the-error practice and dictogloss practice (also known as "Grammar Dictation"; Wajnryb, 1990), before the students performed the story-telling task. Does what was labelled *Task-Supported Language Teaching* in Li et al. (2016) not, in fact, resemble a PPP lesson?

Individual or Collaborative Practice?

In almost all the empirical studies reviewed in this chapter, the participants did language-focused practice individually. From the perspective of researchers interested in how much learning happens through a certain procedure, this is helpful because it reduces the number of variables over which they have no control. In real classrooms, however, teachers may encourage their students to tackle language-focused exercises collaboratively, in pairs or in small groups. This should have 2 advantages. One is that it increases the likelihood of correct responses in the exercise (under the assumption that 2 brains are better than one). The other is that students may discuss their choices, thus increasing their engagement with the exercise and the response options at hand. Nassaji and Tian (2010) and Teng (2020), both about English phrasal verbs, have furnished some evidence in support of collaborative language-focused practice. This raises the question whether the outcomes of the experiments described in this chapter might have been better had the procedures been implemented as pair work. That said, might there also be a downside to doing language-focused exercises collaboratively?

References

Alali, F. A., & Schmitt, N. (2013). Teaching formulaic sequences: The same as or different from teaching single words? *TESOL Journal*, 3, 153–180. https://doi.org/10.1002/tesj.13

Anderson, J. (2005). *Cognitive psychology and its implications* (6th ed.). Worth Publishers.

Bahrick, H. P., & Hall, L. K. (2005). The importance of retrieval failures to long-term retention: A metacognitive explanation of the spacing effect. *Journal of Memory and Language*, 52, 566–577. https://doi.org/10.1016/j.jml.2005.01.012

Bahrick, H. P., & Phelps, E. (1987). Retention of Spanish vocabulary over 8 years. *Journal of Experimental Psychology: Learning, Memory, and Cognition*, 13, 344–349.

Barcroft, J. (2007). Effects of opportunities for word retrieval during second language vocabulary learning. *Language Learning*, 57, 35–56. https://doi.org/10.1111/j.1467-9922.2007.00398.x

Barcroft, J. (2015a). Can retrieval opportunities increase vocabulary learning during reading? *Foreign Language Annals*, 48, 236–249. https://doi.org/10.1111/flan.12139

Barcroft, J. (2015b). *Lexical input processing and vocabulary learning*. John Benjamins.

Bird, S. (2010). Effects of distributed practice on the acquisition of second language English syntax. *Applied Psycholinguistics*, 31, 635–650. https://doi.org/10.1017/S0142716410000172

Bjork, E. L., & Bjork, R. A. (2014). Making things hard on yourself, but in a good way: Creating desirable difficulties to enhance learning. In M. A. Gernsbacher & J. Pomerantz (Eds.), *Psychology and the real world: Essays illustrating fundamental contributions to society* (2nd ed., pp. 59–68). Worth Publishers.

Bjork, R. A. (1994). Memory and metamemory considerations in the training of human beings. In J. Metcalfe & A. Shimamura (Eds.), *Metacognition: Knowing about knowing* (pp. 185–205). Massachusetts Institute of Technology Press.

Bjork, R. A. (2018). Being suspicious of the sense of ease and undeterred by the sense of difficulty: Looking back at Schmidt and Bjork (1992). *Perspectives on Psychological Science*, 13, 146–148. https://doi.org/10.1177/1745691617690642

Bloom, K. C., & Schuell, T. J. (1981). Effects of massed and distributed practice on the learning and retention of second-language vocabulary. *Journal of Educational Research*, 74, 245–248. https://doi.org/10.1080/00220671.1981.10885317

Boers, F., Dang, T. C. T., & Strong, B. (2017). Comparing the effectiveness of phrase-focused exercises. A partial replication of Boers, Demecheleer, Coxhead, and Webb (2014). *Language Teaching Research*, 21, 362–380. https://doi.org/10.1177/1362168816651464

Boers, F., Demecheleer, M., Coxhead, A., & Webb, S. (2014). Gauging the effects of exercises on verb-noun collocations. *Language Teaching Research*, 18, 54–74. https://doi.org/10.1177/1362168813505389

Candry, S., Decloedt, J., & Eyckmans, J. (2020). Comparing the merits of word writing and retrieval practice for L2 vocabulary learning. *System*, 89. https://doi.org/10.1016/j.system.2020.102206

Candry, S., Elgort, I., Deconinck, J., & Eyckmans, J. (2017). Word writing vs. meaning inferencing in contextualized L2 vocabulary learning: Assessing the effect of different vocabulary learning strategies. *Canadian Modern Language Review*, 73, 293–318. https://doi.org/10.3138/cmlr.3688

Cepeda, N. J., Coburn, N., Rohrer, D., Wixted, J. T., Mozer, M. C., & Pashler, H. (2009). Optimizing distributed practice: Theoretical analysis and practical implications. *Experimental Psychology*, 56, 236–246. http://wixtedlab.ucsd.edu/publications/wixted2/Optimizing_distributed_practice.pdf

Collins, L., Halter, R. H., Lightbown, P. M., & Spada, N. (1999). Time and the distribution of time in L2 instruction. *TESOL Quarterly, 33*, 655–680. https://doi.org/10.2307/3587881

Collins, L., & White, J. (2011). An intensive look at intensity and language learning. *TESOL Quarterly, 45*, 106–133. https://doi.org/10.5054/tq.2011.240858

Crace, A., & Acklam, R. (2011). *New Total English, upper intermediate: Students' book*. Pearson Education.

Criado, R. (2016). Insights from Skill Acquisition Theory for grammar activity sequencing and design in Foreign Language Teaching. *Innovation in Language Learning and Teaching, 10*, 121–132. https://doi.org/10.1080/17501229.2015.1090996

Cunningham, S., Moor, P., & Bygrave, J. (2013). *Cutting Edge, intermediate: Students' book* (3rd ed.). Pearson Education.

de Jong, N., & Perfetti, C. A. (2011). Fluency training in the ESL classroom: An experimental study of fluency development and proceduralization. *Language Learning, 61*, 533–568. doi:10.1111/j.1467-9922.2010.00620.x.

DeKeyser, R. (1998). Beyond focus on form: Cognitive perspectives on learning and practicing second language grammar. In C. Doughty & J. Williams (Eds.), *Focus on form in classroom second language acquisition* (pp. 42–63). Cambridge University Press.

DeKeyser, R. (2010). Practice for second language learning: Don't throw out the baby with the bath water. *International Journal of English Studies, 10*, 155–165.

Eckerth, J., & Tavakoli, P. (2012). The effects of word exposure frequency and elaboration of word processing on incidental L2 vocabulary acquisition through reading. *Language Teaching Research, 16*, 227–252. https://doi.org/10.1177/1362168811431377

Erten, I. H., & Tekin, M. (2008). Effects on vocabulary acquisition of presenting new words in semantic sets versus semantically unrelated sets. *System, 36*, 407–422. https://doi.org/10.1016/j.system.2008.02.005

Finkbeiner, M., & Nicol, J. (2003). Semantic category effects in second language word learning. *Applied Psycholinguistics, 24*, 369–383. https://doi.org/10.1017/S0142716403000195

Folse, K. S. (2006). The effect of type of written exercise on L2 vocabulary retention. *TESOL Quarterly, 40*, 273–293. https://doi.org/10.2307/40264523

Gatbonton, E., & Segalowitz, N. (2005). Rethinking communicative language teaching: A focus on access to fluency. *Canadian Modern Language Review, 61*, 325–353. https://doi.org/10.3138/cmlr.61.3.325

Griffin, G. F., & Harley, T. A. (1996). List learning of second language vocabulary. *Applied Psycholinguistics, 17*, 443–460. https://doi.org/10.1017/S0142716400008195

Hashemi, M. R., & Gowdasiaei, F. (2005). An attribute-treatment interaction study: Lexical-set versus semantically-unrelated vocabulary instruction. *RELC Journal, 36*, 341–361. https://doi.org/10.1177/0033688205060054

Hoshino, Y. (2010). The categorical facilitation effects on L2 vocabulary learning in a classroom setting. *RELC Journal, 41*, 301–312. https://doi.org/10.1177/0033688210380558

Hulstijn, J. H., & Laufer, B. (2001). Some empirical evidence for the involvement load hypothesis in vocabulary acquisition. *Language Learning, 51*, 539–558. https://doi.org/10.1111/0023-8333.00164

Ishii, T. (2015). Semantic connection or visual connection: Investigating the true source of confusion. *Language Teaching Research, 19*, 712–722. https://doi.org/10.1177/1362168814559799

Joe, A. (1998). What effects do text-based tasks promoting generation have on incidental vocabulary acquisition? *Applied Linguistics, 19*, 357–377. https://doi.org/10.1093/applin/19.3.357

Johnson, K. (1996). *Language teaching and skill learning.* Blackwell.

Kang, S. H., Lindsey, R. V., Mozer, M. C., & Pashler, H. (2014). Retrieval practice over the long term: Should spacing be expanding or equal interval? *Psychonomic Bulletin and Review*, 21, 1544–1550. https://doi.org/10.3758/s13423-014-0636-z

Karpicke, J. D., Lehman, M., & Aue, W. R. (2014). Retrieval-based learning: An episodic context account. *Psychology of Learning and Motivation*, 61, 237–284. https://doi.org/10.1016/B978-0-12-800283-4.00007-1

Karpicke, J. D., & Roediger, H. L., III. (2008). The critical importance of retrieval for learning. *Science*, 319, 966–968. https://doi.org/10.1126/science.1152408

Kasprowicz, R. E., Marsden, E., & Sephton, N. (2019). Investigating distribution of practice effects for the learning of foreign language verb morphology in the young learner classroom. *The Modern Language Journal*, 103, 580–606. https://doi.org/10.1111/modl.12586

Keating, G. D. (2008). Task effectiveness and word learning in a second language: The involvement load hypothesis on trial. *Language Teaching Research*, 12, 365–386. https://doi.org/10.1177/1362168808089922

Kerr, P., & Jones, C. (2012). *Straightforward, intermediate: Student's book* (2nd ed.). Macmillan Education.

Kim, Y. (2008). The role of task-induced involvement and learner proficiency in L2 vocabulary acquisition. *Language Learning*, 58, 285–325. https://doi.org/10.1111/j.1467-9922.2008.00442.x

Kornell, N. (2009). Optimising learning using flashcards: Spacing is more effective than cramming. *Applied Cognitive Psychology*, 23, 1297–1317. https://doi.org/10.1002/acp.1537

Küpper-Tetzel, C. E., Erdfelder, E., & Dickhäuser, O. (2014). The lag effect in secondary school classrooms: Enhancing students' memory for vocabulary. *Instructional Science*, 42, 373–388. https://doi.org/10.1007/s11251-013-9285-2

Laufer, B. (2003). Vocabulary acquisition in a second language: Do learners really acquire most vocabulary by reading? Some empirical evidence. *Canadian Modern Language Review*, 59, 567–587. https://doi.org/10.3138/cmlr.59.4.567

Laufer, B., & Girsai, N. (2008). Form-focused instruction in second language vocabulary learning: A case for contrastive analysis and translation. *Applied Linguistics*, 29, 694–716. https://doi.org/10.1093/applin/amn018

Laufer, B., & Hulstijn, J. H. (2001). Incidental vocabulary acquisition in a second language: The construct of task-induced involvement. *Applied Linguistics*, 22, 1–26. https://doi.org/10.1093/applin/22.1.1

Laufer, B., & Rozovski-Roitblat, B. (2011). Incidental vocabulary acquisition: The effects of task type, word occurrence and their combination. *Language Teaching Research*, 15, 391–411. https://doi.org/10.1177/1362168811412019

Laufer, B., & Rozovski-Roitblat, B. (2015). Retention of new words: Quantity of encounters, quality of task, and degree of knowledge. *Language Teaching Research*, 19, 687–711. https://doi.org/10.1177/1362168814559797

Li, S., Ellis, R., & Zhu, Y. (2016). Task-based versus task-supported language instruction: An experimental study, *Annual Review of Applied Linguistics*, 36, 205–229. https://doi.org/10.1017/S0267190515000069

Lightbown, P. (2008). Transfer appropriate processing as a model for class second language acquisition. In Z. Han (Ed.), *Understanding second language process* (pp. 27–44). Multilingual Matters.

Lindstromberg, S., & Boers, F. (2008). *Teaching chunks of language.* Helbling Languages.

Lu, M. (2013). Effects of four vocabulary exercises on facilitating learning vocabulary meaning, form, and use. *TESOL Quarterly*, 47, 167–176. https://doi.org/10.1002/tesq.79

Lynch, T., & Maclean, J. (2000). Exploring the benefits of task repetition and recycling for classroom language learning. *Language Teaching Research*, 4, 221–250. doi:10.1177/136216880000400303

Lyster, R., & Sato, M. (2013). Skill Acquisition Theory and the role of practice in L2 development. In M. d. P. García Mayo, M. J. Gutierrez Mangado, & M. Martínez Adrián (Eds.), *Contemporary approaches to second language acquisition* (pp. 71–91). John Benjamins.

Mahmoudi-Gahrouei, V., Youhanaee, M., & Nejadanasari, D. (2020). Targeting accuracy in foreign language teaching: The role of practice type in learning unsalient grammatical aspects. *International Journal of Applied Linguistics*. https://doi.org/10.1111/ijal.12292

McNamara, D. S., & Healy, A. F. (1995). A generation advantage for multiplication skill training and nonword vocabulary acquisition. In A. F. Healy & L. E. J. Bourne (Eds.), *Learning and memory of knowledge and skills: Durability and specificity* (pp. 132–169). Sage. https://doi.org/10.4135/9781483326887

Miles, S. W. (2014). Spaced vs. Massed distribution instruction for L2 grammar learning. *System*, 42, 412–428. https://doi.org/10.1016/j.system.2014.01.014

Min, H. T. (2008). EFL vocabulary acquisition and retention: Reading plus vocabulary enhancement activities and narrow reading. *Language Learning*, 58, 73–115. https://doi.org/10.1111/j.1467-9922.2007.00435.x

Mondria, J.-A., & Wiersma, B. (2004). Receptive, productive and receptive + productive L2 vocabulary learning: What difference does it make? In P. Bogaards & B. Laufer (Eds.), *Vocabulary in a second language: Selection, acquisition, and testing* (pp. 79–100). John Benjamins.

Morris, C. D., Bransford, J. D., & Franks, J. J. (1977). Levels of processing versus transfer appropriate processing. *Journal of Verbal Learning and Verbal Behavior*, 16, 519–533. https://doi.org/10.1016/S0022-5371(77)80016-9

Nakata, T. (2011). Computer-assisted second language vocabulary learning in a paired-associate paradigm: A critical investigation of flashcard software. *Computer Assisted Language Learning*, 24, 17–38. https://doi.org/10.1080/09588221.2010.520675

Nakata, T. (2015). Effects of expanding and equal spacing on second language vocabulary learning: Does gradually increasing spacing increase vocabulary learning? *Studies in Second Language Acquisition*, 37, 677–711. https://doi.org/10.1017/S0272263114000825

Nakata, T. (2016). Effects of retrieval formats on second language vocabulary learning. *International Review of Applied Linguistics*, 54, 257–289. https://doi.org/10.1515/iral-2015-0022

Nakata, T. (2017). Does repeated practice make perfect? The effects of within-session repeated retrieval on second language vocabulary learning. *Studies in Second Language Acquisition*, 39, 653–679. https://doi.org/10.1017/S0272263116000280

Nakata, T., & Suzuki, Y. (2019a). Effects of massing and spacing on the learning of semantically related and unrelated words. *Studies in Second Language Acquisition*, 41, 287–311. https://doi.org/10.1017/S0272263118000219

Nakata, T., & Suzuki, Y. (2019b). Mixing grammar exercises facilitates long-term retention: Effects of blocking, interleaving, and increasing practice. *The Modern Language Journal*, 103, 629–647. https://doi.org/10.1111/modl.12581

Nakata, T., Tada, S., Mclean, S., & Kim, Y. A. (2020). Effects of distributed retrieval practice over a semester: Cumulative tests as a way to facilitate second language vocabulary learning. *TESOL Quarterly*. Online early view. https://doi.org/10.1002/tesq.596

Nakata, T., & Webb, S. (2016). Does studying vocabulary in smaller sets increase learning? Effects of part and whole learning on second language vocabulary acquisition. *Studies in Second Language Acquisition*, 38, 523–552. https://doi.org/10.1017/S0272263115000236

Nassaji, H., & Tian, J. (2010). Collaborative and individual output tasks and their effects on learning English phrasal verbs. *Language Teaching Research*, 14, 397–419. https://doi.org/10.1177/1362168810375364

Pan, S. C., Tajran, J., Lovelett, J., Osuna, J., & Rickard, T. C. (2019). Does interleaved practice enhance foreign language learning? The effects of training schedule on Spanish verb conjugation skills. *Journal of Educational Psychology*, 111, 1172–1188. https://doi.org/10.1037/edu0000336

Peters, E. (2012). The differential effects of two vocabulary instruction methods on EFL word learning: A study into task effectiveness. *International Review of Applied Linguistics*, 50, 213–238. https://doi.org/0019042x/2012/050-213

Peters, E., Hulstijn, J. H., Sercu, L., & Lutjeharms, M. (2009). Learning L2 German vocabulary through reading: The effect of three enhancement techniques compared. *Language Learning*, 59, 113–151. https://doi.org/10.1111/j.1467-9922.2009.00502.x

Peters, E., & Pauwels, P. (2015). Learning academic formulaic sequences. *Journal of English for Academic Purposes*, 20, 28–39. https://doi.org/10.1016/j.jeap.2015.04.002

Plonsky, L., & Kim, Y. (2016). Task-based learner production: A substantive and methodological review. *Annual Review of Applied Linguistics*, 36, 73–97. https://doi.org/10.1017/S0267190516000015

Pyc, M. A., & Rawson, K. A. (2007). Examining the efficiency of schedules of distributed retrieval practice. *Memory and Cognition*, 35, 1917–1927. https://doi.org/10.3758/BF03192925

Richards, J. C., Hull, J., & Proctor, S. (2017). *Interchange 3: Student's book* (5th ed.). Cambridge University Press.

Richards, J. C., & Reppen, R. (2014). Towards a pedagogy of grammar instruction. *RELC Journal*, 45, 5–25. https://doi.org/10.1177/0033688214522622

Roediger, H. L., III, & Butler, A. C. (2011). The critical role of retrieval practice in long-term retention. *Trends in Cognitive Sciences*, 15, 20–27. https://doi.org/10.1016/j.tics.2010.09.003

Rogers, J., & Cheung, A. (2020a). Input spacing and the learning of L2 vocabulary in a classroom context. *Language Teaching Research*, 24, 616–641. https://doi.org/10.1177/1362168818805251

Rogers, J., & Cheung, A. (2020b). Does it matter when you review? Input spacing, ecological validity, and the learning of L2 vocabulary. *Studies in Second Language Acquisition*. Online early view. https://doi.org/10.1017/S0272263120000236

Schneider, V. I., Healy, A. F., & Bourne, L. E. (2002). What is learned under difficult conditions is hard to forget: Contextual interference effects in foreign vocabulary acquisition, retention, and transfer. *Journal of Memory and Language*, 46, 419–440. https://doi.org/10.1006/jmla.2001.2813

Serrano, R. (2011). The time factor in EFL classroom practice. *Language Learning*, 61, 117–145. https://doi.org/10.1111/j.1467-9922.2010.00591.x

Serrano, R., & Muñoz, C. (2007). Same hours, different time distribution: Any difference in EFL? *System*, 35, 305–321. https://doi.org/10.1016/j.system.2007.02.001

Smith, M. A., Roediger, H. L. III, & Karpicke, J. D. (2013). Covert retrieval practice benefits retention as much as overt retrieval practice. *Journal of Experimental Psychology: Learning, Memory, and Cognition*, 39, 1712–1725. https://doi.org/10.1037/a0033569

Sobel, H. S., Cepeda, N. J., & Kapler, I. V. (2011). Spacing effects in real-world classroom vocabulary learning. *Applied Cognitive Psychology*, 25, 763–767. https://doi.org/10.1002/acp.1747

Steinel, M. P., Hulstijn, J. H., & Steinel, W. (2007). Second language idiom learning in a paired-associate paradigm: Effects of direction of learning, direction of testing, idiom imageability, and idiom transparency. *Studies in Second Language Acquisition*, 29, 449–484. https://doi.org/10.1017/S0272263107070271

Strong, B., & Boers, F. (2019a). The error in trial and error: Exercises on phrasal verbs. *TESOL Quarterly*, 53, 289–319. https://doi.org/10.1002/tesq.478

Strong, B., & Boers, F. (2019b). Weighing up exercises on phrasal verbs: Retrieval versus trial-and-error practices. *The Modern Language Journal*, 103, 562–579. https://doi.org/10.1111/modl.12579

Suzuki, Y. (2017). The optimal distribution of practice for the acquisition of L2 morphology: A conceptual replication and extension. *Language Learning*, 67, 512–545. https://doi.org/10.1111/lang.12236

Suzuki, Y., & DeKeyser, R. M. (2017). Effects of distributed practice on the proceduralization of morphology. *Language Teaching Research*, 21, 166–188. https://doi.org/10.1177/1362168815617334

Suzuki, Y., & Sunada, M. (2020). Dynamic interplay between practice type and practice schedule in a second language: The potential and limits of skill transfer and practice schedule. *Studies in Second Language Acquisition*, 42, 169–197. https://doi.org/10.1017/S0272263119000470

Suzuki, Y., Yokosawa, S., & Aline, D. (2020). The role of working memory in blocked and interleaved grammar practice: Proceduralization of L2 syntax. *Language Teaching Research*. Online early view. https://doi.org/10.1177/1362168820913985

Szudarski, P. (2012). Effects of meaning- and form-focused instruction on the acquisition of verb–noun collocations in L2 English. *Journal of Second Language Teaching and Research*, 1, 3–37. https://pops.uclan.ac.uk/index.php/jsltr/article/view/32/15

Tavakoli, P., & Uchihara, T. (2020). To what extent are multiword sequences associated with oral fluency? *Language Learning*, 70, 506–547. https://doi.org/10.1111/lang.12384

Teng, M. F. (2020). The effectiveness of group, pair and individual output tasks on learning phrasal verbs. *The Language Learning Journal*, 48, 187–200. https://doi.org/10.1080/09571736.2017.1373841

Thai, C. & Boers, F. (2016). Repeating a monologue under increasing time pressure: Effects on fluency, accuracy and complexity. *TESOL Quarterly*, 50, 369–393. https://doi.org/10.1002/tesq.232

Thomas, M. H., & Dieter, J. (1987). The positive effects of writing practice on integration of foreign words in memory. *Journal of Educational Psychology*, 79, 249–253. https://doi.org/10.1037/0022-0663.79.3.249

Tinkham, T. (1993). The effect of semantic clustering on the learning of second language vocabulary. *System*, 21, 371–380. https://doi.org/10.1016/0346-251X(93)90027-E

Ur, P. (1996). *A course in language teaching. Practice and theory*. Cambridge University Press.

Van den Broek, G. S. E., Takashima, A., Segers, E., & Verhoeven, L. (2018). Contextual richness and word learning: Context enhances comprehension but retrieval enhances retention. *Language Learning*, 68, 546–585. https://doi.org/10.1111/lang.12285

Wajnryb, R. (1990). *Resource books for teachers: Grammar dictation*. Oxford University Press.

Waring, R. (1997). The negative effects of learning words in semantic sets: A replication. *System*, 25, 261–274. https://doi.org/10.1016/S0346-251X(97)00013-00014

Waterman, J. (2012). *Straightforward, intermediate: Workbook* (2nd ed.). Macmillan Education.

Webb, S. (2005). Receptive and productive vocabulary learning: The effects of reading and writing on word knowledge. *Studies in Second Language Acquisition*, 27, 33–52. https://doi.org/10.1017/S0272263105050023

Webb, S. (2009). The effects of pre-learning vocabulary on reading comprehension and writing. *Canadian Modern Language Review*, 65, 441–470. https://doi.org/10.3138/cmlr.65.3.441

Webb, S., & Kagimoto, E. (2009). The effects of vocabulary learning on collocation and meaning. *TESOL Quarterly*, 43, 55–77. https://doi.org/10.1002/j.1545-7249.2009.tb00227.x

Webb, S., & Kagimoto, E. (2011). Learning collocations: Do the number of collocates, position of the node word, and synonymy affect learning? *Applied Linguistics*, 32, 259–276. https://doi.org/10.1093/applin/amq051

Webb, S., & Piasecki, A. (2018). Re-examining the effects of word writing on vocabulary learning. *ITL-International Journal of Applied Linguistics*, 169, 72–94. https://doi.org/10.1075/itl.00007.web

Wilcox, A., & Medina, A. (2013). Effects of semantic and phonological clustering on L2 vocabulary acquisition among novice learners. *System*, 41, 1056–1069. https://doi.org/10.1016/j.system.2013.10.012

Wood, D. (2010). *Perspectives on formulaic language: Acquisition and communication*. Continuum.

Yang, Y., Shintani, N., Li, S., & Zhang, Y. (2017). The effectiveness of post-reading word-focused activities and their associations with working memory. *System*, 70, 38–49. https://doi.org/10.1016/j.system.2017.09.012

Zhang, X. (2017). Effects of receptive-productive integration tasks and prior knowledge of component words on L2 collocation development. *System*, 66, 156–167. https://doi.org/10.1016/j.system.2017.03.019

Zou, D. (2017). Vocabulary acquisition through cloze exercises, sentence-writing and composition-writing: Extending the evaluation component of the involvement load hypothesis. *Language Teaching Research*, 21, 54–75. https://doi.org/10.1177/1362168816652418

7.

MAKING IT STICK

Introduction

In the preceding chapters I have discussed ways of improving conditions for incidental learning from input texts and from communicative output activities, ways of helping learners work out form–meaning connections during language-focused study and ways of consolidating newly acquired knowledge through practice. In the present chapter, I will consider what teachers and materials writers can do to help learners remember new items or patterns. What can teachers tell their students about a given word, phrase or pattern to make it stick? Items or patterns that are made memorable during a study episode stand a good chance of being recalled successfully during subsequent practice, and so in theory the process of knowledge consolidation may then be smoother. If so, the investment of a little extra time in metalinguistic processing to make new declarative knowledge stick can be worthwhile—provided, of course, that what is done with this extra time truly helps to remember the item or pattern. In this chapter I will review research on diverse instructional techniques that have been proposed for this purpose.

In essence, what all these techniques have in common is that they create connections in the mind. The connection may concern elements or features *within* a given item/pattern (e.g., how a certain affix contributes to the meaning of a word) or *between* the item/pattern and something else (e.g., using visuals to elucidate a word's meaning or pointing out similarities or contrasts between L2 words and L1 counterparts). The general idea is to engage students in mental operations regarding (facets of) newly learned form-meaning correspondences that provide a richer or deeper appreciation of their properties. In *Levels of Processing Theory* (Cermak & Craik, 1979; Craik & Lockhart, 1972; Craik & Tulving, 1975) those mental operations are called *elaborations*. A distinction can be made between elaborations concerning the *meaning* of items (semantic elaborations) and elaborations concerning *formal features* (structural elaborations), although many of the mnemonic techniques discussed further below involve both. It is nonetheless useful to determine whether the focus of the mental operation is on the semantic or on the structural features of an item or pattern, because what one focuses on is what one remembers best (Barcroft, 2015; Morris et al., 1977). For example, a teacher may point out to students that the phrase *turn the tide* displays alliteration and this may help the students remember its composition, but it will take other steps to help the students to remember its meaning. In this chapter I will also use the term elaboration, but in the less technical sense of "saying a bit more about something". After the form-meaning relation of an item, a phrase or a pattern is established by or for students, how can teachers or materials writers elaborate on it to foster strong memories? In what follows, I will discuss various possibilities.

Comparing and Contrasting with L1 Counterparts

Teachers who share (or are familiar with) their students' L1 may find it useful to alert the students to differences between L2 items or patterns and their L1 counterparts. This compare-and-contrast operation is one of several avenues available for students to engage a little more with a freshly learned L2 form-meaning correspondence. To be clear, this involves more than merely giving a translation in L1 through codeswitching (e.g., Lee & Levine, 2020; Tian & Macaro, 2012; Zhouhan & Webb, 2020). Codeswitching is an efficient means to establish a new form-meaning pair, but the compare-and-contrast steps discussed here serve as further, metalinguistic elaboration. In the case of vocabulary, for example, teachers may point out so-called false friends (i.e., deceptive lookalikes, such as English *eventually* [meaning 'in the end'] and Dutch *eventueel* [meaning 'possibly']), explain a lexical distinction in L2 that is absent from L1 (e.g., that English distinguishes between *borrow* and *lend*, while Dutch has one word for both meanings; that English distinguishes between *house* and *home*, while French has one word for both) and alert students that the lexical makeup of an L2 expression differs from that of the L1 counterpart (e.g., that the verb in *make an effort* is different from the verb in the Dutch counterpart expression, which would translate as 'do an effort'). In the case of grammar, teachers may want to point out that a tense in L2 (e.g., the present perfect in English) serves a function that is different from a similar-looking tense in L1, and so on.

There is no doubt that many teachers around the world at least occasionally make such comparisons with L1 (see Cook, 2001; Hall & Cook, 2012; and Lightbown & Spada, 2019, for arguments against a radical L2-only classroom policy, which was introduced in the early 1900s under the banner of the *Direct Method*—and which was in fact already questioned at that time [e.g., Morgan, 1917]). Some contemporary, internationally marketed, course books even include the occasional translation exercise (e.g., Jones & Kerr, 2012; Waterman, 2012). It is rather surprising, then, that few empirical studies have tested the effectiveness of teacher-led L1-L2 compare-and-contrast elaborations. Perhaps this is because discussing L1-L2 contrasts and similarities calls up associations with the *Grammar-Translation Method*, a method which is now generally frowned upon. And yet, it is now also widely recognized that L1 influences L2 acquisition (see chapter 2 on the role of interlingual factors in incidental L2 acquisition), and this recognition could be expected to prompt research into ways of raising learners' awareness of L1-L2 contrasts (Horst, et al., 2010), especially since there are indications that this awareness benefits learners' proficiency in the target language (Ammar et al., 2010).

In the area of vocabulary, one of the few available studies is Laufer and Girsai (2008). Three groups of students of English read the same text containing 10 low-frequency words (e.g., *laudable*) and 10 collocations whose composition differs from counterparts in the students' L1, Hebrew (e.g., the Hebrew counterpart of *meet expectations* is 'answer expectations'), the meanings of which were clarified to the students. One group then engaged further with the contents of the text. The second group did multiple-choice and gap-fill exercises concerning the target vocabulary, without explicit comparisons with L1. The third group was given translation exercises, which naturally involve L1 to L2 comparisons. With this group, the teacher also elaborated on the contrasts between the English items and their L1 counterparts. In both a near-immediate and a one-week delayed posttest, the latter group performed significantly better than the group that had done vocabulary exercises without any explicit focus on the contrasts with L1. Unsurprisingly, the group that had not done any vocabulary-focused exercises performed the worst (see chapter 6). While these findings support the thesis that elaborating on the contrasts between L1 and L2 items helps students remember the L2 items, it is difficult to separate the effect of this teacher-led elaboration from the effect of doing translation exercises, which inherently create L1-L2 connections. It needs to be acknowledged as well that the posttests used by Laufer and Girsai (2008) were translation tests, and this may have given an edge (owing to practice–test congruency) to the students who had done the translation exercises. That said, a more recent and larger-scale study, by Zhang and Graham (2020), lends further support to the usefulness of compare-and-contrast elaborations for vocabulary retention. Students in that experiment engaged in a series of intensive listening comprehension activities (altogether 6 sessions) that were accompanied for most of the students by vocabulary clarifications. For one group of students these were clarifications of meaning given in the target language (English), for another group they were L1 translations, and for a third group the teacher explicitly contrasted features of the items with their L1 (Chinese) counterparts. There were 60 target items altogether (43 words and 17 collocations). Near-immediate and 2-week delayed posttests, which in this experiment did not involve translation, showed that the contrastive elaborations again led to the best meaning recall. There was also a group of students who had not received any explicit vocabulary clarifications, and their learning gains were negligible.

The finding that alerting students to the difference in lexical composition of L2 collocations and their L1 counterparts (e.g., that in English one says *do your homework* while the counterpart in the students' L1 in the case of Dutch is 'make your homework') can be effective is particularly interesting, because this non-congruency with L1 counterparts is known to be a hindrance even during language-focused work. In Peters (2016), for example, students did various exercises (e.g., fill-in-the-blank practice) on 18 collocations. Half of these were congruent with counterpart expression in the learners' L1 while the other half were not. Despite the focused exercises, which did not involve explicit L1-L2 comparisons, non-congruency emerged as a predictor of incorrect responses in a productive recall test, a finding which illustrates just how strong L1 interference at the level of phraseology can be and which invites the question whether explicit contrastive elaboration will make a difference.

Turning now to grammar patterns, several intervention studies which included contrastive elaboration are available, but the effectiveness specifically of the contrastive component of the instructional procedures is difficult to assess. For example, White and Ranta (2002) and White et al. (2007) examined the effectiveness of an instructional program which included explicit L1-L2 contrasts as one of its components to improve French, Catalan and Spanish students' accurate use of the English possessive pronouns *his* and *her*, but this was in comparison to a program without any explicit instruction about these pronouns. While the findings provide robust evidence of the usefulness of explicit language-focused instruction—the groups of students who received the focused instruction made significant progress in their command of the grammar feature, while those in the comparison groups showed little improvement—, they do not reveal whether it was the contrastive component of the instructional program in particular that made it so effective. To determine the latter, one would need to compare 2 explicit teaching procedures that differ in the presence or absence of contrastive elaboration. Such a comparison was made by Kupferberg (1999). L1 Hebrew students of English received explicit explanations about the past perfect tense, which tends to be under-used by these students because its meaning is expressed differently in Hebrew. They were also provided with examples of its use in narratives and were given the opportunity to use the past perfect tense in their own story telling. In one condition, approximately 13 minutes were spent on translating sentences with past perfect tense into Hebrew and for the teacher to raise the students' awareness of the L1-L2 contrast. Tallies of past perfect tense instances in the written stories produced by these students after the intervention revealed more frequent use of the target pattern in comparison to the stories produced by the students who had not been explicitly alerted to the L1-L2 contrast, a finding which indicates that adding a contrastive perspective to the instructional intervention was worth the investment.

More recently, experiments by McManus and Marsden (2017, 2018) have revealed that raising learners' metalinguistic awareness of patterns in their L1 can accelerate their L2 learning. In these experiments, English learners of French received explanations about the *imparfait* tense and engaged in the type of sentence-interpretation practice that is used in *Processing Instruction* (see chapter 5), such as deciding whether or not an activity described by a sentence is completed. The *imparfait* can easily be mistaken as the equivalent of English simple past tense, but its use often corresponds to other English tenses. McManus and Marsden found that, if the learners also received explanations about the corresponding tenses in English and did the same kind of interpretation practice with English sentences, they would master the use of French *imparfait* better. These experiments did not include explicit contrastive information, but it may be assumed that receiving explanations about L1 tenses in addition to explanations about L2 tenses prompted the participants to make comparisons implicitly (McManus, 2019). L2 teachers and students may wonder, however, if it is justified to spend class time on exercises concerning the students' L1 while their expectation is to practise L2. They will almost certainly feel hesitant to spend the amount of time on L1-focused exercises that was invested in McManus and Marsden's experiments—which included as many as 160 English interpretation items. Instead, they may find it more realistic to simply clarify the differences between L1 and L2 regarding a target grammar pattern, illustrate this through a couple of translation exercises and remind their students of these differences over the course of further activities in the target language.

Going Back to the Roots

The preceding section discussed ways of creating *inter*lingual connections (i.e., connections between languages). The present section turns to *intra*lingual connections, that is, connections within the target language. Often, these are connections between current abstract meanings of words or phrases and the more concrete meanings that the abstract uses are derived from. This is typical of polysemy, where one language form has different but related meanings. Learners may encounter a polysemous word in an abstract context before having learned its more concrete sense (or without recognizing the word as one whose concrete meaning they already know). For instance, learners may come across abstract phrases such as *tackle a problem, wield power, forge an alliance* and *overcome hurdles*. It is well documented that abstract meanings are harder to remember than concrete ones (see chapter 2). However, a teacher can link these abstract (figurative) uses to the concrete ones from which they are extended (i.e., their literal underpinnings): one can *tackle* an opponent in sports such as rugby and soccer, *wield* an axe, *forge* a sword and clear *hurdles* in a steeplechase competition. Making these connections can make the abstract uses more imageable (i.e., evoking mental pictures) and as a result easier to remember. This was demonstrated, for example, by Verspoor and Lowie (2003). Students who were presented with both a literal and a figurative use of words (e.g., *The gardener raked up the pile of weeds* and *Relief foundations raked in $16m*) recalled the latter use better than learners who were presented with 2 abstract uses (e.g., *We've been raking through her papers* and *Relief foundations raked in $16m*). As polysemy is very common in language, there may be regular opportunities for teachers to briefly elaborate on abstract word uses by linking them to more concrete uses of the same word, thus helping students appreciate that the abstract uses are in fact figurative and thus imageable.

In addition, students can be helped to appreciate the literal-to-figurative meaning extensions at a more general level. For example, *economic recovery, a chronic budget deficit,* a *financial injection* and *a healthy economy* indicate a more general metaphor—personification—according to which systems (in this case economies) are likened to human beings, including their health (e.g., Boers, 2000a). Such systematic correspondences between one (concrete) "source domain" of experience and another (abstract) "target domain" are called *conceptual metaphors* in the school of thought called *Cognitive Semantics* (e.g., Kövecses, 2010; Lakoff, 1987; Lakoff & Johnson, 1980). These metaphors are not merely a surface phenomenon of language but reflect the way people try to understand abstract concepts and non-tangible experience through analogies with concrete, better-understood things (Gentner & Bowdle, 2008). Of interest here is that raising learners' awareness of these *source-domain* to *target-domain* correspondences can again make it easier to remember figuratively used words and expressions. Boers (2000b) presented students of English with a list of words and phrases to describe states of anger and angry behaviour. For one group these were organized by metaphors, including "anger is a hot liquid in a container" (e.g., *I was boiling with anger, please simmer down* and *she erupted*), "anger is fire" (e.g., *an inflammatory remark, adding fuel to the fire* and *she exploded*) and "angry people are dangerous animals" (e.g., *she snapped at me, don't bite my head off* and *he has a ferocious temper*). For another group, the same items were organized instead according to whether they describe sudden anger, anger as a gradual process or angry people. After the study phase, the vocabulary lists were taken away and later on in the lesson the students were given a text about anger management with blanks for them to complete with the studied words and phrases. The group that had studied the vocabulary organized by metaphors outperformed the other group. Similar results have been reported by Beréndi et al. (2008) and by Li (2009). In another experiment, Boers (2000b) presented students with vocabulary to describe upward and downward trends in the domain of economics. For one group, this vocabulary was organized by the source domains, such as mountaineering (e.g., *peak, slide* and *go downhill*) and aircraft (e.g., *soar, skyrocket* and *crash*), while for another group the organization was according to whether the changes described by the words were, for example, fast or gradual. When the students afterwards wrote a report based on information presented in graphs, the former group used a wider range of the studied vocabulary. These classroom experiments confirm that connecting abstract word uses to the original contexts in which they are used in a literal sense can help students retain them in memory.

A segment of vocabulary likely to lend itself well to this approach are figurative idioms, because many idioms can be traced back to the context in which they were (or still are) used with a literal meaning. Examples of figurative idioms include *a shot in the arm, take a back seat, jump the gun, go with the flow, cut corners, play it by ear, sit on the fence, turn over a new leaf* and *a wet blanket*. Expressions such as these can be made more memorable by informing students about their original use—provided the original use and the current idiomatic meaning are semantically congruent. For example, students can be informed that *a shot in the arm* evokes the image of an injection with helpful medicine, that *taking a back seat* literally means sitting in the back seat of a car and thus leaving the driving to someone else, that the gun in *jump the gun* refers to the pistol used to signal the start of a race and so on. Boers et al. (2004) created a bank of computer-assisted exercises on idioms for English majors and found that inclusion of information about their literal underpinnings often helped the students to remember the expressions (Li, 2009, for similar positive evidence). Information about the original, literal use has also been found to help students guess the figurative meaning of idioms where contextual clues did not suffice (Boers et al., 2007).

Notes about the origin of idioms are included in many recent idiom dictionaries, which suggests that dictionary makers believe that dictionary users find this kind of information interesting. That said, it is likely that not all such elaborations about the literal origin of idioms will be perceived as helpful by students if they find the link between the original use and the contemporary meaning of the expression far-fetched. In a study by Wang et al. (2020), the meaning of a collection of English idioms was explained in association with their literal underpinnings to Chinese students (25 idioms per student), who were then asked to rate for each expression how transparent they found the connection between the figurative meaning and its proposed literal underpinning. One week later, the students were presented with the same idioms again and were asked to recall their meanings. Overall, recall rates were high (>75%), and, interestingly, when students recalled the idiomatic meaning, they almost invariably also remembered the literal underpinning they had been told about. However, meaning recall tended to be poorer in the case of idioms whose connection to the literal underpinnings had been rated as non-transparent.

It needs to be said that the examples of polysemous words given further above and the idioms mentioned just now are unlikely learning targets for pre-intermediate L2 learners. However, items of higher frequency than these lend themselves to creating intralingual connections as well, and so the approach should also be feasible when teaching less advanced learners. *Hard* in the sense of 'difficult' can be connected to its basic sense of 'rigid', by pointing out that it is difficult (or hard) to break a hard object. The use of *bright* in the sense of 'clever' can be connected to its meaning of 'full of light' because light helps to see well. Metaphorically, understanding or knowing something is being able to see it (as reflected also in expressions such as *I see what you mean* and *being in the dark* about something). Polysemy is in fact especially common in high-frequency vocabulary (which is why dictionary entries for high-frequency words often have so many sub-entries). Take modal auxiliaries, for example. These have root meanings (e.g., ability, permission and obligation) and so-called epistemic meanings that are historically derived from the root meanings (Sweetser, 1990). The root meaning of *may* is permission, but if someone receives permission to do something, then it is quite possible it will happen, and hence *may* has over time developed the meaning of possibility. The root meaning of *must* is obligation, and if a person in authority obliges someone to do something, then it is almost certain to happen, and so *must* has developed the meaning of high probability (e.g., *That must be Jack at the door*) and so on. Additionally, past tense modal verbs such as *might* can be re-connected to their present tense relatives such as *may*. That *might* expresses a more tentative possibility than *may* reflects metaphor again: the present is where we are currently situated in time, whereas the past is at some distance. By using *might* (e.g., *She might agree*) rather than *may* (e.g., *She may agree*), speakers create a greater metaphorical distance between themselves and the proposition being expressed. This proximity versus distance metaphor is also reflected in phrases such as *a remote possibility*. I will say more about this further below.

One word class that is particularly notorious for its polysemy is the class of prepositions. Even a moderately polysemous preposition, such as *under*, has different literal uses and numerous abstract ones, as illustrated by the following examples: *under the table, under the blanket, under his coat, under age, under stress, under pressure, under the influence, under investigation, under control, under arrest, under supervision, under sedation, under a pretext, under a cloud, under fire, under your thumb, under her wing, under your breath, under cover, under way*. Again, many of the abstract uses can be made imageable by connecting them to a literal meaning through conceptual metaphors, such as "more is up; less is down" (e.g., *You're not allowed to drive here if you're under 18*), "visible is known; invisible is unknown" (e.g., *under a pretext*), and "having control/power is up; being subjected to control/power is down" (e.g., *under arrest*). Proposals for teaching the abstract uses of prepositions along such ways almost invariably include visual representations of the literal, spatial meanings of the items (e.g., Lindstromberg, 2010; Tyler & Evans, 2004), and I will return to this topic further below when I review studies involving the use of visuals to mediate learning. The reason why I already mention prepositions here is that these items also figure as "particles" in a class of phrases which have attracted a fair amount of attraction in this line of inquiry about linking abstract senses to more basic ones—phrasal verbs. For example, the particles *up* and *down* in *turn the volume up/down* reflect the metaphor "more is up; less is down", in *set up a business* and *the car broke down* they reflect the metaphor "active is up; inactive is down", and in *cheer up* and *feel down* they reflect "happy is up; sad is down". The particle *out* in *find out the truth* and *figure it out* may reflect the aforementioned metaphor "visible is known; invisible is unknown", because when something is out of a container it is visible. Note again that these metaphors make intuitive sense because they are grounded in physical experience: adding objects to a pile makes the pile grow, active people tend to be up and about, and so on. Boers (2000b), Condon (2008), Kövecses and Szabó (1996) and Yasuda (2010) conducted classroom experiments where one group of students studied English phrasal verbs accompanied by the metaphors underlying the choice of particles, while another group studied the same phrasal verbs without this information. Raising students' awareness of the metaphors was in general found to be beneficial for the students' recall of the phrasal verbs, although the effectiveness varies from one phrasal verb to another (Condon, 2008). Kövecses and Szabó (1996) and Yasuda (2010) also report evidence that students may put their enhanced awareness of metaphors to good use as they study additional phrasal verbs even if these are presented without this information (also see Strong, 2013), but such evidence of transfer to new phrasal verbs did not emerge in the studies by Boers (2000b) and Condon (2008).

In this *Cognitive Semantic* approach to phrasal verbs, students are essentially invited to analyse the phrases and to evaluate the role of a specific constituent (here, the particle). Similar suggestions have been made regarding the lexical composition of collocations (e.g., Lindstromberg & Boers, 2008a, p. 74). For example, it is easy to appreciate why the verb *commit* is used in *commit fraud*, because *commit* collocates with crime-related nouns in general (*commit murder*, etc.), why *perform* is used in *perform a song*, because *perform* collocates with public entertainment nouns in general (*perform a play*, etc.) and why *conduct* is used in *conduct an interview*, because *conduct* collocates with research-related nouns in general (*conduct an investigation*, etc.). Even what at first sight appear to be exceptions can lend themselves to elaboration with a view to making the collocations stick in memory. For example, *commit* collocates with *suicide* because in Catholic religion suicide is a crime (against God), and *perform* collocates with *surgery* because in the past famous surgeons practised their craft in the presence of spectators (which is probably also why operating rooms are still sometimes referred to as operating *theatres* in British English). In the case of semantically less distinct words, such as highly polysemous verbs (e.g., *hold* and *keep*) and so-called delexicalized verbs (e.g., *make* and *do*), finding such explanations is far less straightforward, but it has been suggested that reminding students of the original, basic meaning of such items can nonetheless be helpful (e.g., Csábi, 2004; Liu, 2010; Tsai, 2020; Walker, 2011). For example, the literal meaning of *make* is 'create' or 'produce', and so it might be possible to highlight this as students learn new collocations with *make* which seem to focus on the outcome of an activity, whereas collocations with *do* tend to focus on the activity itself.

If it is sometimes feasible to analyse phrases and elaborate on the role of their specific constituents, then this may also be feasible for single words made up of different parts. Clearly both *arm* and *chair* contribute to the meaning of *armchair*, and both *rain* and *bow* contribute to the meaning of *rainbow*. Affixes and word stems with a known etymology have attracted particular attention in this regard (e.g., Sasao & Webb, 2017). For example, the prefix *pre* in *precede* comes from Latin and means 'before'. It has the same meaning in numerous other words, such as *precedent, prediction, prehistory, prelude, premature* and *premeditated*. If, in addition, a learner knows that the stem 'cede' comes from Latin *cedere*, literally meaning 'go', then the form-meaning connection of *precede* becomes more transparent and the meaning more imageable. This type of word-part analysis can be applied to many Latinate words (e.g., the meaning contribution of *inter* in *interaction*, of *anti* in *antidote*, of *in* in *inexplicable* and so on). A large proportion of the English vocabulary is of Latinate origin (mostly imported into English through French) and this proportion is of course even larger in Romance languages (Italian, French etc.), which evolved directly from Latin. Steps to help learners appreciate the role of word parts have been strongly recommended in publications for teachers (e.g., Wei & Nation, 2013). Surprisingly, there appears to be little empirical research to evaluate how well such steps in fact help students remember the words. A rare classroom study addressing this question is Wei (2015). Chinese students of English were asked to memorize new words which were presented to them in association with a familiar word containing the same stem. For example, they studied *addendum* in association with *add* and they studied *simulate* in association with *similar*. A comparison group was simply told to memorize the words using any strategy of their own choice (although they were advised that they could read the words and their meanings, then close their eyes and try to retrieve the words and their meanings from memory—which, according to the research on retrieval practice, is very sound advice; see chapter 6). Posttests showed no marked differences between the 2 groups' learning gains and thus no compelling evidence for the effectiveness of the "word-part technique", at least as implemented in this study (see further below for additional discussion). More research is required to determine the conditions in which the word-part mnemonic will work best.

Visualizing Abstract Meaning

The preceding section looked at ways to make abstract meanings more imageable (and thus easier to remember) but where "imageable" refers to pictures in the mind. The techniques discussed involve *verbal* explanations of the links between abstract meanings of items and their concrete-meaning roots. A more direct way to lend imageability to meanings is to present learners with actual visual representations. These will often be drawings or pictures, but meanings can of course also be made visual through animation, gestures and mime (e.g., Lindstromberg & Boers, 2005). Recall that, according to *Dual Coding Theory* (Paivio, 1986), concrete-meaning words are easier to process and learn than abstract-meaning words because the referents of the former are readily imageable (provided you are familiar with the referents, of course). If you already know what squirrels look like, then hearing or seeing the word *squirrel* is likely to call up a mental picture of this animal (even though that mental picture may for some of us also resemble the animated character Scrat in *Ice Age* movies). Learning the L2 word *squirrel* in association with a picture of a squirrel may therefore be a more direct means of encoding the meaning of the word than learning the word in association with its L1 translation. The use of visuals instead of translations to clarify L2 words was already advocated in the early 1900s by proponents of the *Direct Method* (e.g., Bovée, 1919). When applied to concrete-meaning words, it does not necessarily mean the words will also be better *remembered* after elucidation with a visual (Carpenter & Olson, 2012) because an L1 translation can conjure up the familiar picture before the mind's eye as well (also see chapter 3 on multimodal glosses). Visuals are therefore more likely to make a mnemonic difference if they are used to represent abstract-meaning items, since the latter do not on their own evoke images, according to *Dual Coding Theory*. Presenting abstract meaning pictorially is of course far from self-evident, but sometimes it can be done. For example, Farley et al. (2012) had students of Spanish learn words referring to emotions (e.g., sadness) and attitudes (e.g., laziness) either paired with their L1 translations or with translations *and* a picture exemplifying the abstract meaning, such as a picture of a sad face to represent sadness and a picture of a fat cat to represent laziness. The students who studied the words in association with the pictures recalled the word meanings better than did their peers in the non-picture group. Using pictures with a set of concrete-meaning words did *not* make a significant difference in their study. Similar findings are reported by Shen (2010), who investigated the role of visuals to help students remember Chinese words. For example, the concept of dilemma was visualized as a figure standing at a crossroads. Again, the use of visuals was found to help the students recall a set of abstract words, but it made little difference when it came to a set of concrete words.

In the preceding section I briefly mentioned the *Cognitive Semantic* approach to polysemy whereby abstract language use is reconnected to concrete, root meanings. Recall, for example, how the epistemic meanings (e.g., possibility) of modal verbs are derivable through inferencing from their root meanings (e.g., permission) and how, in addition, the more tentative meaning of past modals (e.g., *might* relative to *may*) reflects metaphorical distancing. In a classroom experiment by Tyler et al. (2010), one group of students was taught English modal verbs with explanations of this kind. Another group of students received instruction about the same verbs in a way that imitates the way many mainstream textbooks present modal verbs, that is, organized by function (e.g., "to express possibility, use *may* ..."; "to express obligation, use *must* ..." etc.). The former group outperformed the latter in the posttest, suggesting again that "going back to the roots" can be beneficial. It needs to be mentioned, though, that the learning gains were far from impressive in this experiment: the scores on a 32-item posttest were on average just 2 points better relative to the pretest, and this after approximately 3 hours of instruction and practice. Surprisingly, the comparison group made no progress at all from pretest to posttest. The reason why I mention this study by Tyler et al. (2010) in the present section is that the intervention included schematic drawings meant to illustrate the meanings of the modal verbs. For example, *may* was explained in association with a drawing of one person opening a door for another, suggesting the latter is given permission to enter/leave, *must* came with a drawing of a person physically directing someone else's movement, and *can* was illustrated by means of a drawing of someone with big biceps. Since these schematic drawings were part of an instructional ensemble that differed from the comparison treatment in various ways, it is unfortunately impossible to tell how much they contributed to the overall outcome.

Creating visuals to clarify the meaning of items such as modal verbs is not straightforward. Items that may lend themselves more readily to this include spatial prepositions (*in, on, over* etc.). Drawings representing the meaning of prepositions (e.g., a figure crawling *over* a wall) have been used in several interventions to help learners appreciate how abstract or figurative uses of prepositions (e.g., *It took her a long time to get over her divorce*) derive from their basic meanings (Cho, 2010; Lam, 2009; Tyler, 2012; Wong et al., 2018). The results have not always been very encouraging. Cho (2010), who focused on the prepositions *in, at* and *on* in a classroom experiment with Japanese students of English, found the approach effective relative to a comparison condition, but the average delayed posttest score was only marginally better than the pretest score. The comparison group in fact obtained *poorer* scores on the delayed posttest than on the pretest. Lam (2009) taught 2 confusable Spanish prepositions (*para* and *por*) with visuals and clarifications of the connections among the various uses of each preposition, but found no significantly better learning gains relative to a comparison group. Tyler (2012) conducted a classroom experiment with Vietnamese students of English receiving instruction about the prepositions *to, for* and *at*, and did find a statistically significant advantage for the *Cognitive Semantic* approach relative to a comparison condition. The former improved their scores from a 40-item pretest to the immediate posttest by on average 9.2 points, while the comparison group improved by 6.8 points. It should be mentioned that these gains were the result of close to 3 hours of instruction and practice, and that the posttest scores were still far from excellent (<60%) despite this amount of work. Wong et al. (2018) focused on *in, at* and *over* in a computer-based experiment. The participants were given a series of 84 picture-sentence-matching exercises where they had to decide which of 2 prepositions corresponded to the given picture (an exercise format resembling the interpretation practice that is part of *Processing Instruction*; see chapter 5). After each choice, they were given feedback. In one condition, this feedback included a schematic diagram representing the meaning of the preposition. In another condition, it included a verbal explanation and a few more examples of use. In the former condition, the exercise items were sequenced such that the students would more easily connect the literal meaning of each preposition to its figurative meanings. This is reminiscent of the experiment about the learning of polysemous words by Verspoor and Lowie (2003), which I reviewed in the previous section. Wong et al. (2018) found slightly better learning gains for the treatment with the diagrams, but this difference fell short of statistical significance. The average improvement in scores from the pretest to the posttest after this treatment was less than 20%, which seems not especially encouraging considering the substantial amount of practice the students had done. Contrary to what Wong et al. (2018) claim in their article, the type of practice where learners are required to choose which of 2 words is appropriate in a given context is perhaps not optimal when it comes to highly confusable words. This echoes the concerns I expressed in chapters 5 and 6 about certain exercises in textbooks. Also echoing a concern expressed there, it is worth noting that the pretest in Wong et al. (2018) required the participants to choose from sets of options to complete 68 gapped sentences, and (since this was a pretest in an experimental study) they did not receive feedback at that stage. The learners in Wong et al.'s experiment thus contemplated a very large number of potential form–meaning associations and were subsequently expected to remember only the correct ones. This also holds true for some of the other experiments discussed above. For example, the comparison treatment in Cho (2010) included a lot of find-and-correct-the-error exercises. The potential interference from seeing so many incorrect instances may help to explain why the students made no progress.

The use of imagery discussed so far concerned vocabulary and items at the lexis-grammar interface (such as modal auxiliaries). The effectiveness of using visuals to make *grammar* easier to remember has less often been examined. In some respects, this is surprising, because teachers and textbooks make use of drawings, for example to explain the function of tenses, (e.g., Cunningham et al., 2013; Kerr & Jones, 2012). A typical example is the drawing of a horizontal time line running from the past (typically on the left) to the future (typically on the right) and on which the simple past and the past perfect are visually situated relative to the present. On the same time line one can then also indicate visually that the present perfect tense in English signals a link between a past event and the present, while the simple past does not. A wavy line may be drawn to suggest progressive aspect (the event or activity is ongoing in the time span indicated), and so on. While such representations intuitively seem helpful, not all textbooks include them, which suggests that not all textbook authors are convinced of their usefulness. There seems to be little available empirical research on this topic, let alone research that compares different implementations of the technique (for instance, see McManus, 2019, and Niemeier, 2008, for alternative ways of depicting progressive aspect). One of the rare studies about the use of visuals for grammar teaching was conducted by Jacobson (2018), who applied ideas from *Cognitive Semantics* (more specifically from Dancygier & Sweetser, 2005) to the teaching of English conditionals. In essence, the different conditional patterns (*If you do…, I will…; If you did…, I would…; If you had done…, I would have…*) were explained according to the aforementioned proximity versus distance metaphor. The reasoning is as follows. The present tense refers to events here and now, and, given their "proximity" to us, we may be able to influence them. The present tense form in the if-clause therefore presents a scenario as a possibility. The past tense, by contrast, refers to events that are over and thus outside the space where we can influence events. Using the past tense form in the conditional clause therefore presents a scenario as hypothetical or imaginary. Events reported in the past perfect tense are even more distant from the here and now and so definitely unalterable. This is how the past perfect tense form in a conditional clause presents a proposition as counterfactual. Jacobson (2018) explained the English conditional patterns along these lines to one group of students, while another group "received a traditional presentation informed by L2 textbooks". The presentation along *Cognitive Semantic* lines included visuals to illustrate the proximity versus distance metaphor. After the explicit explanations, both groups did various practice activities with a focus on conditionals. The learning gains of the group that received the *Cognitive Semantic* explanations were better than the gains of the comparison group: test scores improved on a 49-item test between the pretest and a (10-day) delayed posttest by 11 and by 5 points, respectively. There was also a control group, who received no instruction about conditionals in the period in which the study was conducted. Their test scores also improved a little bit, by 2 points, which puts the learning gains of the instructed groups into perspective. What is worth mentioning as well is that the whole treatment (explicit presentations and practice activities) took a total of 7.5 hours. In that light, the learning gains of the students whose instruction was said to be based on L2 textbooks seem very meagre. That said, few details about the presentations used with these students are included in Jacobson's (2018) article, and so it is impossible to speculate as to why these students made so little progress despite the time invested.

Visuals can depict the referents of words or phrases and so they can be expected to elucidate *meaning* well, but visuals alone cannot be expected to help learners take in the phonological or orthographic *form* of language items. Put differently, visuals serve the purpose of semantic elaboration, not structural elaboration. A couple of experiments focusing on figurative idioms illustrate this. It is not unusual for study materials about idioms to include pictures, often of a humorous kind, that depict a literal reading of the expression, and research suggests that well-chosen visuals (i.e., depicting scenes that point to the figurative meaning of the idioms) can indeed help learners recall their meaning (Ramonda, 2019). If the idioms are made up of words which the learners are already familiar with, such illustrations can help productive recall as well (Szczepaniak & Lew, 2011). However, if the expressions contain as yet unfamiliar words, visual illustrations are less helpful for productive recall. Boers et al. (2009) created study materials about idioms where some of the expressions were accompanied by a picture and others were not. Idioms with low-frequency content words (e.g., *at the end of your tether, pass muster* and *rap someone on the knuckles*) were recalled more accurately in a productive recall test when these had *not* been presented with a picture. It is possible that the pictures attracted attention which the students would otherwise have given to the precise wording of the expressions. Students would remember the referents depicted in the visuals but substitute the words in the recall test by more familiar synonyms. For example, they substituted *fiddle* in *play second fiddle to someone* by the word *violin*, and *rein* in *keep a tight rein on someone* by the word *rope*. Fostering accurate productive knowledge may therefore require supplementary kinds of elaboration. The next couple of sections look at some possibilities.

Attending to Phonological Repetition

When word partnerships (such as compounds and collocations) are forged, this is influenced not only by the semantics of the words but often also by their phonological compatibility. In English, alliteration (i.e., repetition of the same word-initial consonant) has been a major driving force in the creation of word partnerships (e.g., *baby boom, beer belly, below the belt, cut corners, by common consent, curiosity killed the cat, fast food, from pillar to post, a sight for sore eyes, a slippery slope, turn the tables* and *wage war*). Tallies in idiom dictionaries reveal that about 17% of English idioms manifest alliteration; tallies in a general English dictionary suggest that alliteration is a feature of well over 10% of English lexicalized phrases more generally (Boers & Lindstromberg, 2009, pp. 106–125). Some types of phrase, most notably binomials (e.g., *first and foremost, toss and turn*), similes (e.g., *good as gold, blind as a bat*) and aphorisms (e.g., *better safe than sorry, all that glitters isn't gold*) are particularly prone to the phenomenon. In addition, a substantial proportion of English phrases exhibit rhyme or near-rhyme or, to use an umbrella term, assonance (e.g., *brain drain, cook the books, fair and square, high five, hot spot* and *small talk*). A combination of alliteration and assonance (e.g., *fight or flight response, busy bee, through thick and thin* and *part and parcel*) can make an expression even more catchy. The potential catchiness of alliteration and assonance is one explanation for this "words-of-a-feather-flock-together" phenomenon. Even though the meaning of *time will tell* could in theory just as well be expressed as "time will show" or "the future will reveal", it is the alliterative phrase that has become the standard expression. Even though the meaning of *it takes two to tango* could in theory also be expressed by "it takes two to waltz", it is the former wording that caught on. An additional explanation is that phonological repetition can reduce articulatory effort; e.g., saying *small talk* takes slightly less effort thanks to the repetition of the same vowel than "little talk'. The examples given here concern English, but there is no reason to suppose that phonological repetition plays no such role in the makeup of other languages' stocks of phrases. What is likely to vary across languages, though, is the types of phonological pattern that are especially common (Boers & Stengers, 2008). In English (a language where prosodic stress is often on the first syllable of a word) it is alliteration, but in a language where the final syllable receives prosodic stress, such as French, rhyme is likely to be the more common pattern. It is also worth noting that phonological repetition of course not only occurs in multiword expressions but also within single (compound) words (e.g., *skyscraper, tiptoe, zigzag, catnap* and *namesake*).

While alliteration and assonance increase the chances of a word sequence catching on in a language, this does by no means imply that the presence of such a pattern is always noticed. Language users naturally focus on communicative content, not on the precise packaging of this content. Research suggests that L2 learners may not unlock the mnemonic potential of alliteration and assonance unless their attention is directed to these patterns (Boers et al., 2014; Eyckmans & Lindstromberg, 2017). To give just one example of a study which illustrates this, in Eyckmans et al. (2016), students were given a list of 32 English verb-noun phrases, half of which alliterate (e.g., *set a standard*) and the other half do not (e.g., *run a business*), and they were given 15 minutes to study the expressions together with their translations. The students were divided into 3 groups, and 2 of these were given an additional task to perform while they studied the phrase list. One group was instructed to tick phrases in the list that alliterate, and the second group was asked to tick phrases in the list whose verbs do not correspond to the L1 translation (the phrase list was compiled such that half of the phrases were congruent with L1 while the other half were not). The third group received no additional instructions for their study task. Ten days later, the students were given gapped sentences where they needed to supply the appropriate verbs before the given nouns. The students whose task it had been to detect alliteration obtained the highest overall score. They outperformed the other 2 groups especially markedly on the set of alliterative items. In the other groups, the alliterative phrases were not better recalled than the non-alliterative ones. These findings demonstrate that raising students' awareness of alliteration in phrases can indeed make these more memorable. Rather surprisingly, the group of students in Eyckmans et al. (2016) that had been asked to compare the lexical makeup of the English phrases with the L1 translations obtained the poorest overall score— poorer than the group that had simply been told to study the list without any further guidelines. This seems to contradict the findings of Laufer and Girsai (2008) and Zhang and Graham (2020) discussed earlier, which indicated that L1-L2 contrastive analysis *is* beneficial for phrase learning. It is possible that memorizing as many as 32 phrases while also performing the task of evaluating their congruency with L1 counterparts was too demanding in the 15 minutes the students were given to study the list. Detecting alliteration is a more straightforward task. It might therefore be worth replicating Eyckmans et al.'s (2016) experiment with smaller sets of phrases. More work would be welcome to test what other sound patterns in vocabulary and phraseology have a mnemonic potential, not only in English but in other languages.

At the same time, it needs to be acknowledged that such catchy sound patterns are not equally common in all discourse types (Lindstromberg, 2020a), and so opportunities for directing students' attention to them will vary between instructional contexts. Instructors working in an English-for-academic-purposes program, for example, will not encounter a great abundance of alliterative expressions in their course materials.

Exploring Iconicity

Most form-meaning associations in language are arbitrary, that is, the outcome of mere convention within the given language community. Occasionally, however, language forms do seem to reflect what they refer to—a phenomenon called *iconicity*. The best-known illustration of this phenomenon is onomatopoeia, where a word mimics the sound made by an animal (e.g, *hiss* for a snake and *meow* for a cat) or the sound made by an event or action (e.g., *splash* and *kaboom!*). Iconicity extends beyond onomatopoeia, however (Nuckolls, 1999; Ramachandran & Hubbard, 2001). Experiments have demonstrated, for example, that people around the world are inclined to match the pseudoword *kiki* with a thin or jagged shape and *bouba* with a round shape. If you were presented with the unfamiliar word *fluwel* and asked to guess if this word refers to a soft or a rough substance, you would probably opt for the former. If you were asked to guess whether the verb *spuck* means to show love or to show disgust, my bet is that you will think it is the latter. In many cases it will not be clear whether these intuitions are truly the result of iconicity or the result of associations with known words which show formal resemblance to the new word. For example, English has numerous words with the onset sw–, including *sway, sweep, swing, swipe, swirl* and *swoop*, and these all broadly refer to the same kind of movement. Meeting a new word with this same onset (e.g., *swivel*) is then likely to call up associations with this meaning. This also applies to sets of words sharing the onsets cr– (e.g., *crack, crash* and *crush*), gl– (e.g., *glow, glimmer* and *glisten*) and sl– (e.g., *slip, slide* and *slither*). Parault and Schwanenflugel (2006) presented adult speakers of English with unfamiliar words which were either "sound-symbolic" or "nonsound-symbolic" in the above way, and to match the words with the appropriate definition in a multiple-choice task—similar to what I invited you to do just above with the pseudowords *fluwel* and *spuck*. As expected, the participants were better able to identify the matched meanings in the case of sound-symbolic words. Similar findings have been reported for L1 Japanese (Imai et al., 2008). Importantly, sound symbolism has been found to help L2 learners remember words as well (Kantartzis et al., 2011; Nygaard et al., 2009).

The next question is whether teachers can harness the occasional impression that certain words match their meanings rather well in order to make them easier to remember. One option is to use pitch, prosody and other articulatory means to emphasize the phonological features of the item that reflect its meaning. Words such as *teeny-weeny* and *mini* can be spoken in an exaggerated high pitch—a high pitch being associated with smallness (probably because small creatures tend to produce high-pitched sounds). The opposite can be done with words such as *humongous* and *bombastic*. *Whisper* can be articulated softly and with lengthening of the onset, so it begins to sound like a whisper, and so on. These are undoubtedly things that many teachers do spontaneously in their classes—when telling stories to young learners, for instance. It would be interesting to know how much of a difference for learners' retention of new words this playful use of articulation can make. Another possibility is to simply ask the students to consider whether a given word form might match its meaning rather well. This was tried by Deconinck et al. (2010), who presented a group of English majors with sets of unfamiliar words and their translations and asked them to rate each word for how well or how poorly its form corresponds to its meaning. These students later recalled the words better than students in other groups who were given the same sets of words to study but who did not do the same rating task. The form-meaning correspondence ratings varied widely across the words, and—as expected—it was the words which were perceived by the students as exhibiting a good form-meaning correspondence that were particularly well remembered. Importantly, evidence of a comparative advantage for these words did not emerge from the test data of the other participant groups, which indicates that inviting learners to consider the possibility of iconicity in vocabulary can make a difference.

A certain amount of iconicity may also be discernable in logographic scripts, such as the written characters in Chinese. Some of the radicals that make up Chinese characters can be traced back in history to pictograms representing concrete referents. In the contemporary Chinese script, these pictograms have been simplified to the extent that they are no longer recognizable without assistance. With assistance to reconnect radicals to their original pictograms, however, some Chinese characters may become easier to remember. This was found in a study by Li and Tong (2020), where students of Chinese learned sets of concrete compound words and their written characters either in association with their original pictograms or in association with pictures of the referents of the words. For example, one group of students would be shown the character for fruit in combination with its ancestor pictogram, while another group would be shown the character in combination with a picture of fruit. The former group obtained the better posttest scores. It is unclear what proportion of the vast collection of contemporary Chinese characters lends itself to this mnemonic technique, but Li and Tong's (2020) findings certainly suggest that it is worth applying the technique where it is feasible. The test used in their study did not require participants to reproduce the characters from memory, however. It is not clear whether teaching characters in conjunction with their pictographic ancestors is as beneficial for productive knowledge as it is for receptive knowledge. After all, remembering a contemporary character in conjunction with its ancestor pictogram logically leaves 2 mental representations of the written form of the character, and it is conceivable that a strong memory of the pictogram—strong owing to its iconic nature—may interfere with learners' accurate reproduction of the contemporary character. A replication study addressing this question could be interesting.

The instances of iconicity discussed so far concern vocabulary. Finding instances of iconicity beyond the realm of vocabulary is much harder, although a general iconic principle seems to be this: the more form, the less basic the meaning. This may be reflected, for example, in the various types of conditional sentences where *If I have time, I'll do it* is both formally and conceptually simpler than *If I'd had time, I would have done it.* Iconicity can also be detected in some of the features of polite or tentative requests (and other speech acts). The syntagmatic distance between the requester and the actual request in an utterance such as *I was wondering if it might be possible for you to reconsider my course grade* corresponds to a metaphorical distance between the requester and the request, suggesting the requester considers being granted the request only a *remote* possibility. The use of the past tense in such polite requests is another way of indicating this metaphorical distance (as discussed further above). However, while there are interesting proposals along these lines (e.g., Littlemore, 2009), there is little empirical research to assess whether raising learners' metalinguistic awareness at this abstract level helps learners to remember the taught language patterns. In the next section, I turn to a mnemonic technique (for vocabulary again) which *has* attracted a lot of attention from researchers.

Spotlight on a Specific Mnemonic Technique: The Keyword Method

The *Keyword Method* (Atkinson, 1975) is a mnemonic technique which combines the features of interlingual connections and imagery. To help them remember a new L2 word, learners are given (or asked to look for) a word in L1 that bears phonological resemblance to the L2 word, and they are then given (or asked to invent) an image which combines the meanings of the 2 words. When the L2 is encountered again afterwards, the L1 word can then serve as a mnemonic "key" to the L2 word's meaning. For example, Dutch learners of English could use the Dutch word *puntje* (sharp end) as a keyword to recall the English word *puncture* through conjuring up an image of a flat tyre punctured by the sharp end of a nail. In the case of closely related languages, L1 keywords may be available that bear not only phonological but also semantic resemblance to the L2 target words. For instance, Dutch learners of English may relate the English word *bleach* to their L1 word *bleek* ('pale') and create an image of a colourful Hawaiian shirt that was accidentally dropped into a bucket containing bleach. Oftentimes, however, there will be no intrinsic semantic relatedness between the L1 keyword and the L2 target word, and it is the creative thinking that goes into linking the 2 items in one way or another that is believed to make the target word memorable. For example, to remember the English verb *frolic* Dutch learners might think of the L1 word *vrolijk* ('merry') and then think of puppies frolicking merrily in the garden. Should they want to remember *steering wheel* they could think about the L1 word *stier* ('bull') and picture a bull with a steering wheel around its head, and so on. Some readers may find this a rather roundabout mnemonic technique—I remember I did when I first read about it after having been a certified language teacher for several years. They may then also be surprised that it is a technique that has attracted far more attention from researchers than any of the other mnemonic techniques discussed in this chapter—generating over 100 published studies since the 1970s, according to Lindstromberg (2020b). In many of these studies, the effectiveness of the keyword method is compared to a rote-learning condition, that is, a condition where learners are simply told to try and memorize the words and their L1 translations, without any instruction to use a mnemonic strategy. Lack of space prevents an in-depth systematic review of so many studies, but it is safe to say that, overall, the results have been mixed (e.g., Pressley et al., 1982; Wang & Thomas, 2005). This is not unexpected, because there are multiple variables that can influence the relative effectiveness of any mnemonic technique, and this holds certainly true for the keyword method as well.

One such variable is the characteristics of the words. Given its reliance on imagery, the keyword method is easiest to apply to concrete-meaning words. Another is the availability of a keyword in L1 with sufficient phonological similarity to the target word—which is not straightforward when the L1 and the target language belong to distant language families. It is also worth noting in this context that the posttests used in experiments on the keyword method almost always assess the learners' ability to remember the meaning of the target words, not their form. It cannot be assumed that remembering the L1 keyword will help accurate recall of the pronunciation or the spelling of the L2 word, since the phonological or orthographic overlap between the 2 is partial—in fact, there may even be a risk of the L1 word form causing interference with accurate L2 word form recall (a possibility I also mentioned above when discussing the use of pictographs to teach logographic script). The Dutch keyword *bleek* might lead a learner to write *bleech* instead of *bleach*. An English speaker learning Spanish may find *messy* a helpful keyword to remember the *meaning* of Spanish *mesa* ('table') by picturing a messy table, but the learner then needs to avoid writing *messa* instead of *mesa*. Another factor is how much time participants are given to study a set of words with the keyword method. It is indeed a rather roundabout route of memorization, after all, and so it can only work well if learners have enough time to travel it. To save time, researchers have in several studies opted to supply learners with L1 keywords and the images to combine them with the L2 target words instead of asking the learners to generate these themselves. This is also what teachers might do in class if they decided to make a given L2 word easier to remember through this technique. A problem here is that keyword associations can be quite idiosyncratic, and so what the teacher believes to be a helpful mnemonic may not resonate with the students. A solution explored by Campos et al. (2004) is to have a cohort of students generate their own keywords and images for sets of L2 target words, and then select the most common keywords from that collection for the teacher to use with subsequent cohorts of similar-profile students.

What inevitably matters as well is precisely when and how the technique is applied. It seems commonsensical to offer the keyword and the interactive image as a mnemonic *after* the students have already encoded the meaning of the target word. For example, students may have been introduced to a number of new words over the course of a lesson, and at the end of the lesson the teacher may remind the students of these words and then suggest a mnemonic to help entrench them in long-term memory (e.g., "One of the words we met today is *puncture*. Something that may help you remember this word is to think of *puntje* in your own language, because a tyre can be punctured by the sharp end— *puntje*—of a nail"). However, in experiments testing the merits of the keyword method, it is not unusual for the keyword mnemonic to be applied at the stage when new words are introduced to the learners and thus simultaneously to encoding their meaning. For example, Campos et al. (2003) presented their Spanish participants with Latin words and their translation, with the suggested keyword in parentheses between them. For example, the target word *puella* was followed by its translation ('girl'), but between the target word and the translation the participants would see the Spanish keyword *puerto*, a word bearing phonological resemblance to *puella* but having an unrelated meaning ('door'). Some participants were in addition shown a picture of a girl standing by a door. The learners were thus introduced to the real meaning of the word and a different meaning (the meaning of the keyword) *at the same time*. The participants would thus have had to constantly remind themselves that the word adjacent to the new L2 word was *not* its translation. Displaying the keyword in between the L2 word and its actual meaning may reflect the metaphor of the keyword acting as "mediator" between the L2 word and its meaning. This is but a metaphor, however, and should not be taken literally. Inserting the keyword between the L2 word and its meaning at the initial learning stage, when learners are only just encoding the L2 word meaning, may be misguided because it risks creating competition between the L1 keyword and the correct L1 translation of the L2 word. The same presentation of keywords, that is, in between the L2 words and their L1 translations, was used in Wei (2015), a study already mentioned earlier in connection with the "word-part-technique". It is perhaps not surprising that these experiments are among those which found the keyword method to be *less* effective than rote learning.

What makes interpreting the overall findings from the body of research about the keyword method difficult as well is how the comparison condition labelled "rote learning" was operationalized. One can tell participants in an experiment to just try and memorize a set of words without resorting to any particular memory strategies, but post-childhood learners are likely to have developed such strategies, and simply switching these off on command is far from straightforward. One strategy, whose effectiveness I discussed in chapter 6, is to study form–meaning pairs, try to retrieve them from memory and then check if the retrieval was accurate. For example, learners may cover the L1 translations in a bilingual word list and see if they can recall them, or they may read information and then close their eyes to try and recall what they have read. This is actually what was suggested to the students in the rote-learning condition in Wei (2015), which was found to be as effective as the word-part technique and more effective than the keyword condition. In an effort to restrict participants' mental operations in the rote-learning condition, Sagarra and Alba (2006) instructed the participants to look at L2-L1 word pairs on a screen and to "write continuously and to read silently the word-translation pair and not to try to find any links other than what was written (participants would see '*sobaco* = armpit' on the screen and would write and silently read '*sobaco* = armpit' repeatedly in their booklet for 1 minute)"

(p. 234). It needs to be said that, while repeated copying is certainly something that some learners habitually do when they try to memorize words, it is not generalizable to learners at large. Besides, copying does not necessarily engage learners with the meaning of words (Barcroft, 2006; Candry et al., 2020). This is relevant because (as in most research about the keyword method) the posttests in Sagarra and Alba (2006) concerned meaning rather than word form. In their keyword condition, the learners were given one minute to generate and write down a keyword and its connection with the target word (e.g., *sobaco* sounds like *tobacco*; tobacco smells bad, as do armpits). The keyword method yielded better posttest scores than the rote-learning condition *as implemented in the above way*. Interestingly, the authors mention that one minute per word was not long enough for several participants to create keywords as instructed. The data of these participants were excluded from the analysis. Data from participants who did not adhere to the instructions given in the rote-learning conditions were excluded as well. What Sagarra and Alba's (2006) results show, then, is that, *provided* learners are successful at finding a helpful keyword, they are likely to remember the meaning of an L2 word comparatively well, at least when the comparison is with a condition (repeated copying) that is known not to be particularly effective in the first place. What cannot be concluded from their results is that the keyword method is more effective (let alone more efficient) than a condition where students are asked to memorize words *in their own way*.

A multitude of published studies concerning the keyword method is available, and I have only reviewed a few studies here. My impression from browsing the major journals in our discipline is that interest in the keyword method has dwindled in recent years (but this may possibly reflect a more general trend where incidental vocabulary acquisition has been attracting more attention than deliberate, decontextualized vocabulary learning). What I wanted to illustrate with these reviews is that the outcomes of research studies will inevitably depend on precisely how learning conditions are operationalized. The effectiveness (and the efficiency) of any instructional method ultimately depends on the quality of its implementation, and this holds true not only for the instructional treatment whose merits a study aims to assess, but also for the comparison treatment against which its merits are weighed—which is a comment that I have made before and that I will reiterate in the next chapter.

Moderation in All Things

When I was planning the present chapter, I pictured a language class with a primary focus on content, with a teacher present to clarify new language items or patterns. The question I had in mind was what steps teachers can take to make newly learned language items/patterns stick *as the opportunity arises*. For example, a text used in class might contain an idiom that may be better remembered by students if their teacher briefly tells them about the origin of the expression, or if the teacher directs their attention to a sound pattern such as alliteration if the expression happens to exhibit this. Each of the mnemonic techniques discussed in this chapter has its own action radius, so to speak, and so it seems sensible to employ them in a complementary manner. Sometimes explicit L1-L2 comparisons may be helpful, at other times some sort of etymological elaboration will make items more imageable, at yet other times, iconicity may be exploited and so on. However, virtually all the empirical research studies on the effectiveness of mnemonic techniques apply one or the other mnemonic technique intensively during one-off experiments, for example by asking learner-participants to apply a technique during word-list memorization. It is not certain whether the findings of such studies can readily be generalized to a scenario where a teacher occasionally uses a mnemonic technique in an existing language course. It is understandable that researchers tend to shy away from experiments about the effect of a given teaching procedure when the procedure is used in moderation over an extended period of time. Not only can longitudinal classroom studies be difficult to organize (unless the researcher is the students' regular teacher), but the chances of finding a significant effect of this or the other teaching technique if it is used in moderation may be considered slim—and researchers may then feel worried that non-significant outcomes will not be publishable. The perspective of teachers is almost certain to be different from that of researchers anxious about their publication record, however. Teachers may (sensibly) feel reluctant to subject their students to certain of the experimental procedures described in the research literature, but they may nonetheless be curious to know if the occasional addition of a particular element to their instructional routine is likely to benefit their students. An example of a classroom study conducted from this perspective is reported in Lindstromberg and Boers (2008b). Throughout an English course, students in 2 parallel groups regularly worked with authentic reading and listening texts that served as input for subsequent content-focused output activities. Unfamiliar words and phrases in the texts were clarified by the teacher. Unsurprisingly (given what was said earlier about phonological repetition), the texts included alliterative phrases (e.g., *from pillar to post, mind over matter, get short shrift* and *wage war*). For one of the 2 groups of students, the teacher would not only clarify the meaning of the new words and phrases but also direct these students' attention to alliteration where it occurred. At the end of the course, both groups took a vocabulary test which elicited both non-alliterative and alliterative expressions from the course texts. No difference between the 2 groups emerged for the non-alliterative items, but the alliterative expressions were recalled better by the students whose attention had been directed to the sound pattern during classwork. Although no statistical significance was reached—and it is indeed doubtful if this experiment would have been published had it not been accompanied in the same manuscript by another experiment which did yield statistical significance—, the results suggests that creating the occasional mnemonic episode in a primarily content-oriented course has the potential to make a difference. It is worth noting that such episodes need not be long. For example, pointing out an instance of alliteration takes less than 10 seconds. Also, this classroom study investigated the occasional use of only one technique. It could be interesting to examine the cumulative effect of applying diverse mnemonic techniques as opportunities for using one and then another naturally arise in an existing language course.

Further Reflection

What Does Your Textbook Do to Make New Language Stick?

Browsing through a textbook (or another resource for language learning), do you discern any of the means for helping students remember language items or patterns along ideas discussed in this chapter? Can you detect any missed opportunities where the textbook author(s) could have applied these ideas?

How Are Idioms Presented in Study Materials?

Examine study materials with a focus on idioms. This could be an Internet resource or a book for independent study. Are the idioms organized by topic that they are used to talk about (e.g., a set of idioms to talk about relationships) or rather per domain that they originate from (e.g., a set of expressions derived from seafaring)? According to Zyzik (2011), the former grouping (i.e., by target domain) does not help much in comparison to grouping them without any thematic connection. However, according to the research reviewed in this chapter, grouping idioms by source domain may be more helpful. Is that the approach taken in the study materials you have examined? Another question concerns the use of visuals. If these materials feature drawings or pictures representing the idioms, are the visuals congruent with the meaning of the expressions? If, for example, *looking for a needle in a haystack* is represented by a haystack with a huge needle sticking through it and thus clearly visible, does this capture the meaning of the idiom (i.e., that something is impossible to find)?

Can There Be Too Much Baggage?

An experimental study by Barcroft et al. (2011) found that learners who had memorized L2 words through the keyword method (see above) not only performed comparatively poorly on a posttest but also needed more time to respond to test prompts than did learners in a comparison group. The authors attribute this to the learners' efforts to employ the keywords as mediators to recollect the target words instead of activating the target words directly. Put differently, after hooking new knowledge to a mnemonic association, it may be difficult to detach it from that association. This also seems to hold true for the technique discussed further above where the contemporary meaning of figurative words or phrases is made imageable by evoking the contexts in which the expressions were (or still are) used in a literal sense (e.g., *toe the line* can be made more imageable by evoking the scene of track-and-field athletes standing in a row with their toes just behind the starting line waiting for the signal to start running). When Boers et al. (2006) re-tested students' ability to recall the meaning of figurative idioms they had learned through this mnemonic technique 2 years earlier, they found that when the students remembered the idiomatic meaning they almost always remembered the literal underpinning as well (also Wang et al., 2020). While this testifies to the mnemonic power of the association, one may wonder how useful recall of the mnemonic association still is *after* it has served its purpose and is no longer needed. This question could be asked about metalinguistic knowledge more generally. Metalinguistic information may foster a richer episodic memory of a language item or pattern than simply telling learners "X means Y". It is clearly knowledge of the declarative kind, though, and it will take additional steps for the newly acquired knowledge to become smoothly deployable in real-time communication. I once used the following analogy in a review article about mnemonics based on *Cognitive Semantics* (Boers, 2013): "[The] approach may serve as a high-speed train to Word City, but its terminus is in a suburb. That's okay, as long as one realises it's still a bit of a stroll downtown, where the real action is" (p. 219). If more evidence were to emerge that activation of metalinguistic associations slows you down, then perhaps this analogy should be extended: Your visit to the downtown area will be more relaxed if you leave your bags with metalinguistic content in a locker at the train station. Still, would it not depend on the learners' needs and aspirations? Automaticity characterizes much of L1 speakers' language use, but is automaticity also the aspiration of all L2 learners? After all, not all learners expect to be using the target language for impromptu, high-paced communication.

References

Ammar, A., Lightbown, P. M., & Spada, N. (2010). Awareness of L1/L2 differences: Does it matter? *Language Awareness*, 19, 129–146. https://doi.org/10.1080/09658411003746612

Atkinson, R. C. (1975). Mnemotechnics in second-language learning. *American Psychologist*, 30, 821–828. https://doi.org/10.1037/h0077029

Barcroft, J. (2006). Can writing a new word detract from learning it? More negative effects of forced output during vocabulary learning. *Second Language Research*, 22, 487–497. https://doi.org/10.1191/0267658306sr276oa

Barcroft, J. (2015). *Lexical input processing and vocabulary learning*. John Benjamins.

Barcroft, J., Sommers, M. S., & Sunderman, G. (2011). Some costs of fooling Mother Nature: A priming study on the Keyword Method and the quality of developing L2 lexical representations. In P. Trofimovich & K. McDonough (Eds.), *Applying priming methods to L2 learning, teaching and research* (pp. 49–72). John Benjamins.

Beréndi, M., Csábi, S., & Kövecses, Z. (2008). Using conceptual metaphors and metonymies in vocabulary teaching. In F. Boers & S. Lindstromberg (Eds.), *Cognitive Linguistic approaches to teaching vocabulary and phraseology* (pp. 65–99). De Gruyter Mouton.

Boers, F. (2000a). Enhancing metaphoric awareness in specialised reading. *English for Specific Purposes*, 19, 137–147. https://doi.org/10.1016/S0889-4906(98)00017-9

Boers, F. (2000b). Metaphor awareness and vocabulary retention. *Applied Linguistics*, 21, 553–571. https://doi.org/10.1093/applin/21.4.553

Boers, F. (2013). Cognitive linguistic approaches to second language vocabulary: Assessment and integration. *Language Teaching*, 46, 208–224. https://doi.org/10.1017/S0261444811000450

Boers, F., Demecheleer, M., & Eyckmans, J. (2004). Etymological elaboration as a strategy for learning figurative idioms. In P. Bogaards & B. Laufer (Eds.), *Vocabulary in a second language: Selection, acquisition and testing* (pp. 53–78). John Benjamins.

Boers, F., Eyckmans, J., & Stengers, H. (2006). Motivating multiword units: Rationale, mnemonic benefits, and cognitive style variables. In S. H. Foster-Cohen, M. M. Krajnovic, & J. M. Djigunovic (Eds.), *EUROSLA yearbook* 6 (pp. 169–190). John Benjamins.

Boers, F., Eyckmans, J., & Stengers, H. (2007). Presenting figurative idioms with a touch of etymology: More than mere mnemonics? *Language Teaching Research*, 11, 43–62. https://doi.org/10.1177/1362168806072460

Boers, F., & Lindstromberg, S. (2009). *Optimizing a lexical approach to instructed second language acquisition*. Palgrave Macmillan.

Boers, F., Lindstromberg, S., & Eyckmans, J. (2014). Is alliteration mnemonic without awareness-raising? *Language Awareness*, 23, 291–303. https://doi.org/10.1080/09658416.2013.774008

Boers, F., Piquer-Píriz, A. M., Stengers, H., & Eyckmans, J. (2009). Does pictorial elucidation foster recollection of idioms? *Language Teaching Research*, 13, 367–382. https://doi.org/10.1177/1362168809341505

Boers, F., & Stengers, H. (2008). Adding sound to the picture: An exercise in motivating the lexical composition of metaphorical idioms in English, Spanish and Dutch. In L. Cameron, M. Zanotto, & M. Cavalcanti (Eds.), *Confronting metaphor in use: An applied linguistic approach* (pp. 63–78). John Benjamins.

Bovée, A. G. (1919). Teaching vocabulary by the Direct Method. *The Modern Language Journal*, 4, 63–72.

Campos, A., Amor, A., & González, M. A. (2004). The importance of the keyword-generation method in keyword mnemonics. *Experimental Psychology*, 51, 125–131. https://doi.org/10.1027/1618-3169.51.2.125

Campos, A., González, M. A., & Amor, A. (2003). Limitations of the mnemonic-keyword method. *The Journal of General Psychology*, 130, 399–413. https://doi.org/10.1080/00221300309601166

Candry, S., Decloedt, J., & Eyckmans, J. (2020). Comparing the merits of word writing and retrieval practice for L2 vocabulary learning. *System*, 89. https://doi.org/10.1016/j.system.2020.102206

Carpenter, S. K., & Olson, K. M. (2012) Are pictures good for learning new vocabulary in a foreign language? Only if you think they are not. *Journal of Experimental Psychology: Learning, Memory, and Cognition*, 38, 92–101. https://doi.org/10.1037/a0024828

Cermak, L. S., & Craik, F. I. M. (1979). *Levels of processing in human memory*. Lawrence Erlbaum.

Cho, K. (2010). Fostering the acquisition of English prepositions by Japanese learners with networks and prototypes. In S. De Knop, F. Boers, & A. De Rycker (Eds.), *Fostering language teaching efficiency through Cognitive Linguistics* (pp. 259–276). De Gruyter Mouton.

Condon, N. (2008). How Cognitive Linguistic motivations influence the learning of phrasal verbs. In F. Boers & S. Lindstromberg (Eds.), *Cognitive Linguistic approaches to teaching vocabulary and phraseology* (pp. 133–158). De Gruyter Mouton.

Cook, V. (2001). Using the first language in the classroom. *Canadian Modern Language Review*, 57, 402–423. https://doi.org/10.3138/cmlr.57.3.402

Craik, F. I. M., & Lockhart, R. S. (1972). Levels of processing: A framework for memory research. *Journal of Verbal Learning and Verbal Behavior*, 11, 671–684. https://doi.org/10.1016/S0022-5371(72)80001-X

Craik, F. I. M., & Tulving, E. (1975). Depth of processing and the retention of words in episodic memory. *Journal of Experimental Psychology: General*, 104, 268–294. https://doi.org/10.1037/0096-3445.104.3.268

Csábi, S. (2004). A cognitive linguistic view of polysemy in English and its implications for teaching. In M. Achard & S. Niemeier (Eds.), *Cognitive Linguistics, second language acquisition, and foreign language teaching* (pp. 233–256). De Gruyter Mouton.

Cunningham, S., Moor, P., & Bygrave, J. (2013). *Cutting Edge, intermediate: Students' book* (3rd ed.). Pearson Education.

Dancygier, B., & Sweetser, E. (2005). *Mental spaces in grammar: Conditional constructions*. Cambridge University Press.

Deconinck, J., Boers, F., & Eyckmans, J. (2010). Helping learners engage with L2 words: The form–meaning fit. *AILA Review*, 23, 95–114. https://doi.org/10.1075/aila.23.06dec

Eyckmans, J., Boers, F., & Lindstromberg, S. (2016). The impact of imposing processing strategies on L2 learners' deliberate study of lexical phrases. *System*, 56, 127–139. https://doi.org/10.1016/j.system.2015.12.001

Eyckmans, J., & Lindstromberg, S. (2017). The power of sound in L2 idiom learning. *Language Teaching Research*, 21, 341–361. https://doi.org/10.1177/1362168816655831

Farley, A. P., Ramonda, K., & Liu, X. (2012). The concreteness effect and the bilingual lexicon: The impact of visual stimuli attachment on meaning recall of abstract L2 words. *Language Teaching Research*, 16, 449–466. https://doi.org/10.1177/1362168812436910

Gentner, D., & Bowdle, B. (2008). Metaphor as structure-mapping. In R. Gibbs (Ed.), *The Cambridge handbook of metaphor and thought* (pp. 109–128). Cambridge University Press.

Hall, G., & Cook, G. (2012). Own-language use in language teaching and learning. *Language Teaching*, 45, 271–308. https://doi.org/10.1017/S0261444812000067

Horst, M., White, J., & Bell, P. (2010). First and second language knowledge in the language classroom. *International Journal of Bilingualism*, 14, 331–349. https://doi.org/10.1177/1367006910367848

Imai, M., Kita, S., Nagumo, M., & Okada, H. (2008). Sound symbolism facilitates early verb learning. *Cognition*, 109, 54–65. https://doi.org/10.1016/j.cognition.2008.07.015

Jacobson, N. D. (2018). The best of both worlds: Combining Cognitive Linguistics and pedagogic tasks to teach English conditionals. *Applied Linguistics*, 39, 668–693. https://doi.org/10.1093/applin/amw030

Jones, M., & Kerr, P. (2012). *Straightforward, pre-intermediate: Workbook* (2nd ed.). Macmillan Education.

Kantartzis, K., Kita, S., & Imai, M. (2011). Japanese sound symbolism facilitates word learning in English speaking children. *Cognitive Science*, 35, 626–630. https://doi.org/10.1111/j.1551-6709.2010.01169.x

Kerr, P., & Jones, C. (2012). *Straightforward, intermediate: Student's book* (2nd ed.). Macmillan Education.

Kövecses, Z. (2010). *Metaphor: A practical introduction* (2nd ed.). Oxford University Press.

Kövecses, Z., & Szabó, P. (1996) Idioms: A view from Cognitive Semantics. *Applied Linguistics*, 17, 326–355. https://doi.org/10.1093/applin/17.3.326

Kupferberg, I. (1999). The cognitive turn of contrastive analysis: Empirical evidence. *Language Awareness*, 8, 210–222. https://doi.org/10.1080/09658419908667130

Lakoff, G. (1987). *Women, fire and dangerous things: What categories reveal about the mind.* University of Chicago Press.

Lakoff, G., & Johnson, M. (1980). *Metaphors we live by.* University of Chicago Press.

Lam, Y. (2009). Applying cognitive linguistics to teaching the Spanish prepositions por and para. *Language Awareness*, 18, 2–18. https://doi.org/10.1080/09658410802147345

Laufer, B., & Girsai, N. (2008). Form-focused instruction in second language vocabulary learning: A case for contrastive analysis and translation. *Applied Linguistics*, 29, 694–716. https://doi.org/10.1093/applin/amn018

Lee, J. H., & Levine, G. S. (2020). The effect of instructor language choice on second language vocabulary learning and listening comprehension. *Language Teaching Research*, 24, 250–272. https://doi.org/10.1177/1362168818770910

Li, J.-T., & Tong, F. (2020). The effect of cognitive vocabulary learning approaches on Chinese learners' compound word attainment, retention, and learning motivation. *Language Teaching Research*, 24, 834–854. Online early review. https://doi.org/10.1177/1362168819829025

Li, T. F. (2009). *Metaphor, image, and image schemas in second language pedagogy.* Lambert Academic Publishing.

Lightbown, P. M., & Spada, N. (2019). Teaching and learning L2 in the classroom: It's about time. *Language Teaching*. https://doi.org/10.1017/S0261444819000454

Lindstromberg, S. (2010). *English prepositions explained* (2nd ed.). John Benjamins.

Lindstromberg, S. (2020a). Surplus interword phonological similarity in English multiword units. *Corpus Linguistics and Linguistic Theory*, 16, 95–118. https://doi.org/10.1515/cllt-2017-0013

Lindstromberg, S. (2020b). Intentional L2 vocabulary learning. In S. Webb (Ed.), *The Routledge handbook of vocabulary studies* (pp. 240–254). Routledge.

Lindstromberg, S., & Boers, F. (2005). From movement to metaphor with manner-of-movement verbs. *Applied Linguistics*, 26, 241–261. https://doi.org/10.1093/applin/ami002

Lindstromberg, S., & Boers, F. (2008a). *Teaching chunks of language.* Helbling Languages.

Lindstromberg, S., & Boers, F. (2008b). The mnemonic effect of noticing alliteration in lexical chunks. *Applied Linguistics*, 29, 200–222. https://doi.org/10.1093/applin/amn007

Littlemore, J. (2009). *Applying Cognitive Linguistics to second language learning and teaching.* Palgrave Macmillan.

Liu, D. (2010). Going beyond patterns: Involving cognitive analysis in the learning of collocations. *TESOL Quarterly*, 44, 4–30. https://doi.org/10.5054/tq.2010.214046

McManus, K. (2019). Awareness of L1 form-meaning mappings can reduce crosslinguistic effects in L2 grammatical learning. *Language Awareness*, 28, 114–138. https://doi.org/10.1080/09658416.2019.1620756

McManus, K., & Marsden, E. (2017). L1 explicit instruction can improve L2 online and offline performance. *Studies in Second Language Acquisition*, 39, 459–492. doi:10.1017/S027226311600022X2018

McManus, K., & Marsden, E. (2018). Online and offline effects of L1 practice in L2 grammar learning. A partial replication. *Studies in Second Language Acquisition*, 40, 459–475. doi:10.1017/S0272263117000171

Morgan, B. Q. (1917). In defence of translation. *The Modern Language Journal*, 1, 235–241.

Morris, C. D., Bransford, J. D., & Franks, J. J. (1977). Levels of processing versus transfer appropriate processing. *Journal of Verbal Learning and Verbal Behavior*, 16, 519–533. https://doi.org/10.1016/S0022-5371(77)80016–80019

Niemeier, S. (2008). The notion of boundedness/unboundeness in the foreign language classrooom. In F. Boers & S. Lindstromberg (Eds.), *Cognitive Linguistic approaches to teaching vocabulary and phraseology* (pp. 309–328). De Gruyter Mouton.

Nuckolls, J. B. (1999). The case for sound symbolism. *Annual Review of Anthropology*, 28, 225–252. https://doi.org/10.1146/annurev.anthro.28.1.225

Nygaard, L. C., Cook, A. E., & Namy, L. L. (2009). Sound to meaning correspondences facilitate word learning. *Cognition*, 112, 181–186. https://doi.org/10.1016/j.cognition.2009.04.001

Paivio, A. (1986). *Mental representations: A dual coding approach.* Oxford University Press.

Parault, S. J., & Schwanenflugel, P. J. (2006). Sound–symbolism: A piece in the puzzle of word learning. *Journal of Psychological Research*, 35, 329–351. https://doi.org/10.1007/s10936-006-9018-7

Peters, E. (2016). The learning burden of collocations: The role of interlexical and intralexical factors. *Language Teaching Research*, 20, 113–138. https://doi.org/10.1177/1362168814568131

Pressley, M., Levin, J. R., & Miller, G. E. (1982). The keyword method compared to alternative vocabulary-learning strategies. *Contemporary Educational Psychology*, 7, 50–60. https://doi.org/10.1016/0361-476X(82)90007–90008

Ramachandran, V. S., & Hubbard, E. M. (2001). Synaesthesia: A window into perception, thought and language. *Journal of Consciousness Studies*, 8, 3–34.

Ramonda, K. (2019). A double-edged sword: Metaphor and metonymy through pictures for learning idioms. *International Review of Applied Linguistics.* https://doi.org/10.1515/ira l-2018-0336

Sagarra, N., & Alba, M. (2006). The key is in the keyword: L2 vocabulary learning methods with beginning learners of Spanish. *The Modern Language Journal*, 90, 228–243. https://doi.org/10.1111/j.1540-4781.2006.00394.x

Sasao, Y., & Webb, S. (2017). The Word Part Levels Test. *Language Teaching Research*, 21, 12–30. https://doi.org/10.1177/1362168815586083

Shen, H. H. (2010). Imagery and verbal coding approaches in Chinese vocabulary instruction. *Language Teaching Research*, 14, 485–499. https://doi.org/10.1177/1362168810375370

Strong, B. (2013). A cognitive semantic approach to L2 learning of phrasal verbs. *The Language Teacher*, 37, 27–31. https://jalt-publications.org/files/pdf-article/37.5tlt_art09.pdf

Sweetser, E. (1990). *From etymology to pragmatics: Metaphorical and cultural aspects of semantic structure.* Cambridge University Press.

Szczepaniak, R., & Lew, R. (2011). The role of imagery in dictionaries of idioms. *Applied Linguistics*, 32, 323–347. https://doi.org/10.1093/applin/amr001

Tian, L., & Macaro, E. (2012). Comparing the effect of teacher codeswitching with English-only explanations on the vocabulary acquisition of Chinese university students: A lexical focus-on-form study. *Language Teaching Research*, 16, 367–391. https://doi.org/10.1177/1362168812436909

Tsai, M.-H. (2020). The effects of explicit instruction on L2 learners' acquisition of verb–noun collocations. *Language Teaching Research*, 24, 138–162. https://doi.org/10.1177/1362168818795188

Tyler, A. (2012). *Cognitive Linguistics and second language learning: Theoretical basics and experimental evidence.* Routledge.

Tyler, A., & Evans, V. (2004). Applying cognitive linguistics to pedagogical grammar: The case of *over.* In M. Achard & S. Niemeier (Eds.), *Cognitive Linguistics, second language acquisition, and foreign language teaching* (pp. 257–280). De Gruyter Mouton.

Tyler, A., Mueller, C. M., & Ho, V. (2010). Applying cognitive linguistics to instructed L2 learning: The English modals. *AILA Review*, 23, 30–49. https://doi.org/10.1075/aila.23.03tyl

Verspoor, M., & Lowie, W. (2003). Making sense of polysemous words. *Language Learning*, 53, 547–586. https://doi.org/10.1111/1467-9922.00234

Walker, C. P. (2011). A corpus-based study of the linguistic features and processes which influence the way collocations are formed: Some implications for the learning of collocations. *TESOL Quarterly*, 45, 291–312. https://doi.org/10.5054/tq.2011.247710

Wang, A. Y., & Thomas, M. H. (2005). Effect of keywords on long-term retention: Help or hindrance? *Journal of Educational Psychology*, 87, 468–475. https://doi.org/10.1037/0022-0663.87.3.468

Wang, X., Boers, F., & Warren, P. (2020). Using literal underpinnings to help learners remember figurative idioms: Does the connection need to be crystal-clear? In A. Piquer-Píriz & R. Alejo-González (Eds.), *Metaphor in foreign language instruction* (pp. 221–239). De Gruyter Mouton.

Waterman, J. (2012). *Straightforward, intermediate: Workbook* (2nd ed.). Macmillan Education.

Wei, Z. (2015). Does teaching mnemonics for vocabulary learning make a difference? Putting the keyword method and the word part technique to the test. *Language Teaching Research*, 19, 43–69. https://doi.org/10.1177/1362168814541734

Wei, Z., & Nation, P. (2013). The word part technique: A very useful vocabulary teaching technique. *Modern English Teacher*, 22, 12–16.

White, J., Muñoz, C., & Collins, L. (2007). The *his/her* challenge: Making progress in a 'regular' L2 programme. *Language Awareness*, 16, 278–299. https://doi.org/10.2167/la419.0

White, J., & Ranta, L. (2002). Examining the interface between metalinguistic task performance and oral production in a second language. *Language Awareness*, 11, 259–290. https://doi.org/10.1080/09658410208667060

Wong, M. H. I., Zhao, H., & MacWhinney, B. (2018). A Cognitive Linguistics application for second language pedagogy: The English preposition tutor. *Language Learning*, 68, 438–468. https://doi.org/10.1111/lang.12278

Yasuda, S. (2010). Learning phrasal verbs through conceptual metaphors: A case of Japanese EFL learners. *TESOL Quarterly*, 44, 250–273. https://doi.org/10.5054/tq.2010.219945

Zhang, P., & Graham, S. (2020). Vocabulary learning through listening: Comparing L2 explanations, teacher codeswitching, contrastive focus-on-form and incidental learning. *Language Teaching Research*, 24, 765–784. https://doi.org/10.1177/1362168819829022

Zhouhan, J., & Webb, S. (2020). Incidental vocabulary learning through listening to teacher talk. *The Modern Language Journal*, 104, 550–566. https://doi.org/10.1111/modl.12661

Zyzik, E. (2011). Second language idiom learning: The effects of lexical knowledge and pedagogical sequencing. *Language Teaching Research*, 15, 413–433. https://doi.org/10.1177/1362168811412025

PART IV

CONCLUSIONS AND FUTURE DIRECTIONS

8.

TAKING STOCK

Focus on Content and Focus on Language

My synthesis of the research on L2 vocabulary and grammar instruction distinguished 2 broad approaches. One approach, discussed in Part II of the book, is to find ways of *improving the chances of incidental acquisition* of words, phrases and patterns. This can be done through modifying textual input, such as making certain lexical items or grammar patterns more noticeable and comprehensible (chapter 3), and through designing communicative output activities that help learners notice and fill lacunae in their L2 repertoire (chapter 4). What the activities under this first broad approach have in common is that the learners are expected to be engaged mostly with communicative content (i.e., what is said) rather than the linguistic packaging of that content (i.e., how it is said). It is expected in this approach that the learners will acquire or fine-tune their knowledge of lexical items and grammar patterns as a by-product of compre-hending and expressing messages. The conditions created under this approach are different from naturalistic conditions, however, because the input materials and communicative tasks are designed such that preselected items/patterns stand a better chance of attracting the learners' interest. The other broad approach, discussed in Part III of the book, is to *overtly engage learners with the language code.* This can be done by giving centre stage to a segment of the lexicon or to a certain grammar feature and either clarify the form–meaning correspondences and usage patterns directly or invite learners themselves to figure them out with the necessary guidance (chapter 5), by engaging learners in language-focused practice to consolidate knowledge so it becomes easier to retrieve from memory (chapter 6) and by elaborating about certain properties of the items/patterns that can make them easier to remember (chapter 7).

The question is sometimes asked whether language-focused learning is really more efficient than interventions of the kind discussed in Part II, where the main focus is on communicative content but where steps are taken to increase the likelihood that learners will shift their interest to certain elements or features of the language code. There is no straightforward answer to this question. Within each of the 2 broad approaches, I have found studies that produced only marginal learning outcomes as well as studies yielding encouraging outcomes. Within the realm of research on language-focused interventions, I have found studies which compared one intervention to another, and which showed very encouraging outcomes of one but dismal outcomes of the latter—despite it being language focused as well. It would therefore be unwarranted to claim that language-focused interventions are always more effective for vocabulary and grammar learning than activities that are more oriented to communicative content. What does seem to be safe to say is this:

1. Using input materials that have been modified with a view to helping learners notice and comprehend certain items/patterns is usually more effective (for learning those items/patterns) than using non-modified input for the same content-oriented activities (see chapter 3).
2. Content-oriented output activities that stimulate use of certain items/patterns from "model" input is usually more effective (for learning those items/patterns) than only receptive content-oriented engagement with the input material (see chapter 4).
3. Giving learners explicit explanations about certain items/patterns before they engage in content-oriented activities is usually more effective (for learning those items/patterns) than doing only the content-oriented activities (see final parts of chapters 3 and 4).
4. Some language-focused interventions can be highly effective for vocabulary/grammar learning and will trump activities that are mostly content oriented; however, not all language-focused interventions are quite effective and so their outcomes are not necessarily better than the outcomes of well-designed content-oriented activities (see chapters 5 to 7).

When weighing the benefits of content-oriented and language-oriented activities, it is important to appreciate that the perspective taken here is narrow—assessing the extent to which learners improve their knowledge of vocabulary and grammar. There are several other dimensions of learning that are served by content-oriented activities: improving reading, listening and interactional skills, as well as increasing learners' depth of knowledge of items/patterns which they are already somewhat familiar with. These other dimensions are seldom captured by the assessment instruments used in the research strands discussed in this book, and so the broader benefits of content-oriented activities have probably been underestimated. Turning specifically to the learning of items/patterns, however, it seems that relatively substantial learning gains can be obtained from content-oriented activities, if the following conditions are met:

1. The learner experiences the item/pattern as highly relevant to accomplish the given communicative activity (i.e., it is experienced as vital for understanding or expressing a certain message). For example, this condition may be met in a reading activity when text-comprehension questions can only be answered correctly if the students adequately process the meaning of certain target words or phrases. It is likely to be met also in an output activity when the students realize there are gaps in their L2 repertoire that prevent them from conveying a certain message, and they are given the opportunity to fill these gaps in order to meet the communicative need.

2. The circumstances are such that the learner successfully establishes the form–meaning connection of the item/pattern that is felt to be highly relevant. This condition is likely to be met if supportive comprehensible context is available, if glosses are added to textual input, if dictionaries (or other resources) are available *and* consulted adequately, and if assistance (including feedback) is provided by a more proficient interlocutor—such as the teacher.

3. The learner considers the item/pattern *useful beyond the immediate purpose* it serves, and so considers it worth remembering for future occasions. The likelihood of this can be enhanced, for example, by increasing the number of occurrences of the item/pattern in the texts which the learner is exposed to. In addition, making an item/pattern more visually salient in a text (e.g., using boldface, underlining or italics) can increase interest, at least if the learner realizes this was done by their teacher or by the materials designer to flag useful language. In the context of output activities, repeating the same task or doing a sequence of tasks that invite use of the same lexical items or grammar patterns can also demonstrate the relevance of remembering them.

When a learner considers a given lexical item or grammar pattern vital enough to make a mental note about it for potential future use, this entails a shift in focus from content to language. Even though chapters 3 and 4 were about ways of improving the chances of incidental language learning (which I defined in this book as language learning from *primarily* content-focused activities), it is during episodes where the learner temporarily considers certain words, phrases or patterns as worthy study objects in their own right that these stand a relatively good chance of being remembered. For example, presenting students with a short text accompanied by glosses which repeatedly clarify the same words (e.g., Rott, 2007) or with multiple-choice glosses that ask learners to decide which proposed meaning is correct (e.g., Nagata, 1999) likely shifts the students' engagement with the textual input from its content to the selected words as study objects. In a similar vein, presenting students with a model example of an output task *and* directing the students' attention to certain wordings before asking them to perform a very similar task themselves (e.g., Van de Guchte et al., 2017) likely indicates to the students that the task is not just about conveying content, but about doing this with specific properties of the language code in mind. Similarly, asking students to reconstruct short texts flooded with instances of a grammar pattern, and then comparing the reconstructions with the original text in which the pattern is visually enhanced (e.g., Izumi, 2002), must shift the students' attention from text content to the language code. Even though I included such experiments under the umbrella of "incidental" learning, the materials and interventions used in them are clearly different from more naturalistic opportunities for incidental learning (discussed in chapter 2). Granted, they resemble naturalistic conditions in the sense that there was no forewarning of a test on specific language items or features. Still, it cannot be ruled out that the students either suspect there is going to be a test or simply decide the items/patterns whose presence in the input is made conspicuous deserve to be studied. Researchers rarely ask the participants in their studies how they perceived or experienced the materials and tasks they were given. Did they suspect a test might follow about the lexical items that occurred remarkably often in a reading text? Did they interpret the highlighting of certain segments of the text as invitations to study the highlighted wordings? Did they realize that the glosses in the margin of a text were not just meant to assist text comprehension, but to promote vocabulary learning? It is for such reasons that it is hard to distinguish between incidental and intentional learning in practice, and why some have argued that the easiest way of operationalizing this distinction in experimental research is by deciding whether or not to explicitly forewarn participants that a test will follow (e.g., Hulstijn, 2003, for a review). This operationalization is not straightforward in the case of classroom-based studies which are conducted with students enrolled in a real language course because assessment is normally an integral part of a course, and so the students expect to be tested sooner or later. Besides, if students attend a language course, they presumably do this with the purpose of getting more proficient in the target language, and so they will hopefully engage deliberately with the language code regardless of any anticipated tests. (At the other extreme, of course, there may be students who did not enrol voluntarily and for whom test announcement makes little difference because they cannot be bothered anyway.) In any case, the fact that studies on ways of improving the chances of incidental acquisition (see chapters 3 and 4) have yielded a range of learning outcomes most probably reflects—in addition to other differences among the studies—the varying degrees to which the participants felt inclined to shift their attention from a focus on communicative content to a focus on the language code. Researchers may design activities with a view to examining incidental learning, but these activities may not always be experienced that way by the study participants. What I have called incidental learning in this book should certainly *not* be equated with "unconscious" learning.

What also matters for the outcomes of those experiments is the aspect of the language code the researcher is interested in. For example, when I reviewed the research on the effects of text modification in chapter 3, these effects were consistently positive for learners' uptake of lexical items. Although often on the small side, the learning gains after working with modified input were usually greater than the gains attested after working with non-modified input—the latter gains typically being negligible. When it came to grammar, however, the benefits of modified input were not as consistent. For example, Lee (2007) found a (moderate) positive learning effect of flooding texts with typographically enhanced instances of the passive voice, but a replication study by Winke (2013) did not. The observation that lexical items are more amenable to being learned from activities that are content oriented is not surprising, for reasons that were discussed in chapter 2. For one, content words are more crucial conveyers of meaning than grammar patterns. If learners struggle with either text comprehension or with getting their own message across, this will often be due to lacunae in their lexical knowledge, and so content words will attract more spontaneous interest than grammar. Moreover, the contribution to meaning by grammar features is often overshadowed in natural discourse by the contribution made by vocabulary (e.g., past tense morphology does not require attending to if time adverbs are available which situate the event in the past). It is also worth reiterating that the target words which are used in experiments about incidental learning are often concrete-meaning words. In comparison, grammar features have abstract meanings, and this makes them more elusive. Altogether, it is thus probably easier to learn new form-meaning connections from modified input when it comes to (concrete) lexical items than when it comes to grammar. In sum, learning gains from content-oriented activities supported by modified input tend to be modest especially in the case of grammar.

However, when content-focused activities are preceded by explicit language-focused instruction, the gains are far greater. This was demonstrated by Indrarathne and Kormos (2017), reviewed in chapter 3, and by Li et al. (2016), reviewed in chapter 4. In these studies, explaining the target grammar patterns to the students before they embarked on content-oriented activities with modified input texts led to learning gains that were more than twice as great as the gains obtained from doing only the content-oriented activities. Similar evidence of the benefits of pre-teaching is also available in the realm of vocabulary learning (e.g., Khezrlou et al., 2017; Pujadas and Muñoz, 2019). Clearly, language-focused instruction can accelerate learning considerably—which must be reassuring (but probably not surprising) to the many teachers who regularly invest time and effort in explaining words, phrases and patterns to their students. Popular L2 textbooks also treat content-oriented and language-focused activities as complementary. For example, they typically use input texts for both purposes, but in a sequential manner (e.g., Crace & Acklam, 2011; Kerr & Jones, 2012; Richards et al., 2017; Soars & Soars, 2016): a text is typically read first with a focus on its content and then again to find examples of certain lexical items, phrases or grammar patterns (which may in some cases be highlighted in the text). Sometimes, these are clarified to the students after the reading (or listening) activity, and the text is revisited for the purpose of exemplification. At other times, it is the students' task to work out the form–meaning connections or usage patterns themselves, with the assistance of guiding questions (see chapter 5). After this, the textbook will typically provide activities (exercises or tasks of a more communicative nature) inviting learners to apply the new knowledge. Popular textbooks thus use a combination of language-focused and content-focused activities, which according to the aforementioned research can indeed be expected to generate a cumulative effect.

If multiple variables influence the effectiveness for vocabulary and grammar learning from content-oriented activities, this will of course hold true for language-focused work as well. Although the impression may be that the latter brings about measurable learning gains faster, this does certainly not mean that language-focused work will *always* be quite effective. Several of the studies that I reviewed in Part III of the book revealed only very modest learning gains (e.g., Boers et al., 2014; Kasprowicz et al., 2019; Tyler et al. 2010; Wong et al., 2018), despite the time invested in language-focused work. It would thus be naïve to claim that items and patterns will always be better remembered from language-focused activities than from content-oriented ones, because *within* each of the 2 broad approaches the activities and materials vary widely. As shown in chapter 6, for example, language-focused exercises which engage learners repeatedly with instances of incorrect language (e.g., error-correction and multiple-choice exercises) tend to generate learning outcomes that are *not* better than the outcomes of some of the incidental learning activities discussed in chapters 4 and 5. I also illustrated (in chapter 7) that there are diverse ways of elaborating about language items and patterns during language-focused instruction, some of which may be more fruitful than others. In short, when asked whether language-focused learning is more efficient than learning from content-oriented activities, the cautious answer must therefore be that *it depends*. As I have said before, the effectiveness of any method depends on the quality of its implementation. The quality of implementation is sometimes difficult to assess (see below), but one factor must certainly be whether the intervention matches the profile of the learner group. For example, it is perhaps no coincidence that the studies on the effectiveness of *Processing Instruction* that I reviewed in chapter 5 showed only very modest learning gains when they were conducted with young learners (e.g., Kasprowicz et al., 2019; Marsden, 2006). This particular learning procedure requires good metalinguistic and analytic skills, which young learners may not yet have sufficiently developed to benefit from it as much as adult learners do—although there is evidence that analytic ability varies even within groups of young learners (Roehr-Brackin & Tellier, 2019), and so it is difficult to tell at the individual level what age is too soon to implement language-focused interventions whose effectiveness depends on such abilities and on the learners' readiness more generally.

In any case, a comparison of learning gains between the collections of studies reviewed in Parts II and III of the book is not quite meaningful, because the studies within and across the 2 collections vary in numerous respects (e.g., varying targets for learning, varying participant profiles, varying educational contexts, varying amounts of time invested, varying types of instruments used to measure learning, varying time lags between learning and assessment, and so on), and so one could end up comparing apples and oranges. Comparing the different learning conditions *within* a single experiment (Indrarathne & Kormos, 2017; Li et al., 2016; Pujadas & Muñoz, 2019) is more valid, and it is these comparisons which indicate more directly that explicit language-focused explanations can accelerate learning—provided, of course, that the explanations are accurate and comprehensible.

A Need for Nuance

When researchers design an experiment to compare the learning outcomes from 2 (or more) instructional methods, the outcome will inevitably be influenced by precisely how these methods were implemented. Consequently, a study which claims superiority of method X over method Y should be cautiously interpreted as superiority of method X over method Y *as implemented in this study*. This is a point I have made on various occasions throughout the book, but it is worth reiterating it here. A first example to illustrate this point again is a classroom study by Hummel (2010) about using translation exercises to help students remember new words. According to the abstract and the conclusion of this article, what is referred to as "active translation" by the author turned out less effective than exercises where the students simply copied sentences. This finding is at odds with the outcomes of some of the studies reviewed in chapter 7 that assessed the usefulness of translation. However, on closer inspection of the article, it transpires that the students in the translation condition were *not* in fact required to "actively" translate the target words at all. The students were asked to translate sentences that included the target words, but the translation of each target word (i.e., the words that the students were later tested on) was already given on their worksheet. So, if translation practice did not live up to its promise in this experiment, this is possibly due to the way it was implemented—or, rather, *not* implemented regarding the lexical items of interest. This example illustrates that it can be risky to rely solely on the information provided in the abstracts of research articles. It is when you inspect an article more closely that you may realize that how the researcher implemented a given method is not how you (as a teacher or researcher) would have done it yourself.

To illustrate this point just once more, let's consider a study by Benati (2020), who compared a modified version of *Processing Instruction* (see chapter 5 for discussion of this method) to what he labelled "traditional instruction". The experiment is an interesting example of how eye-tracking can help researchers ascertain whether a certain instructional intervention affects the way learners process language. Here, however, I will focus just on the learning outcomes. The target grammar pattern was the causative *have* construction, and learning gains were assessed by how well the students understood sentences of this kind, notably that in a sentence such as *Jane had her car washed* it was not Jane herself but someone else who washed the car. In what was found to be the most effective procedure for this purpose, students interpreted a series of sentences exhibiting the causative construction and they received corrective feedback on their answers regarding who performed the actions. Through the corrective feedback, they gradually came to understand that they should not mistake the subject of the sentences for the agent or 'doer' of the action. In the so-called traditional instruction, by comparison, students were presented with a model sentence such as *Jane had her car washed* and with the prompts *Paul/his dress/ mended*. They were then expected to produce *Paul had his dress mended*. No information was provided to these students about the meaning of the construction. Note also that this exercise requires no understanding of the causative construction; it just requires imitating a pattern and substituting the words. It is thus not quite surprising that the students who were neither informed of nor invited to engage with the meaning of the target pattern were found not to have improved their understanding of the pattern. The question must be asked, though, how many teachers would have their students do just this substitution-drill practice *while withholding information about the meaning or function of the pattern being practised*? Is that really what "traditional" teachers do? Popular textbooks that include exercises on the causative construction most certainly include notes about its meaning (e.g., Richards et al., 2017, pp. 58–59). When reading classroom research, practitioners must occasionally wonder, "Okay, so learning procedure X generated better results than procedure Y in this experiment, but as a teacher I would never have considered using procedure Y in the first place; what I'd like to know is whether procedure X is more efficient than the procedure that *my colleagues and I* have been using."

On the positive side, it is when reports of classroom studies such as Benati (2020) include detailed information about the instructional procedures that readers can properly evaluate them. This level of detail cannot always be taken for granted. For example, reporting that the comparison group "received a traditional presentation informed by L2 textbooks" (Jacobson, 2018, p. 679) is not particularly informative if it is not mentioned what these L2 textbooks were and what is meant by "informed by". Another example is an article by Gorman and Ellis (2019) reporting an experiment focusing on the effect of metalinguistic explanations, which, oddly enough, says almost nothing about the metalinguistic explanations that were used. In this study, young learners (aged 9–11) did a series of brief writing activities (based on the dictogloss or "grammar dictation" procedure; see chapter 4) and the researchers were interested in whether these learners would get better at producing the English present perfect tense. Little evidence of improvement emerged, regardless of whether the learners received metalinguistic explanations about the present perfect tense in between the writing activities. The authors therefore conclude that metalinguistic explanations have little effect on young learners' writing accuracy. This finding appears at odds with what was found in the studies that I mentioned earlier, which did furnish evidence in favour of grammar explanations (Indrarathne & Kormos, 2017; Li et al., 2016), but, as argued by Gorman and Ellis (2019), the lack of effect in their experiment may well be due to the relatively young age of the students. The findings are somewhat difficult to interpret, however, because it is not stated what explanations about the meaning of the present perfect tense were given to these young learners. The functions of the present perfect tense are explained *to the reader* of the article in technical jargon (e.g., "Universal/continuative: A state continues throughout a time period whose upper boundary is the time of speaking [...]", p. 65), but presumably this was not the wording used with the actual participants, since it would probably not have been comprehensible to them. The article does provide some information about the procedure that was used with the students: "The teacher asked questions to clarify the difference in meaning and use of the 2 structures [present perfect vs. simple past] and to highlight the difference in auxiliary form for singular and plural subjects" (p. 66). This still remains vague about how the meanings were clarified to these young learners. It seems to be presupposed in publications such as this that there is a standard way of explaining a given grammar pattern, and that readers know and agree on what that standard way is. It is true that popular course books for students of English resemble each other and that new editions look very similar to previous ones when it comes to the presentation of grammar. There is nonetheless some divergence as well, suggesting there is no single standard. For example, the functions of the present perfect tense are described in varying ways in textbooks for intermediate-level learners of English, as illustrated by the following excerpts (with example sentences omitted to save space):

From Crace & Acklam (2011, p. 33):

> We use the Present Perfect to talk about things which started in the past, but continue to the present, or are finished, but have an effect on the present.

From Kerr & Jones (2012, p. 24):
We use the present perfect...

> – when the time is not stated. The event happened in the past, but the time is not important. We often use present perfect to talk about general experience.
> – with time expressions that do not specify the exact time (e.g. ever, never, already)
> – when we talk about actions in the past that happened in a period of time that is unfinished.

Some books apply guided inductive learning to help students match the present perfect to its functions, as in the following example, from Cunningham et al. (2013, unit 4):

We use the present perfect when a past action is connected to the present in some way. Choose the correct form in the rules below and find an example of each rule in exercise 3.

1. If an action started in the past but continues into the present, we use the *Past Simple / Present Perfect*.
2. If we want to show that an action in the past is still relevant now, we use the *Past Simple / Present Perfect*.
3. If an action happened in a finished time period, or if we say when it happened, we use the *Past Simple / Present Perfect*.

To my knowledge, there is no empirical research to help determine if one way of explaining the meaning of the present perfect tense is more helpful than another. Each of the above is arguably a little ambiguous in some regards. For instance, what does it mean for a finished event to "have an effect on the present", for a past action to be "connected to the present in some way" or for an action in the past to be "relevant now"? Take, for example, the discovery of the American continent by Europeans as a past event. Nobody will deny that this has had consequences that continue into the present. Does this then imply that we should use the present perfect tense in a sentence such as "Columbus has discovered America"? Apparently not. Perhaps the distinction between "finished time period" and "unfinished time period" may help to prevent students from over-extending the use of the present perfect where the simple past tense is the appropriate choice, but what are the boundaries of a "time period" if the period is not stated? Neither is it clear which of 2 guidelines, such as guidelines 2 and 3 in Cunningham et al. (2013), should be given precedence when they conflict. Additional interpretation challenges may be posed by statements (in Kerr & Jones, 2012) such as "We often use present perfect to talk about general experience" (what qualifies as general experience?) and "time expressions that do not specify the exact time" (what qualifies as the exact time? Yesterday? 2:30pm yesterday? Last week? Last Tuesday? 2005? October 14, 2005?). In some resources, the term "indefinite past" is used to describe the use of present perfect tense, which potentially leaves students puzzled about how past events can possibly be indefinite. Because different metalinguistic explanations concerning a given grammar pattern are available and because it is not certain whether they are all equally helpful (or helpful for a specific learner group), it would be useful for the sake of (partial) replication if reports of studies which examine the role of metalinguistic explanations were more transparent about precisely what those explanations were.

An Ensemble

Although research studies often focus on either incidental or intentional learning, these 2 broad approaches are, of course, complementary. They can (and should) be combined in actual practice. Relying on incidental L2 learning alone would create a pace of learning that is too frustratingly slow for many learners, while spending too much time on the intentional study of the language code would leave insufficient time for activities that foster communication skills. Even if language-focused activities are often more efficient than content-focused activities for vocabulary and grammar learning, this does not mean that vocabulary-focused and grammar-focused activities should predominate in a language program. Nation (2007), for example, suggests that a well-balanced language learning program should devote only about 25% of available time to language-focused learning, so that sufficient space is available for meaning-focused activities and fluency development—although he concedes that the precise proportions recommended are inevitably somewhat arbitrary. It is important to appreciate that creating a balanced language learning program concerns the totality of learning opportunities for a given group of learners, both inside and outside the language classroom. If learners have ample opportunity to use the language for content-focused purposes outside the language classroom, then this may free up more time for language-focused work inside the language classroom. This may be the case, for example, when L2 learners are immersed (e.g., as exchange students) in the L2 community. It may also be the case in content-and-language-integrated learning contexts, where students receive instruction about half of their school subjects in the second language. In contexts where L2 students have little exposure to the target language outside the language class, instructors may need to find ways to increase the out-of-class exposure (e.g., through extensive reading and the use of audiovisual resources such as movies in the target language). Alternatively, instructors in such contexts could instead allocate a fair proportion of language-focused learning to independent study outside the classroom, in order to free up time for content-oriented communicative activities inside the classroom.

The next question is how to create an ensemble of language-focused and content-focused activities to help language students (a) develop initial knowledge of a certain segment of vocabulary or of a certain grammar pattern, (b) retain this knowledge, and (c) use it smoothly for communicative purposes. Because there are so many variables, it is probably wise to adopt an eclectic approach, and let's consider the following sequence of teaching steps:

1. Draw the learners' attention to a target words/phrases/pattern.
2. Explain the meaning or function of the items/pattern with the aid of examples, or, if deemed feasible without a high risk of confusion, ask the learners to work them out themselves with the aid of examples, and then confirm (see chapter 5).
3. Engage the learners in content-oriented activities with input texts that further illustrate the use and meaning of the items/pattern (see chapter 3).
4. Possibly elaborate briefly about a property that may make the items/pattern easier to remember (see chapter 7).

5. Provide opportunities for the students to retrieve the items/pattern from memory. This can be done in diverse ways (see chapter 6). For example, a modified version of the input texts from step 3 could be used to cue recall of missing items. In the case of certain grammar features, it could be done through the kind of interpretation practice proposed in *Processing Instruction* (see chapter 5). Recall of meaning can be given precedence if the aim is to foster receptive knowledge; recall of form will be useful if the aim is to foster productive knowledge.

6. Engage the students in a series of communicative tasks likely to elicit the target items/pattern (see chapter 4). Ensure opportunities for improvement (e.g., feedback episodes) between the tasks or task repetitions.

Note that, although there are more language-focused steps in this ensemble (steps 1, 2, 4 and 5), the content-focused activities (steps 3 and 6) would by their very nature take up more time, thus creating a balance overall between the 2 broad approaches.

Few teachers will find the above ensemble original. It indeed looks commonsensical rather than informed by decades of research. And yet, it is compatible with conclusions from that research, including the following:

1. Introducing target items or patterns prior to content-focused activities can accelerate learning of these items or patterns during the content-focused activities.

2. The form-meaning pairings can simply be presented to the learner or the learner can be invited to work them out with the necessary assistance. The jury is still out on the question whether the latter (i.e., guided inductive learning) is the better choice and, if so, under what conditions.

3. Focusing simultaneously on content and on language is hard. It is therefore helpful to process the same input text more than once. It is also helpful to perform the same (or similar) output activity more than once. When content is familiar, more attention can be given to language.

4. Retrieval of newly learned items or patterns from memory is highly effective for the consolidation of knowledge.

5. Talking about certain striking or intriguing features of the target language can help to make items/patterns which exhibit these features more memorable.

6. You get better at what you practise. If the aim of language learning is to use the target language for real communication, then practice should enhance (micro-)skills that contribute to the skill set that is orchestrated during communicative use of the language. Although some types of practice (e.g., find-and-correct-the-errors exercises) are quite common in existing language courses, they are unlikely to serve that purpose well, and so should probably be used in moderation. Instead, it is the errors that are made by the learners themselves—not ones invented by the course writer—that invite corrective feedback and remedial teaching.

While the ensemble of teaching and learning steps proposed above seems to reflect research findings rather well, many readers will consider it totally conventional and even traditional. Does this mean, then, that too few new insights have emerged from the research on instructional procedures to push innovation in vocabulary and grammar teaching? After all, the notion that each of the components of the above ensemble contributes to learning in one way or another is commonsensical, and research seems to have merely confirmed this. However, it is probably *within* each of the components of the ensemble that research findings have the potential to push innovation. We now know more about the factors which influence learning at each of the stages and which together contribute to the learning process at large. More is now known about how learners engage with items/patterns in modified reading texts, the effects of guessing and retrieval, the merits of certain mnemonic techniques, the importance of task repetition and so on. At the same time, more research is needed—especially research that addresses the practical concerns of teachers. That is the topic of the next (and final) chapter.

Further Reflection

What is "Conventional"?

All too often do researchers in our discipline casually label the comparison treatments in their classroom experiments "traditional" or "conventional", without explaining why these should be considered so. What is conventional in one educational context need not be so in another. Besides, there have been many traditions in the discipline of language teaching (Richards & Rodgers, 2014), and what is embraced as innovative by one generation gets deemed traditional by later generations. Browsing through the archives of journals such as *The Modern Language Journal* (going back as far as the early 1900s) and *ELT Journal* (going back to the 1940s) can be revealing of such changes in mindsets. It is true that quite a few academics who publish about language teaching—including myself—were language teachers at some earlier stage of our careers and so may remember what was considered conventional then. This may be a long time ago and situated in a specific context, though. So, it is worth reflecting what teaching methods are considered conventional in *your* context, and whether they match what is labelled conventional in the research literature. Can you tell from the authors' descriptions?

The Right Time?

In experiments such as the ones reviewed in this book, the researchers are usually interested in how certain "treatments" foster the development of *new* knowledge. In vocabulary studies, target items which were already known by some of the learners at pretest will often be excluded from the analysis. In some lines of inquiry about grammar learning (e.g., research on *Processing Instruction*), it is customary to exclude from the analysis the data from participants who, according to the pretests, already had some familiarity with the target pattern. These methodological decisions make it more straightforward to calculate and compare learning gains (although it is in fact perfectly possible to incorporate the variation in pretest scores in the statistical analyses). At the same time, these decisions arguably create an artificial picture, because in real classrooms it *is* probable that some lexical items that a teacher draws the students' attention to are already known by some of the students, and it *is* probable that some of the students already have some familiarity with a supposedly new grammar pattern (thanks to an earlier L2 course or thanks to exposure outside the language classroom). It is the skill of building on previous knowledge that is one of the characteristics of successful teachers. The practice of extending prior knowledge is also reflected in popular textbook series, where certain grammar patterns (e.g., the use of tenses) are introduced in simple terms in one book (e.g., the book for pre-intermediate level) and revisited and elaborated upon in a subsequent one (e.g., the book for intermediate level). Interestingly, experimental studies which do not eliminate data indicating prior familiarity suggest that it is when learners already have some familiarity with a target grammar pattern that they tend to benefit from interventions such as textual enhancement (e.g., Lee, 2007) and corrective recasts (e.g., Li et al., 2016). Learning gains in vocabulary studies have been found to be more substantial for learners with some prior knowledge as well (e.g., Bui et al., 2020). Zooming in on items that are unfamiliar to all the participants or zooming in on the participants who were totally unfamiliar with the grammar pattern of interest may thus produce a picture that underestimates the amount of learning that might have happened for the group of learners at large. It might therefore be worth replicating some of the experiments with participants who are not learning the chosen target patterns from scratch. Because researchers deliberately select target items or patterns that are highly unlikely to be as yet familiar to the given learner groups, it could even be argued in the case of some experiments that the learners were simply not yet "ready" to learn these—or, to use a term from *Sociocultural Theory*, they were beyond the learners' "Zone of Proximal Development" (Lantolf & Poehner, 2014). Looking back at *your* experience as a language learner or language teacher, can you remember any classes where you thought certain aspects of the target language were introduced too soon, and that little learning occurred because of this?

References

Benati, A. (2020). The effects of structured input and traditional instruction on the acquisition of the English causative passive forms: An eye-tracking study measuring accuracy in responses and processing patterns. *Language Teaching Research*. Online early view. https://doi.org/10.1177/1362168820928577

Boers, F., Demecheleer, M., Coxhead, A., & Webb, S. (2014). Gauging the effects of exercises on verb-noun collocations. *Language Teaching Research*, 18, 54–74. https://doi.org/10.1177/1362168813505389

Bui, T., Boers, F., & Coxhead, A. (2020). Extracting multiword expressions from texts with the aid of on-line resources: A classroom experiment. *ITL International Journal of Applied Linguistics*, 171, 221–252. https://doi.org/10.1075/itl.18033.bui

Crace, A., & Acklam, R. (2011). *New Total English, upper intermediate: Students' book*. Pearson Education.

Cunningham, S., Moor, P., & Bygrave, J. (2013). *Cutting Edge, intermediate: Students' book* (3rd ed.). Pearson Education.

Gorman, M., & Ellis, R. (2019). The relative effects of metalinguistic explanation and direct written corrective feedback on children's grammatical accuracy in new writing. *Language Teaching for Young Learners*, 1, 57–81. https://doi.org/10.1075/ltyl.00005.gor

Hulstijn, J. H. (2003). Incidental and intentional learning. In C. Doughty & M. Long (Eds.), *The handbook of second language acquisition* (pp. 349–381). Blackwell Publishing.

Hummel, K. M. (2010). Translation and short-term L2 vocabulary retention: Hindrance or help? *Language Teaching Research*, 14, 61–74. https://doi.org/10.1177/1362168809346497

Indrarathne, B., & Kormos, J. (2017). Attentional processing of input in explicit and implicit learning conditions: An eye-tracking study. *Studies in Second Language Acquisition*, 39, 401–430. https://doi.org/10.1017/S027226311600019X

Izumi, S. (2002). Output, input enhancement, and the noticing hypothesis? An experimental study on ESL relativization. *Studies in Second Language Acquisition*, 24, 541–577. https://doi.org/10.1017/S0272263102004023

Jacobson, N. D. (2018). The best of both worlds: Combining cognitive linguistics and pedagogic tasks to teach English conditionals. *Applied Linguistics*, 39, 668–693. https://doi.org/10.1093/applin/amw030

Kasprowicz, R. E., Marsden, E., & Sephton, N. (2019). Investigating distribution of practice effects for the learning of foreign language verb morphology in the young learner classroom. *The Modern Language Journal*, 103, 580–606. https://doi.org/10.1111/modl.12586

Kerr, P., & Jones, C. (2012). *Straightforward, intermediate: Student's book* (2nd ed.). Macmillan Education.

Khezrlou, S., Ellis, R., & Sadeghi, K. (2017). Effects of computer-assisted glosses on EFL learners' vocabulary acquisition and reading comprehension in three learning conditions. *System*, 65, 104–116. https://doi.org/10.1016/j.system.2017.01.009

Lantolf, J. P., & Poehner, M. E. (2014). *Sociocultural theory and the pedagogical imperative in L2 education. Vygotskian praxis and the theory/practice divide*. Routledge.

Lee, S.-K. (2007). Effects of textual enhancement and topic familiarity on Korean EFL students' reading comprehension and learning of passive form. *Language Learning*, 57, 87–118. https://doi.org/10.1111/j.1467-9922.2007.00400.x

Li, S., Ellis, R., & Zhu, Y. (2016). Task-based versus task-supported language instruction: An experimental study. *Annual Review of Applied Linguistics*, 36, 205–229. https://doi.org/10.1017/S0267190515000069

Marsden, E. (2006). Exploring input processing in the classroom: An experimental comparison of processing instruction and enriched input. *Language Learning*, 56, 507–566. https://doi.org/10.1111/j.1467-9922.2006.00375.x

Nagata, N. (1999). The effectiveness of computer-assisted interactive glosses. *Foreign Language Annals*, 32, 469–479. https://doi.org/10.1111/j.1944-9720.1999.tb00876.x

Nation, I. S. P. (2007). The four strands. *International Journal of Innovation in Language Learning and Teaching*, 1, 2–13. https://doi.org/10.2167/illt039.0

Pujadas, G., & Muñoz, C. (2019). Extensive viewing of captioned and subtitled TV series: A study of L2 vocabulary learning by adolescents. *The Language Learning Journal*, 47, 479–496. https://doi.org/10.1080/09571736.2019.1616806

Richards, J. C., Hull, J., & Proctor, S. (2017). *Interchange 3: Student's book* (5th ed.). Cambridge University Press.

Richards, J. C., & Rodgers, T. S. (2014). *Approaches and methods in language teaching* (3rd ed.). Cambridge University Press.

Roehr-Brackin, K., & Tellier, A. (2019). The role of language-analytic ability in children's instructed second language learning. *Studies in Second Language Acquisition*, 41, 1111–1131. https://doi.org/10.1017/S0272263119000214

Rott, S. (2007). The effect of frequency of input-enhancements on word learning and text comprehension. *Language Learning*, 57, 165–199. https://doi.org/10.1111/j.1467-9922.2007.00406.x

Soars, L., & Soars, J. (2016). *American Headway* 3 (3rd ed.). Oxford University Press.

Tyler, A., Mueller, C. M., & Ho, V. (2010). Applying cognitive linguistics to instructed L2 learning: The English modals. *AILA Review*, 23, 30–49. https://doi.org/10.1075/aila.23.03tyl

Van de Guchte, M., Rijlaarsdam, G., Braaksma, M., & Bimmel, P. (2017). Focus on language versus content in the pre-task: Effects of guided peer-video model observations on task performance. *Language Teaching Research*, 23, 310–329. https://doi.org/10.1177/1362168817735543

Winke, P. (2013). The effects of input enhancement on grammar learning and comprehension: A modified replication of Lee (2007) with eye-movement data. *Studies in Second Language Acquisition*, 35, 323–352. https://doi.org/10.1017/S0272263112000903

Wong, M. H. I., Zhao, H., & MacWhinney, B. (2018). A cognitive linguistics application for second language pedagogy: The English preposition tutor. *Language Learning*, 68, 438–468. https://doi.org/10.1111/lang.12278

9.

AVENUES

Two-Way Traffic

One of the aims of this book was to bring research about language teaching and learning closer to practitioners. Many teachers find the universe of research publications hard to navigate, and they find research articles hard to read due to the excessive use of technical jargon and (in many cases) the use of complex statistics (Marsden & Kasprowicz, 2017). Besides, many teachers simply do not work in institutions such as universities with free library access to such publications. Laudable initiatives have been taken in recent years to make findings from studies published in key peer-reviewed journals more accessible in the form of one-page summaries written for non-specialists (*OASIS—Open Accessible Summaries in Language Studies*). Several journals (e.g., *TESOL Quarterly* and *The Modern Language Journal*) now solicit such transparent summaries from authors whose articles were accepted for publication. Time will tell if these initiatives are successful at increasing practitioners' engagement with research. The fact remains that the number of potentially relevant publications is vast, and even academics (myself included) whose job it is to stay abreast of new developments in their discipline find the perpetual stream of new publications hard to keep up with. It must be even more daunting for language teaching professionals, who can naturally devote only a small fraction of their time to reading research papers.

Alternatively, teachers may look for research-informed recommendations in periodicals for professionals, seek advice from speakers at professional development workshops and symposia, and learn about research findings from instructors on teacher-training programs. However, also professional development providers, whose task it is to translate research findings into recommendations for pedagogy, must feel overwhelmed by the proliferation of empirical studies. It may then be more manageable for them to turn to authoritative "state-of-the-art" review articles instead. A limitation of that type of comprehensive review article is that there is seldom enough space for the authors to include much detail about precisely how the instructional interventions of interest were implemented in the original studies being reviewed. Another limitation is that a systematic review article does of course not stay "state of the art" indefinitely, and so regular updates are necessary. Worth mentioning as well is that such reviews offer an interpretation of the available body of research on a given topic, since it is the author's task to look for trends and cause-effect relations in a complex and diverse assemblage of research reports. They will inevitably do this through a particular (theoretical) lens. As a result, the evaluations presented in such review articles—often called *narrative* reviews—can differ markedly from one author to the next (e.g., Benati, 2019; DeKeyser & Botana, 2015).

A type of systematic review article that has become increasingly popular in recent years and which professional development providers could also turn to as a shortcut into the available research on a given topic is *meta-analysis* (e.g., Shintani, 2015). A meta-analysis collects as many empirical studies on the role of a given factor as possible and then calculates the weighted average effect from that pool of studies. This helps to estimate with greater confidence than any individual empirical study whether the chosen factor of interest is likely to play a role that is not confined to specific contexts and how substantial its role is likely to be (Norris & Ortega, 2006). Because of their quantitative nature, such meta-analytic reviews may look more objective than narrative reviews (but see Oswald & Plonsky, 2010), and so educators (and those advising educators) may feel inclined to rely on their outcomes. The growing availability of meta-analyses is certainly providing a welcome additional channel for knowledge dissemination, even though, again, these reviews will not have enough space for detailed accounts of precisely how instructional methods were implemented in the original studies.

Importantly, meta-analyses need to be interpreted with caution just like any other research report. For one, the outcome of a meta-analysis will be determined by which empirical studies were found eligible for inclusion. For another, the labels used by the authors of a meta-analysis for a certain variable or a certain instructional method need not correspond to what the reader associates with the same labels—an issue I also mentioned in chapter 8. For example, in a rare meta-analytic review about the merits of *Task-Based Language Teaching* (TBLT), Bryfonski and McKay (2019) concluded that the available research "supports the notion that program-wide implementation of TBLT is effective for promoting L2 learning above and beyond the learning found in programs with other, traditional or non-task-based pedagogies" (p. 622). However, when Boers et al. (2020) re-examined the collection of studies used in that meta-analysis, it turned out that what was called TBLT in many of the reports did not at all correspond to how TBLT is described by its leading proponents. Instead, what was called TBLT often amounted to language-focused work rather than the use of language for communication, and these studies in fact compared the outcomes of different language-focused approaches where one was misleadingly labelled TBLT. In the majority of the remaining studies included in the original meta-analysis, the descriptions of the instructional procedures were too vague to determine if they corresponded to TBLT at all, and even less information was provided in these reports about the instructional procedures to which the benefits of so-called TBLT were compared. The comparison treatments were often merely characterized as "conventional" or "traditional", without specifying what those labels might entail in the given educational context (see chapter 8 for similar concerns). Boers et al.'s (2020) re-examination found that there were still far too few empirical studies that compared TBLT to other approaches in a transparent enough manner to justify any generalizations about the superiority of TBLT. In the meantime, however, professional development providers who may have heard about the original meta-analysis—published in a well-established journal—may have spread the news that there was now compelling research evidence of the superiority of TBLT. To find out that, overall, the available evidence was in fact not so compelling, it was necessary to closely inspect all the studies included in the original meta-analysis. This obviously defeats the time-saving purpose of reading a systematic review (be it of the narrative or meta-analytic kind).

If one of the aims of this book was to lay a bridge between the worlds of research and professional practice, the bridge I envisioned was intended to serve two-way traffic. Practitioners' decision making can benefit from being informed by research, but, conversely, researchers who wish to assess the merits of an instructional intervention can certainly benefit from being better informed by what teachers and course designers already do and what choices and dilemmas *they* face. I have had to observe time and again that the instructional procedures used in experimental studies as well as the excessive time invested in these procedures are often a far cry from how teachers would (be able to) implement them in real practice—let alone what their students would be willing to endure. Put differently, there are often issues with "ecological validity", that is, the desirability for experimental treatments to resemble real teaching and real learning conditions. Surely, *if* pedagogy-minded researchers want their work to have an impact on the language teaching profession, then they need to be aware of the perspectives of the stakeholders who have first-hand experience of the profession.

One way of ascertaining that a planned research project is perceived by practitioners as relevant is simply to consult them. Do language teachers find proposed research questions pertinent beyond their relevance to a theoretical debate? For example, is the question whether input-oriented activities and output-oriented activities bring about different learning gains one of the questions that many language teachers are curious about, or do language teachers find it justifiably commonsensical to use a cycle of input and output activities in their classrooms, anyhow? If researchers wish to test the effect of a specific learning procedure and set up an experiment where this procedure is implemented repeatedly, for an extensive period of time, and with a narrow language focus, will language teachers consider such time investment truly ecologically valid? Might language teachers not also comment that they would find a combination of 2 or more activities more suitable? When researchers want to compare the learning outcome of an innovative instructional procedure to that of another, more conventional procedure, then consulting language teachers may also help to verify that the latter is indeed considered conventional and that the way it is designed for the purpose of the experiment resembles how it is normally applied by teachers. If not, chances are that the innovative procedure will be found superior merely because the so-called conventional procedure was implemented in a questionable, *un*conventional way.

A less direct way of investigating how vocabulary and grammar are approached in language courses is to examine popular L2 textbooks or course books. This is an indirect way, because not all teachers use such resources and those who do may not follow them to the letter. Still, textbooks remain the backbone of many language courses, and, for publishers to successfully market a textbook it will need to accord sufficiently with teachers' beliefs about what "works".

An examination of textbooks also makes one realize that it is very rare for a segment of vocabulary or a certain grammar pattern to be tackled through just one single teaching step or one single activity in a language course. As pointed out in chapter 8, textbooks typically make use of an ensemble of teaching steps and activities. Researchers understandably wish to isolate the effect of a specific intervention, and that may be one of the reasons why so many experimental studies implement one single intervention in comparison to a no-intervention condition and/or in comparison to another treatment which also involves just one single intervention. It is quite conceivable, however, that the relative effectiveness of a given treatment changes when it is part of an ensemble. Educators may therefore be especially interested in the cumulative effects of different ensembles, including the ensembles proposed by textbooks. Researching this does not preclude the possibility of isolating the contribution made by a specific component of the ensemble. One could examine how a textbook approaches a given grammar pattern, modify one of the components, and compare learning outcomes from the modified version to those from the original version. For example, the textbook might be one which deals with a given grammar pattern deductively, and a researcher interested in the merits of guided inductive learning might adapt this component so that learners are invited to discover the pattern themselves (chapter 5). The textbook may be one where much of the language-focused practice consists of find-the-error exercises, and a researcher who feels sceptical about the usefulness of such exercises could substitute these by another exercise type (chapter 6). In case target items lend themselves to one or the other mnemonic technique (chapter 7), this could be introduced as a new variable as well. Researchers who feel sceptical of decontextualized practice altogether may want to try replacing this by additional content-focused activities (chapter 4). The textbook may include an activity where learners can simply copy or imitate items from an input text, and a researcher may want to modify this so the learners need to retrieve the items from memory instead (chapter 6). The textbook may suggest 2 communicative output activities with opportunities for using certain lexical items or patterns, and a researcher interested in the benefits of task repetition might decide to have the learners do one of them twice instead of doing each activity once (chapter 4). And so on. An additional research option is to investigate whether changing the sequence of the activities that make up the ensemble makes a difference. What would of course remain crucial to be able to determine cause-effect relations in such research projects is that the ensembles being compared differ in just one clearly defined respect, and that the total amount of time invested in implementing the different versions stays comparable. If the latter condition is not met, then one might be able to make the claim that ensemble X is more *effective* than ensemble Y for a certain purpose, but if the former required considerably more time to complete, then it would not be justified to claim that it is also more *efficient*.

I am by no means suggesting that research of the above kind should supplant existing strands. Researchers may even feel hesitant to embark on it, because the cumulative contribution to learning by the shared components may override the effect of the single component that was manipulated for the comparison, and so the likelihood of finding significantly different outcomes seems slim (and researchers may feel concerned that non-significant findings are hard to publish). However, I believe it is the kind of research that may forge a closer collaboration between researchers and educators.

But Don't Take My Word for it

Above, I mentioned state-of-the-art reviews as one of the sources that professional development providers can turn to in order to stay informed about developments in our discipline. The book you have been reading was intended to be such a state-of-the-art review, albeit with a much broader scope than the typical review articles found in academic journals. It is different from systematic review articles also in the sense that space was available for me to describe empirical studies in enough detail to evaluate the procedures used and to put the findings into perspective.

While I have tried to cover a lot of ground in this book, it is important to realize that it remains far from comprehensive or exhaustive (see chapter 1). Many more studies could have been included, but I have focused on ones published in the key journals of our discipline, and even within that range I must have missed numerous relevant publications. Besides, as explained in the introductory chapter, I have reviewed only studies which included a comparative dimension, that is, studies that evaluate the merits of a certain intervention relative to a control and/or comparison condition. It is also vital to realize that a comment I made above about narrative reviews applies to this work, too—I have not just described research but have also interpreted it and evaluated the practical implications. My interpretations and evaluations are inevitably influenced by my individual history as a language learner, linguist, language teacher, teacher trainer, researcher, parent of multilingual children and much more. They are influenced by the views of scholars and colleagues that I admire and by the reflections about language learning and teaching that many generations of students have generously shared with me. Others may look at the same collections of studies through their own lens and may as a result paint a picture in shades different from mine.

In the time span between publication of this book and the moment you decided (or were told) to read it, many new relevant empirical studies will undoubtedly have become available. The chapters presenting systematic reviews in this book will thus no longer be "state-of-the-art". I hope the book will nonetheless serve as a useful, critical synthesis of the research published between the late 1990s and 2020, and make it easier for you to understand and situate the work that has followed. More importantly, though, I hope the book has left you not only with answers to some questions (be they research questions, practical questions concerning pedagogy or—preferably—both), but also with a healthy curiosity to seek answers to questions which our discipline has not yet properly answered. I mentioned in the introductory chapter that I thought the time was ripe for a research synthesis such as this, because I was (perhaps naïvely) hopeful that, considering the fast proliferation of empirical studies in the past 2 decades, enough progress had been made to answer most of the questions about vocabulary and grammar instruction that I pondered myself as a language teacher and have often been asked as a teacher trainer. Progress has certainly been made, and many questions can now be answered in a cautiously nuanced manner. At the same time, it needs to be recognized that there is plenty of work left to be done.

References

Benati, A. (2019). Classroom-oriented research: Processing Instruction (findings and implications). *Language Teaching*, 52, 343–359. https://doi.org/10.1017/S0261444817000386

Boers, F., Bryfonski, L., Faez, F., & McKay, T. (2020). A call for cautious interpretation of meta-analytic reviews. *Studies in Second Language Acquisition*. Online early view. https://doi.org/10.1017/S0272263120000327

Bryfonski, L., & McKay, T. H. (2019). TBLT implementation and evaluation: A meta-analysis. *Language Teaching Research*, 23, 603–632. https://doi.org/10.1177/1362168817744389

DeKeyser, R., & Botana, G. P. (2015). The effectiveness of Processing Instruction in L2 grammar acquisition: A narrative review. *Applied Linguistics*, 36, 290–305. https://doi.org/10.1093/applin/amu071

Marsden, E., & Kasprowicz, R. (2017). Foreign language educators' exposure to research: Reported experiences, exposure via citations, and a proposal for action. *The Modern Language Journal*, 101, 613–642. https://doi.org/10.1111/modl.12426

Norris, J. M., & Ortega, L. (2006). The value and practice of research synthesis for language learning and teaching. In J. M. Norris & L. Ortega (Eds.), *Synthesizing research on language learning and teaching* (pp. 1–50). John Benjamins.

OASIS—Open Accessible Summaries in Language Studies. https://oasis-database.org/about

Oswald, F. L., & Plonsky, L. (2010). Meta-analysis in second language research: Choices and challenges. *Annual Review of Applied Linguistics*, 30, 85–110. https://doi.org/10.1017/S0267190510000115

Shintani, N. (2015). The effectiveness of Processing Instruction and Production-based instruction on L2 grammar acquisition: A meta-analysis. *Applied Linguistics*, 36, 306–325, https://doi.org/10.1093/applin/amu067

INDEX